IBI International Business Intelligence

1992 - Planning for the Food Industry

ibi
INTERNATIONAL BUSINESS INTELLIGENCE

Other titles in the IBI series

Investment Incentives Worldwide

A practical guide to national funding of capital investment projects

Development Aid

A guide to national and international agencies

1992 – Planning for Financial Services and the Insurance Sector

The first in a series of guides to the implications and impact of the Single European Act.

Forthcoming titles

1992 – Planning for the IT Industries
1992 – Planning for Chemicals, Pharmaceuticals and Biotechnology
1992 – Planning for the Engineering Industries

Butterworths
Borough Green
Sevenoaks
Kent TN15 8PH   Telephone: (0732) 884567

IBI International Business Intelligence

1992 - Planning for the Food Industry

Researched and compiled by Eurofi plc

Butterworths
London Boston Singapore Sydney Toronto Wellington

Eurofi plc
Birmingham Cardiff Edinburgh Manchester Newbury
Brussels New York

PART OF REED INTERNATIONAL P.L.C.

All rights reserved. No part of this publication may be reproduced or transmitted in any form or by any means (including photocopying and recording) without the written permission of the copyright holder except in accordance with the provisions of the Copyright Act 1956 (as amended) or under the terms of a licence issued by the Copyright Licensing Agency Ltd, 33–34 Alfred Place, London, England WC1E 7DP. The written permission of the copyright holder must also be obtained before any part of this publication is stored in a retrieval system of any nature. Applications for the copyright holder's written permission to reproduce, transmit or store in a retrieval system any part of this publication should be addressed to the Publishers.

Warning: The doing of an unauthorised act in relation to a copyright work may result in both a civil claim for damages and criminal prosecution.

This book is sold subject to the Standard Conditions of Sale of Net Books and may not be re-sold in the UK below the net price given by the Publishers in their current price list.

First published 1989

© **Butterworth & Co (Publishers) Ltd and Eurofi plc, 1989**

British Library Cataloguing in Publication Data

1992 – planning for the food industry. –
  (International business intelligence series: 4)
  1. European community countries. Food industries and trades. European Economic community law
  I. Eurofi plc   II. Series
  341.7′54756413

ISBN 0-408-04091-2

Library of Congress Cataloging in Publication Data

1992--planning for the food industry

  (IBI international business intelligence)
  1. Food law and legislation--European Economic Community countries.   I. Eurofi plc
II. Series
  KJE6778.A39A15   1989   344.4′04232   89-655
  ISBN 0-408-04091-2   344.044232

Every care has been taken to ensure the accuracy of the information contained in this publication, but no liability can be accepted by Butterworths or Eurofi plc for errors or omissions of any kind. To ensure that such errors are eliminated from future editions, readers are kindly invited to notify the publishers.

Printed by Unwin Bros., Old Woking, Surrey
Bound by Hartnolls Ltd., Bodmin, Cornwall

CONTENTS

1. INTRODUCTION 1

2. THE SINGLE EUROPEAN MARKET 3
   Achieving the internal market: 1957-1985 3
   The Commission's White Paper proposals 5
      Harmonisation and mutual recognition 6
      Removal of physical barriers 7
      Removal of technical barriers 8
      Removal of fiscal barriers 9
   Implications for industry, commerce and individuals 10
      Industry and commerce 10
      General economic growth 11
      Public procurement 12
      Individuals 12

3. THE SINGLE EUROPEAN ACT 15
   Policy objectives 16
   Reform of the decision-making process 18
   Other institutional reforms 20
   Problems envisaged in completing the
      internal market 21
   The legislative process 22

4. CORPORATE ISSUES 27
   Background 27
   Company law 27
   Mergers and acquisitions 28
   Mutual recognition of professional qualifications
      and employment rights 29
   Corporate taxation 30
   Transport 30
      Border controls 31
      Animal and plant health controls 32

v

4. CORPORATE ISSUES (cntd)
   - Intellectual property 32
   - Product liability 33
   - Community research and development programmes 34
     - ECLAIR 35
     - FLAIR 35

5. THE FOOD INDUSTRY - TOWARDS 1992 37
   - Background 37
   - 1969 harmonisation programme 38
   - 1973 harmonisation programme 39
   - 1985 White Paper proposals 40
     - Public health 41
     - Consumer protection 42
     - Official inspection 42
     - European Agricultural Guidance and
       Guarantee Fund 43
     - Simplified procedure 43
   - Case law of the European Court 44
   - Implications for the food and drink industry 48

6. REMOVAL OF PHYSICAL BARRIERS 51
   - Background 51
     - Fruit, vegetables and cereals 51
     - Meat and meat products 52
     - Other products 52
   - Fruit, vegetables and cereals -
     existing legislation 53
   - Fruit, vegetables and cereals -
     proposed legislation 62
   - Fruit, vegetables and cereals -
     legislation not yet proposed 64
   - Meat and meat products - existing legislation 66
   - Meat and meat products - proposed legislation 112
   - Meat and meat products - legislation not yet
     proposed 128
   - Other products - existing and proposed legislation 128
   - Other products - legislation not yet proposed 137

7. REMOVAL OF TECHNICAL BARRIERS 139
   Background 139
   Labelling - existing legislation 139
   Labelling - proposed legislation 150
   Packaging - existing legislation 157
   Packaging - proposed legislation 171
   Additives and flavourings - existing legislation 174
   Additives and flavourings - proposed legislation 194
   Food for special nutritional uses -
      existing legislation 204
   Food for special nutritional uses -
      proposed legislation 206
   General food legislation - existing 214
   General food legislation - proposed 218
   Composition of foodstuffs - existing legislation 227
   Composition of foodstuffs - proposed legislation 260
   Food legislation not yet proposed 265

8. REMOVAL OF FISCAL BARRIERS 267
   Background 267
   VAT 267
      Abolition of fiscal frontiers 267
      Approximation of VAT rates 268
   Excise duties 268
      Standstill and convergence 269
   Effect of harmonised VAT and excise duties on
      national revenue 270
   VAT legislation 271
      Existing VAT legislation 271
      Proposed VAT legislation 272
      VAT legislation not yet proposed 275
   Excise duties legislation 275
      Existing excise duties legislation 276
      Proposed legislation - structures of
         excise duties 276
      Proposed legislation - rates of
         excise duties 278
      Legislation on excise duties
         not yet proposed 281

9. IMPLICATIONS OF A SINGLE EUROPEAN MARKET FOR
   THE FOOD AND DRINK INDUSTRY 283
   Background 283
   Implications of the internal market programme 283
       Labelling 283
       Materials and articles in contact with food 284
       Packaging 284
       Additives 285
       Foodstuffs for particular nutritional uses 285
       Composition of foodstuffs 286
       Spirit drinks 286
       Official inspection of foodstuffs 286
       Information procedures: standards
           and technical regulations 287
       Metrication 287
       Agricultural products 288
       Transport 289
   Trends in the European food industry 290
       Market restructuring 291
       Implications for retail distribution 292
   Trends in the European drinks industry 293
       Wines and spirits 293
       Beer 294
   Implications for third countries 295
       Import restrictions - impact on third
           countries 296

10. STRATEGIC PLANNING FOR 1992 299
    Original contributions from:
        Minister of Agriculture, Fisheries and Food 300
        Ministry of Agriculture, Fisheries and Food
            (general policy statement) 308
        Food from Britain 311
        Confederation of the Food and Drink
            Industries of the EEC 318
        University of Reading, Department of
            Food Science and Technology 323

10. STRATEGIC PLANNING FOR 1992 (cntd)
    Ministry of Agriculture, Fisheries and Food
       (additives and flavourings) 328
    British Nutrition Foundation 332
    Unilever N.V. 343
    Lloyds Bank 345
    Ralph Howell MP 351
    Tempco Union Ltd 353
    Meat and Livestock Commission 356
    Bacon and Meat Manufacturers' Association 361
    Danish Bacon and Meat Council 362
    Federation of Swiss Food Industries 365
    Federation of Greek Food Industries 368
    Ministry of Agriculture, Fisheries and Food
       (packaging) 372

1. INTRODUCTION

The objective of the European Commission's current legislative programme is the creation of an internal market for goods and services throughout the twelve Member States by 31 December 1992. Achievement of this goal necessitates the removal of all existing barriers to intra-Community trade. In the food sector, barriers to trade exist in the form of complex and detailed national food laws, which in many cases prevent the marketing of products throughout the Community. The origins of national regulations in the food sector can be found in a common desire to maintain standards of health and hygiene for consumers. In practice, the maintenance of divergent national rules has restricted the marketing of food produced in another Member State and prevented the establishment of an internal market for the European food industry.

The aim of Community law has been to remove national restrictions to trade, while at the same time ensuring the maintenance of product standards at the highest possible level. In order to understand the full context of the internal market programme, this book will examine the whole framework of legislation affecting the food industry at the European level.

Technical restrictions in the foodstuffs sector have been a major focus of the Community's harmonisation attempts. Restrictions have commonly taken the form of national food laws relating to labelling, packaging and additives, or restrictions on the composition of particular foodstuffs. All these types of technical restrictions have been subject to extensive Community legislation.

In addition to technical restrictions in the foodstuffs sector, the Community has addressed itself to problems associated with intra-Community trade in agricultural products. While the full extent of the Common Agricultural Policy is outside the scope of this book, the availability agricultural goods does have direct implications for the functioning of the internal market. Community action in this sector has concerned the harmonisation of health and hygiene standards for agricultural products, both in order to ensure the health and safety of consumers and in order to facilitate the free functioning of the market by removing national restrictions. The full implications of Community legislation relating to product standards in fruit and vegetables, meat and meat products, dairy products and fish will be examined in detail.

Commission proposals for the harmonisation of standards for foodstuffs and agricultural products are accompanied by proposals to remove fiscal barriers to trade. Differing rates of VAT on food (in the case of the UK, zero rated) and differing rates of excise duties on alcoholic beverages cause price distortions during trade between the Member States. The Commission has insisted that without the removal of all fiscal barriers to trade, the objective of an internal market cannot be fulfilled. However, industry itself has already expressed its fears about any future fiscal harmonisation. While the full impact of current proposals for fiscal harmonisation is not yet apparent, this book will examine potential developments which would affect the food industry.

An appreciation of the legislative issues which are designed to complete a single European market for food and drink is essential for an understanding of the impact of the 1992 programme. Even so, the implications of an internal market will be more far reaching than legislative changes. Organisations and companies operating in the market are well placed to comment on the issues which will be raised for both Community and third country markets. The views included in the book highlight many of the factors which will influence developments in the European food industry into the 1990s.

2. THE SINGLE EUROPEAN MARKET

When the Treaty of Rome was signed in 1957 it contained as a central goal the creation of a single internal market between the Member States of the European Community (EC). The objective was to remove within twelve years all restrictions on the free movement of goods, services and individuals by removing all frontier controls, taxation differentials and other forms of economic distortion. After initial successes, progress towards an internal market for European goods and services lost impetus for a number of reasons, both political and economic. It was against this background of inertia that the Commission formulated its most recent proposals for completion of the internal market by 31 December 1992.

ACHIEVING THE INTERNAL MARKET: 1957 - 1985

During the early years of the Community significant progress was made towards this goal with the achievement of a common customs tariff. This was successfully achieved eighteen months ahead of the twelve year schedule set out for implementation and was accompanied by the establishment of a single customs barrier applicable to all imports from outside the Community. Attention then focussed upon the harmonisation of indirect taxation in a process of negotiation which resulted in the Sixth VAT Directive of 1977.

Despite these achievements, initial commitment within the Community to the goal of an internal market was lost due to a number of interrelated factors. The initial momentum of the Community had been absorbed by successive enlargements which doubled the number of Member States: the original six being joined by Denmark, Ireland and the UK on 1 January 1973, by Greece on 1 January 1981 and by Spain and Portugal on 1 January 1986, to produce a potential European market of 320 million people.

Economic recession of the late 1970s and early 1980s turned Member States economically inward and reinforced commitment to defending national markets against European competitors. Lack of confidence in the benefit of an internal European market ensured that the physical and technical barriers to intra-European trade remained firmly in place. During the oil crisis and years of recession, protectionist measures became more common as each Member State pursued what it perceived to be in its national interests.

At the Community level this protectionism was most obvious in the Council of Ministers, where ministers or their deputies directly represent the interests of Member State governments. After 1966 the whole process of Community decision-making was characterised by the need to reach unanimous decisions in the Council of Ministers. When agreements were reached they tended to be at the lowest common denominator of "national interests".

The protection of national markets was reinforced by public aid to loss-making companies, and a reluctance to grant public procurement contracts to companies located in other Member States.

The continued use of barriers within the Community caused additional costs to be incurred in a number of areas:

- high administrative costs caused by national bureaucratic requirements;

- high transport costs due to delays at borders;

- high costs due to different national standards for goods;

- the duplication of work on separate Research and Developement (R & D) programmes;

- intervention by national governments, preventing open competition;

- national markets keeping costs artificially high and reducing choice for consumers;

- economic expansion limited by the inability to spread across borders.

By 1982 there was a growing realisation within the Member States that many of these problems were contributing to inadequate market performance in the Community, and that national economies could benefit from achieving a unified European market. The belief was that completion of the internal market would enable Europe to reverse the trend of falling demand and production which had caused the EC to fall behind the economic growth of the United States and Japan, and would allow European economies to compete more effectively. As national governments began to renew their commitment to the goal of an internal market the Commission, formally composed of 17 members appointed by national governments and acting in its capacity as initiator of Community policy, presented to the Member States its "White Paper on Completion of the Internal Market" in March 1985.

THE COMMISSION'S WHITE PAPER PROPOSALS

Lord Cockfield's White Paper envisaged that an integrated economy capable of adapting to changing economic circumstances could be achieved by increasing competition, reducing costs, increasing demand for Community products and ultimately causing a reduction in consumer costs. The Commission's intention was to create a single market which was both expanding and flexible, enabling resources to flow to areas of economic growth within the Community.

In embarking on the largest legislative programme in its history, the Commission proposed measures to remove intra-European barriers to the free movement of goods, services, labour and capital in the form of 300 draft directives to be implemented by 31 December 1992. The proposals concerned the removal of three types of barriers:

- physical barriers;

- technical barriers;

- fiscal barriers.

The 300 proposals have subsequently been reduced to 279 by the withdrawal of proposals no longer required and the grouping of others into single proposals. While some proposals were concerned with the elimination of differences in technical specifications, many others were more general in their impact upon whole sectors of economic activity. The White Paper also proposed complementary action in the fields of monetary capacity, social policy, economic and social cohesion and Research and Development. Those areas of Community activity not subject to proposals in the White Paper were agricultural policy, budgeting matters, monetary union, or the EMS (except indirectly in terms of monetary capacity). Overall, the White Paper had three objectives:

- unifying the twelve national markets into a single European-wide market;

- ensuring that the single market also becomes an expanding and growing market;

- ensuring that the market is flexible so that resources flow into areas of greatest economic advantage.

The intention was to remove all barriers between Member States since the Commission feared that the maintenance of any internal frontier controls could perpetuate the costs and disadvantages of a fragmented European market. In order to achieve this objective, the Commission adopted a new policy of harmonisation and mutual recognition of national laws.

Harmonisation and mutual recognition

The White Paper marked a significant departure from previous Commission attempts to progress towards a single European market, which had relied on the harmonisation of national laws and regulations at every level (Article 100 of the Treaty of Rome). The innovative element of the White Paper was contained in the form of the dual strategy of minimum harmonisation and mutual recognition.

While harmonisation was still envisaged for the standardisation of basic rules, a supplementary concept was that technical standards which differ between Member States should be mutually recognised in order to allow goods and services originating in another Member State free access into a national market. While acknowledging that the internal market cannot be completed by 1992 if the Community relies exclusively on Article 100 of the Treaty of Rome, the intention of the White Paper is that the role of harmonisation will decrease as new approaches lead to quicker and less problematic progress.

In terms of the decision-making capacity of the Community, the fact that harmonisation based on Article 100 requires a unanimous vote in the Council has delayed the adoption of draft directives. Even where Article 100 remains appropriate, the Commission view was that more flexible means of decision-making were necessary.

By extending the idea of mutual recognition to the provision of services, the Commission envisaged that Member States would adopt a procedure of home country control. This would involve the supervision of European-wide activities being the responsibility of an appointed authority in the Member State in which a company has its head office. In moving towards the principle of mutual recognition, the White Paper proposed to speed up the decision-making process and reduce the regulatory burden on companies wishing to operate on a Community-wide basis. This initiative will ultimately require a high level of information exchange and policy co-ordination between national supervisory authorities.

Removal of physical barriers

The Commission's White Paper embodied the belief that a complete internal market requires not only a simplification of harmonisation and mutual recognition of goods and services, but also the abolition of all internal frontier controls. Physical barriers at customs posts and immigration controls remain the most obvious restrictions. For industry and commerce these barriers impose an unnecessary burden in terms of border formalities and transportation costs which damage the competitiveness of goods.

While customs posts were abolished in the early years of the Community, border controls have been retained by Member States as a means of enforcing fiscal, commercial, health and security regulations. In an attempt to abolish all such frontier controls, the White Paper intended that Member States would replace border checks with other methods of control, improving co-operation and information exchange between national authorities.

Control of goods

In an attempt to eliminate border controls the Commission has sought a commitment from the Member States that no new controls on the movement of goods will be introduced. This is known as "standstill". This may be achieved by avoiding the duplication of controls on both sides of the frontier.

Commercial and economic policy

Article 115 of the Treaty of Rome stipulates that the Commission may deny a Member State the right to exclude quota products from free movement within the Community. On the basis of Article 115, the White Paper stressed that the abolition of national and regional quotas could be achieved by 1992 only if the Member States co-operate in renouncing frontier controls completely. However, the Commission acknowledges that there will be a continuing need for some form of control in limited areas, particularly until such time that all national protection measures and regional Community quotas can be abolished. In addition, the Commission has announced its commitment to honour all obligations to GATT.

The Commission further intends to step up the monitoring of exchange control measures which present a potential obstacle to payments for liberalised trades in goods, services or capital. By 1992 any remaining currency controls will have to be applied by means other than frontier controls.

Removal of technical barriers

The Commission envisages that, through the elimination of technical barriers, the internal market will develop its economic and industrial dimension by enabling industries to make economies of scale and become more competitive.

Manufactured goods

The traditional Commission strategy of seeking the adoption of harmonisation directives in order to remove technical barriers has in the past proved difficult. Therefore the White Paper emphasised that a genuine unified market could not be achieved unless mutual recognition of national standards and regulations in general replaces the systematic harmonisation of technical standards. Harmonisation of technical standards is retained only where necessary to ensure public health and safety; elsewhere mutual recognition becomes the norm. The general rule laid down in the White Paper is that if a product is lawfully manufactured and marketed in one Member State, there is no reason why it should not be sold freely throughout the Community.

The Commission considered that barriers created by different national products add extra costs and distort product patterns. As a result the maintenance of these barriers forces manufacturers to focus on national rather than European markets. This principle applies not only to the free movement of goods (as established by the Cassis de Dijon Case, where the Court of Justice ruled that a product manufactured and marketed in one Member State must be also allowed to compete elsewhere in the Community) but also to the free movement of individuals and the freedom to provide services.

Services

The Treaty of Rome established the principle that freedom to provide services should be available throughout the Community. Failure to implement this principle led the Commission to propose that a free market in services could be best achieved by mutual recognition of national regulations, underpinned by the harmonisation of basic rules. In setting out the Commission's intention to open up the whole market, including new markets such as information technology, traditional services such as the financial sector, and public procurement contracts, the White

Paper gave formal recognition to the importance of freedom to provide services in the creation of an internal market.

The White Paper also contained the proposal that Community citizens should be free to engage in their professions throughout the Community without encountering national barriers to their movement. In order to achieve this aim, it is anticipated that the general system of mutual recognition will be applicable to national academic and professional qualifications.

Furthermore, the White Paper envisaged that the removal of internal borders would be accompanied by the strengthening of pan-European research and technology development programmes in order to prevent the duplication of resources caused by fragmented national research programmes.

Removal of fiscal barriers

Since fiscal checks cause significant delays at the Community's internal frontiers, the Commission's objective is that all internal economic frontiers will be removed by 1992. The proposed removal of frontier controls has widespread implications for national indirect taxation, however differing levels of indirect taxation are incompatible with the goal of a single market since both VAT and excise duties enter into the fiscal price of goods and services. Building on the basis provided by the Sixth VAT Directive of 1977, the White Paper suggested three methods of removing fiscal barriers:

- Council agreement to intensify efforts to harmonise the VAT base and structure of excises, using existing Commission proposals as its basis;

- a Commission "standstill" proposal to ensure that existing differences in the number of VAT rates and the coverage of excises are not widened;

- a Commission proposal for target rates/norms, together with proposed ranges of variations. Member States would then have the option of moving indirect taxation towards the common rate immediately or in a series of shifts.

Further progress in the removal of fiscal barriers is likely to result from the abolition of fiscal frontier controls, while on a macroeconomic level the White Paper urged closer co-operation of the Member States within the European Monetary System (EMS).

IMPLICATIONS FOR INDUSTRY, COMMERCE AND INDIVIDUALS

The full implications of a Single European Market remain difficult to quantify. As the Commission has stressed, gains will only be achieved if the programme for removing all barriers to trade is fully implemented. However, the Commission remains optimistic of the potential for achieving substantial benefits.

Industry and commerce

The Commission's own report on the benefits of the completed internal market, "The European Challenge - 1992" (Paolo Cecchini, 1988), highlighted the potential for European industry to improve its competitiveness. The Cecchini Report predicted that the overall economic impact of an internal market for goods and services could amount to approximately 5 % of total EC GNP (200 billion ECU). In the completed internal market, costs and prices for intermediate goods would be reduced, while factors of production provide the opportunity to expand both within the Community and in third-country markets. The potential for expansion would be greatest in markets which have previously been fragmented.

However, this gain will not be felt immediately after the 1992 deadline has been reached. Despite the overall economic gain predicted in a Single Market, the Cecchini Report acknowledges that industry may experience a reduction in short-term profits due to a downward convergence of prices. It is in the long-term that the Commission predicts economic advantages. The stimulus of the completed internal market will create a new competitive environment, a scaling up of production, an increased efficiency and greater product innovation.

The Commission's projected scenario of an expanding European market starts from the assumption that the removal of physical, technical and fiscal barriers to trade will boost competition and act as a stimulus to the market. The Commission anticipates that the overall consequences will be:

- cost reduction as a result of economies of scale operating in both production and business organisation;

- greater efficiency within companies;

- new patterns of competition between industries and a reallocation of resources;

- increased innovation in research and development as new products and manufacturing processes are generated by new market conditions.

In the Commission's model of a Single European Market, increased industrial competitiveness would be the result of lower input costs as labour, capital, equipment and components are obtained at more competitive prices.

It is anticipated that industry and commerce will respond to a new competitive market environment by developing a greater concentration of business activities and reducing overheads. The exploitation of economies of scale would be applicable not only to production costs, but also to business organisation, research and development, marketing and finance. In all these areas a reduction in costs can be expected.

While large firms will seek opportunities to exploit economies of scale, Cecchini suggests that smaller firms will benefit directly from the removal of administrative regulatory burdens which will accompany the internal market programme. The flexibility of small firms would enable them to seize new opportunities in specialised sectors of a new market.

General economic growth

The direct reductions in costs and prices which the Cecchini Report has predicted would lead to increased growth in domestic and international demand. Specifically, projected mid-term economic gains have been highlighted as:

- a major relaunch of economic activity;

- a cooling down of the economy as consumer prices are deflated;

- a relaxation of budgetary and external constraints;

- a reduction in levels of unemployment.

Overall, it is anticipated that the stimuli of increased trade and heightened competition will lead to a reduction in the costs of large-scale production as existing capacity becomes better utilised and each industry is restructured to deal with new market forces.

Public procurement

The Cecchini Report pinpointed the liberalisation of procurement markets as an area which will have a much greater impact on the general economy than will the removal of customs barriers.

Significant potential exists for large reductions in purchasing and investment costs, since capital goods in particular would become cheaper under the pressure of foreign competition in a Single Market.

Individuals

The aim of the internal market programme itself goes much wider than the removal of barriers to trade in the Community. The Commission anticipates direct benefits to the individual in terms of:

- health and safety at work;

- rights of employed persons;

- education;

- travel;

- consumer goods.

The Commission has consistently stressed the importance of the parallel goal of social cohesion. The Commission's intention is to create Community-wide provisions on health and safety at work in order to safeguard employees.

A developing single European market will require a flexible and mobile labour market capable of providing the resources for sustained economic growth. The Commission has proposed that this objective may be achieved by ending restrictions on the free movement of workers and by ensuring freedom of establishment for the professions throughout the Community. This would be achieved by mutual recognition of professional qualifications by the Member States.

Employment opportunities of a single market will be accompanied by job losses in other sectors as a restructuring of European market gathers momentum. Attempts to alleviate economic and social disparities will be coordinated by a Community social policy.

New programmes for educational exchanges in the form of ERASMUS (educational exchanges) and YES (Europe for Youth) are designed to strengthen social links between the peoples of the Community.

Travel opportunities for individuals will improve as a result of the removal of border controls, the removal of transport monopolies, an end to artificially high fares and the provision of health care to individuals throughout the Community.

For consumers, the Commission anticipates that the benefits of the internal market will accrue from a reduction in prices, an increase in product choice and an improvement in quality. Open competition created by the internal market programme will ensure that the consumer will no longer experience large variations in prices between countries.

3. THE SINGLE EUROPEAN ACT

At the Luxembourg European Council meeting of December 1985, the Member States adopted all the main proposals contained in the Cockfield White Paper. In urging the Council of Ministers to work within the Commission's 1992 deadline, the heads of state of the twelve Member States embodied the Commission's proposals for completion of the internal market in the Single European Act (SEA). The Act is "single" in the sense that, after early discussion, it was decided to include in one Act provisions both to complete the internal market and to bring European Political Cooperation formally within the Treaty of Rome.

In providing the first major revision of the Treaty of Rome since 1957, the Single European Act reflects a renewed desire among the Member States to prevent the economic fragmentation of the Community. However, the SEA goes beyond a declaration of intent to achieve economic integration by embodying a political commitment by the Member States to progress towards the goal of a much closer European Union.

The SEA provides both a legal framework and a political commitment by Member States to achieve implementation of draft directives considered necessary for completion of the internal market by 31 December 1992. Furthermore, in acknowledging the economic, social, regional and environmental implications of a single market in Europe, the SEA has provided for progress not only in terms of the removal of barriers to the free movement of goods, services and individuals, but also in associated areas likely to be affected by the internal market programme.

The White Paper had highlighted the institutional and economic problems which the Community faced. The Single European Act now provides a new impetus for progress in these areas and set new policy objectives for the Member States. In an attempt to ensure that the 1992 deadline is adhered to, the SEA amends the Treaty of Rome by:

- introducing new policy objectives for the Community;

- streamlining the decision-making process in order to provide an institutional framework capable of carrying through the Commission's programme for completion of the internal market;

- introducing other institutional reforms.

The Single European Act was ratified by nine Member States on 17 February 1986. Denmark later signed after a national referendum on 27 February. Greece did not ratify the Act until January 1987 and, following a Supreme Court ruling, Irish ratification was received after a referendum in June 1987. The SEA finally came into force on 1 July 1987.

Policy objectives

The SEA introduces new policy objectives for the Community in five main areas:

- formal recognition of the EMS and ECU (monetary capacity of the Community);

- social policy;

- economic and social cohesion;

- research and technological development;

- environmental policy.

The Commission holds responsibility for policy initiation and is anxious to see the adoption of its draft proposals within the self-imposed timescale. In this capacity it has deliberately refrained from attaching different priorities to draft directives in an attempt to prevent the progress of those proposals considered less urgent being hindered.

Monetary capacity

The SEA requires that Member States "shall take account of the experience acquired in co-operation within the framework of the European Monetary System (EMS) and in developing the ECU".

It further stipulates that where economic and monetary policy necessitates institutional changes, unanimous approval will be required by the Member States after prior consultation with the Monetary Committee and the Committee of Governors of the Central Banks.

Social policy

The Commission has stressed that the achievement of an internal market will require freedom of movement for both skilled and unskilled workers throughout the Community. The Single European Act anticipates progress in this area by requiring that Member States give particular attention to basic social provisions by seeking to harmonise health and safety measures.

The Act does not envisage that these measures would impose constraints on small or medium-sized enterprises (SMEs) which would inhibit their development.

Economic and social cohesion

Progress towards a Single Market brings with it implications for industrial competition and technological development. Changes in market conditions will require an improved standard of vocational training, redeployment of workers in new industries and a reappraisal of the economic role of whole regions.

By acknowledging an increased role for EC structural funds, the Single European Act indicates an intention to combat the adverse economic and social consequences of the internal market programme at the EC level.

The SEA proposes that the following structural funds should be used to reduce disparities between better-off and poorer regions of the Community:

- European Agricultural Guidance and Guarantee Fund;

- European Social Fund;

- European Regional Development Fund.

Research and technological development

The SEA stipulates that the Community should have as its aim the strengthening of the scientific and technological basis of European industry in order to encourage competitiveness on an international level. These objectives will be achieved by the following means:

- implementing technological development and development programmes;

- promoting co-operation with third countries;

- information exchange on the results of research;

- encouraging the training and mobility of researchers.

In addition the Community will adopt a multiannual framework programme to involve participation by Member States, third countries and international organisations.

Environment

The SEA lays down the objectives of Community action in the field of environmental policy. On these decisions the Council shall decide which decisions are to be taken by majority voting.

Reform of the decision-making process

The SEA contains reforms of the Community decision-making process in the following areas:

- extending the use of qualified majority voting in the Council;

- increasing the powers of the European Parliament.

Qualified majority voting in the Council

Since 1966, virtually all decision-making in the Council has been on the basis of the "Luxembourg Compromise" whereby, on French insistence, it was agreed that no decision could be taken in the Council if it conflicted with the "vital national interests" of a Member State.

In recognising the need for an accelerated decision-making process in order to facilitate the passage of legislation required to complete the internal market by 1992, the SEA brought an end to much of the institutional deadlock which had characterised the EC legislative process by providing for an increased use of majority voting in the Council. Since the implementation of the Single European Act, qualified majority voting has been used on most issues which have as their objective the completion of the internal market. Unanimity is retained only for issues on which "vital national interests" are at stake, specifically in the fields of taxation, free movement of persons and the rights and interests of employed persons. On environmental issues the Council will decide by unanimity which issues are suitable for decisions by qualified majority voting.

Where qualified majority voting is to apply, each Member State has a weighting according to its population: France, Germany, Italy and the UK have ten votes each; Spain has eight votes; Belgium, Greece, the Netherlands and Portugal have five votes each; Denmark and Ireland have three votes and Luxembourg two votes. A majority decision will constitute fifty-four out of seventy-six votes.

Powers of the European Parliament

The SEA supplements the existing consultation procedure between the Council and the European Parliament (EP), consisting of 518 democratically elected MEPs, which prior to July 1986 acted only as a consultative body on most EC affairs by giving an official Opinion on Commission proposals for legislation. The SEA strengthened the role of the EP, and consequently the democratic legitimacy of the Community, by introducing an additional "co-operation procedure" under which the EP not only gives an Opinion on Commission proposals but also on the common position adopted by the Council on a Commission proposal. The cooperation procedure is applicable to legislative proposals emanating from the following policy areas:

- discrimination on grounds of nationality;

- free movement of persons (excluding rights and interests);

- freedom of establishment;

- mutual recognition of professional qualifications;

- liberalisation of capital movements;

- sea and air transport;

- harmonisation policy;

- improvement of working conditions;

- the European Regional Development Fund;

- measures relating to the implementation on research and development and demonstration programmes.

Within the new co-operation procedure, once the Council has reached a common position on a Commission proposal after obtaining the opinion of the EP, it must then communicate to the Parliament its reasons for doing so. The EP may then either approve the Council's decision, or may reject or amend it. Any rejection or amendment must be by an absolute majority of MEPs. If the decision is approved, the proposal will be adopted. Failure of the EP to act within three months will result in automatic adoption of the proposal. If the proposal is rejected by the EP, the proposal will only be adopted if the Council can reach unanimity. If the EP amends the proposal, it must be re-examined by the Commission within one month. The Commission reviews the EP's amendments and may revise its proposal accordingly. The revised proposal is then returned to the Council, which may adopt it by qualified majority voting, amend it by unanimity, or adopt EP amendments not approved by the Commission by unanimous voting. If the Council does not act within three months, the proposal falls, unless the Council and EP agree to a one month extension of this time limit.

The SEA also gives the EP powers of veto over future applications for membership of the Community and over association agreements with third countries.

Other institutional reforms

European Council

The European Council, the summit meetings between the heads of governments which take place two or three times a year in Brussels and in each Member State holding the presidency of the Council of Ministers, deals with matters of general political and economic cooperation. During the 1970s, while the detail of policy formation remained the function of the Council of Ministers, new policy initiatives increasingly emerged from European Council meetings between the heads of governments.

Despite its increasing role in Community affairs since the first summit meetings in the early 1970s, the Single European Act gives official status to the European Council in the Treaty of Rome for the first time. Beyond the formal recognition of its existence, the SEA contains no implications for the role of the European Council.

Commission

The Committee of Permanent Representatives (COREPER), consisting of permanent representatives of the national governments, developed in both an administrative and a decision-making capacity as the work of the Council became more complex. Despite the increasing involvement of COREPER in the legislative process since the late 1960s, its existence is not recognised by the Treaty of Rome.

The SEA provides a greater role for the Commission in the implementation of Council decisions, taking over many of the routine functions carried out by COREPER. However, the Council may stipulate certain requirements of this involvement and may reserve the right to retain implementing powers itself. This provision reinforces the watchdog role of the Commission, which can ultimately take either national governments or companies to the European Court of Justice for non-compliance with Community legislation.

The Court of First Instance

In order to streamline the enforcement of Community law, the SEA provides for the creation of a Court of First Instance, attached to the European Court of Justice and empowered to deal with disputes arising from competition law (excluding anti-dumping), steel quotas and other ECSC levies, and staff problems of the Community institutions.

European Political Co-operation

The SEA gives formal recognition for the first time to political co-operation between the Member States at the level of meetings between political directors of foreign offices. In addition, provision is made for the establishment in Brussels of a small secretariat to assist the Presidency in the preparation and implementation of political co-operation initiatives.

Problems envisaged in completing the internal market

One of the main successes of Lord Cockfield's White Paper lay in the fact that, by accepting no compromise, the Commission has been able to insist that all barriers to the single market must be removed if the goal is to be reached by 31 December 1992. Once the 1992 deadline was adopted by the Single European Act, it became a positive slogan for achieving completion of the internal market.

However, despite the emergence of a clear consensus on the benefits of unified market and the increased use of majority voting in the Council, as the deadline approaches it will become increasingly difficult to ensure that all proposals are adopted prior to that date.

Once directives have been adopted by the Council, implementation by national authorities may be a slow process. Each directive stipulates a time limit by which Member States must take measures necessary to comply with EC law. However, there is always the possibility that some Member States may either fail to implement directives altogether, or may retain some regulatory controls which fall outside the scope of White Paper proposals.

A Member State which fails to fulfill the requirements of Community legislation will face prosecution in the European Court of Justice. In practice, much will depend on the interpretation of European case law derived from the Cassis de Dijon Case, which ruled that products made and marketed in one Member State must be allowed entry into other Community markets. No quick solution is available when Community law is violated. The Commission is only able to seek rectification in the Court of Justice in a process which could take up to three or four years.

Perhaps a more potent means of ensuring that all Member States comply with Community law lies in the commercial and political pressures imposed on a Member State when eleven other Community members demonstrate their commitment to complete the internal market by the 1992 deadline.

THE LEGISLATIVE PROCESS

At the preliminary stage of the legislative process, the Commission generally initiates an explanatory study in which consultations are held with national experts on the more technical aspects of proposals; a working paper will be issued on the basis of these discussions. Draft legislation can then be drawn up by the Directorate General of the Commission which is responsible for that policy area. The Commission, acting as a collegiate body, can then formally adopt the proposal. The proposal first emerges in public when it appears as a Commission (COM) document and in the "Communication" series of the Official Journal (OJ C).

Once the Council has received the Commission's proposal, it will in turn convey the draft legislation to both the European Parliament (EP) and the Economic and Social Committee for their official Opinions. The

Economic and Social Committee (ECOSOC) consists of 189 representatives of employers' associations, trade unions, consumer associations, and other professional and interest groups. The Committee must be consulted on all Commission proposals affecting issues relating to the EEC and Euratom treaties. Opinions of the EP and ECOSOC are delivered following debate in the monthly plenary sessions of both these bodies. Debate is based on information provided by "rapporteurs" of the specialist committees assigned to scrutinise each proposal in detail. Rapporteurships will have been allocated in proportion to the representation of political groupings in the institutions as a whole. Additional viewpoints may also be taken into consideration by the committees through contact with outside groups and Commission officials. The Opinions of the EP and the Economic and Social Committee are published in the "Communication" series of the Official Journal. Opinions are not binding on the Member States, but must be received before the Council can proceed with the formulation of legislation. Furthermore, the Commission may decide to amend its proposals accordingly.

In theory, Opinions should be received by the Council before it begins to consider the details of a proposal. In practice, there is nothing to prevent the Council from commencing work on a proposal at the same time as it is being discussed by the EP and the Economic and Social Committee.

Consideration of a proposal by the Council is carried out via the twelve permanent representatives of the Member States, supported by a network of national officials. This is the Committee of Permanent Representatives (COREPER). A pyramid of committees from the permanent representatives, through permanent specialist working committees to temporary ad hoc committees, meet to establish a framework within which the Member States can reach agreement, or at the very least pinpoint the main areas of conflict which Council negotiations will encounter. A proposal gradually filters through the COREPER network before discussions take place in the Council. However, despite the involvement of COREPER in the day-to-day business of the Community, it is not recognised within the Treaty of Rome as a formal decision-making body. In practice, many routine decisions are taken by COREPER officials.

When a proposal reaches the Council of Ministers, the Member States are required to reach a decision by qualified majority voting on those issues specified in the Single European Act. Only where a policy concerns issues of a "vital national interest" or fiscal matters will the Council vote on the basis of unanimity.

Under the pre-SEA decision-making procedure, once an agreement had been reached in the Council by unanimous voting draft legislation was deemed to have been adopted. Since 1 July 1987, the Single European Act has introduced a second level of legislative involvement for the EP, broadly speaking those areas in which qualified majority voting now operates in the Council, including those issues relating to completion of the internal market (with the exception of fiscal policy and some derogation for environmental policy).

The legislative process outlined above remains in place for those policy areas in which the SEA does not provide for the new "co-operation procedure" between EP and Council.

The Co-operation Procedure

Under the terms of the SEA, the existing legislative process remains intact, but adds to this what amounts to a second reading of draft legislation for the EP. Once the Council has reached a common position on a proposal, after taking into account the Opinions of the EP and the Economic and Social Committee, the Council is now required to re-submit its proposals to the EP, together with its reasons for adopting that common position. On the basis of this information, the Parliament may either accept, amend or reject the Council's decision. If the EP accepts a proposal, it must be reconsidered by the Commission within one month. The Commission may either incorporate the EP's amendments in a revised proposal or alternatively ignore Parliamentary Opinion. The Commission then re-submits its proposal to the Council, which may accept the proposal by qualified majority voting. The Council may amend the Commission's proposal only on the basis of unanimity. If the Council fails to adopt the proposal within three months, the proposal will fall. This period may be extended by one month by agreement between the Council and the EP.

If the Parliament rejects the Council's proposals outright, the Council may still adopt it on the basis of unanimity.

Types of European Community Legislation

Regulations — are immediately binding on the governments of the Member States. No alteration of national law is required for implementation.

Directives — set out a specific result which must be achieved by the Member States. Member States are required to implement national laws necessary to comply with a Directive within a specified time limit.

Decisions — set out specific rulings applicable to the particular Member States, companies or individuals. Decisions are binding in their entirety upon those to which they refer.

Recommendations and Opinions — are not binding on the Member States. They give a Community view and attempt to encourage good practices.

4. CORPORATE ISSUES

BACKGROUND

In addition to the many specific measures proposed under the internal market programme there are others which are very broad in their application and will affect many industries. While it is beyond the scope of this book to examine these in detail, no account of the single market would be complete if it did not indicate their existence.

The corporate issues which are considered here relate to the Community policy on company law including mergers and acquisitions, mutual recognition of professional qualifications, and corporate taxation. Further general issues of this type are transport, intellectual property and product liability. A brief account is also given to the Community research and development programmes of relevance to the food industry.

COMPANY LAW

The aim of the measures in the field of company law is to simplify and harmonise the organisation and operation of company business throughout the Community. The restructuring of the industry of Europe which is an inevitable consequence of the internal market can be achieved more easily by this means. Co-operation across the Community's internal frontiers is essential if industries are to enhance their market position, particularly in high-technology industries and in financial services. Until now, takeover bids have been the only means of achieving restructuring at the Community level, since it has been legally impossible to merge companies from different Member States, bound by different national laws.

The Commission's approach to the problem has two sides. Firstly a number of measures have been introduced towards the co-ordination of national laws, based on Article 54(3)g of the Treaty of Rome; and seven company law directives were adopted between 1968 and 1984. However, the proposed Fifth Company Law Directive, proposed in 1972 to harmonise the structure of public limited companies, has met considerable difficulties; principally due to fundamental differences on the question of worker participation.

The other harmonisation measures concern single person incorporation, cross-border mergers (the Tenth Company Law Directive), publishing and other requirements for company accounts and consolidated accounts, liquidation, and the relationship of undertakings in a group. The last three proposals are yet to be tabled. The proposed rules governing takeover bids were tabled at the end of December 1988.

The second type of approach has been to propose the European Company Statute, which offers the formation of a transnational company, independent of national laws. The Statute is based on a proposal first moved in 1970, and shelved in 1982 when completion of its first reading by a Council working party was made conditional on the development of proposals for harmonising national laws on groups of companies. It has now been revived in 1988.

The Statute will make provision for coexistence with national systems of company law; for worker participation at the supervisory level and in development of company strategy; for information and consultation of workers; for the operation of groups of companies, whose economic requirements may not match the legal independence of each company; and finally the question of tax treatment of a European company, which will be according to the laws of the state in which it is domiciled.

MERGERS AND ACQUISITIONS

The restructuring of industry associated with the development of the internal market has made it essential for the Community to develop a single, comprehensive policy on company mergers. The 1987 report on competition policy showed that cross-border mergers increased by 45% between mid 1986 and mid 1987; the same rate as national mergers within the Community.

The main proposal on merger control (the regulation on the control of concentration between undertakings) was proposed in March 1988. It is derived from a proposal first made in 1973 but persistently blocked by the UK, West Germany and France; which already have their own merger control provisions. The proposed EC regulation is not specifically a part of the internal market programme, although closely related to it, and requires unanimous approval of the Council of Ministers.

The major innovation of the proposal is to require advance authorisation from the Commission for all larger cross-border mergers with a Community dimension, i.e. two or more of the companies involved have their main operations in different Member States, or if one of them has substantial activities in more than one Member State. Until now, the

Commission has only been empowered to outlaw mergers after they have taken place, under Articles 85 and 86 of the Treaty of Rome.

The 1988 original proposal requires prior notification of proposed mergers except where the combined worldwide turnover of the undertakings is less than ECU 1 billion, or where it is greater than that but the combined worldwide turnover of the undertaking to be acquired is less than ECU 50 million; or where all the undertakings involved have more than three-quarters of their Community turnover within one Member State.

At the end of 1988, there were still substantial obstacles to the adoption of the proposal, principally from the UK and West Germany. The Commission made some moves toward compromise in its removal of the requirement for a month's freeze on merger plans while the Commission decided on whether to launch an enquiry; and also by offering to double to ECU 2 billion the level of combined turnover which triggered the requirement for advance clearance. However, agreement was not reached by Council at the last meeting of the year, and the responsibility now passes from the outgoing competition Commissioner Peter Sutherland, to his successor, Sir Leon Brittan.

MUTUAL RECOGNITION OF PROFESSIONAL QUALIFICATIONS AND EMPLOYMENT RIGHTS

The 1985 White Paper stated that Community citizens "should be free to engage in their professions throughout the Community if they so wish, without the obligation to adhere to formalities which could serve to discourage such movement". Until then, the Commission had tried to achieve harmonisation of training for each profession, and individual directives were adopted for members of a number of sectors of the medical profession, and architects.

However, these directives were extremely difficult to reach adoption (the architects' directive took 17 years), and the White Paper proposed a new approach in the principle of mutual recognition of the degrees and diplomas awarded after comparable university studies in the various Member States.

The proposal will cover about 80 professions, and those already covered by their own specific directives will continue to be so. Members of professions within the scope of the general directive will then be guaranteed recognition of their qualifications in the other Member States. If their education is substantially different from that of the Member State in which they wish to work, they may be required to undertake a test or period of supervised practice; but it will not be necessary to repeat the whole course of training.

European legislation already in operation aims to guarantee rights of geographical and occupational mobility to workers, and rights of social integration. Nationals of Member States may enter and live in another Member State, and take up employment there under the same conditions and terms as nationals of that country.

Further legislation is under development to establish recognition of diplomas, rights of family reunification, and extension of the rights of residence; including the extension of validity of the EC residence permit from five to ten years.

CORPORATE TAXATION

Since 1969 the Commission has made a number of attempts to harmonise company taxation in the Community. The moves have been given greater urgency by the internal market programme, but the area is particularly difficult due to its administration by national governments and the requirement for unanimous agreement in the Council of Ministers. The Commission considers it essential that the varying tax systems of the Member States do not have disproportionate influence on the location of investment by industry, and on production costs; to the detriment of the free movement of capital within the Community.

There are currently five proposals under consideration, but these are being revised and updated. The proposals concern elimination of double taxation, a harmonised taxation system for companies, tax arrangements for the carry-over of losses, the taxation of mergers, and the harmonisation of taxes on transactions in securities.

TRANSPORT

The Treaty of Rome included a requirement for the development of a common transport policy, and the right to provide transport services throughout the Community is vital to such a policy. However, progress has been slow, and the Court of Justice has taken action against the Council of Ministers for its failure to act in this area. Since 1986 a number of major decisions have quickened the pace of change.

The internal market programme includes a large number of measures to remove restrictions and distortions to trade in transport service including air, sea, road and inland waterways.

On air transport, a package of measures adopted in December 1987 makes requirements on fares, market and capacity sharing, and competition. Sea transport is also largely deregulated already by the adoption at the end of 1986 of regulations to stipulate freedom to offer sea transport services between Member States or to third countries (although not within Member States), and on competition, access to cargoes in ocean trade and unfair pricing practices by third country companies.

Of much greater direct relevance to the food industry are the measures on liberalisation of road transport. In June 1988 substantial progress was made by the agreement to remove all quota restrictions on goods transport by 1 January 1993. The licence for road haulage will allow carriers to operate throughout the Community. Requirements on the fixing of rates for the carriage of goods by road between Member State were also adopted in June 1988.

Further measures on road transport which still await adoption concern the operation of road haulage or passenger services within a Member State by non-resident carriers (two separate proposals), common rules for the international carriage of passengers by coach and bus, and the charging of transport infrastructure costs to heavy goods vehicles. A proposal on the conditions for transport services by inland waterway offered in a Member State by non-resident carriers is likely to be adopted in 1989.

Border Controls

The Commission's objective is to eliminate the barriers and controls at the Community's internal frontiers. There are a range of various checks and requirements associated with crossing the national borders, which for the transport of goods include the imposition of VAT and excise duties, the compilation of trade statistics, and regulation of tariff restrictions.

One of the most obvious signs of the coming single internal market is the Single Administrative Document (SAD) which is the one document now required for transport of goods across internal borders, and has been in operation since 1 January 1988. At the completion of the internal market, border controls will cease for all goods at internal frontiers, and for goods of Community origin in trade between Member States. The SAD will then also cease to be required for Community goods being traded between Member States, except for a few special cases of goods in transit.

Most of the legislation relating to the abolition of border controls has already been adopted. This includes the introduction of a single customs check at entry into a Member State in relation to the TIR system;

abolition of the guarantee of payment of customs duties except for high-value or high-charge goods; abolition of postal fees for customs presentation of goods sent between Member States, and the coaches section of legislation on duty-free admission of fuel in the fuel tanks of commercial vehicles: the corresponding section on lorries awaits adoption.

Further legislation has been tabled and awaits adoption on abolition of exit customs formalities for goods apart from those under TIR, and proposing an alternative system for collection of trade statistics after abolition of the internal frontier controls. Finally, a further measure will be necessary to adapt the EC transit legislation on the completion of the internal market.

Animal and plant health controls

Border controls which specifically relate to animal and plant health are examined in detail in Chapter 6: Removal of Physical Barriers.

The general principle observed by the Commission in this area is to seek a rationalisation of the various requirements of the Member States. The question is difficult and sensitive, and a large number of proposals are outstanding.

INTELLECTUAL PROPERTY - PATENTS AND TRADE MARKS

The 1985 White Paper pointed out that differences in the national laws of Member States could cause a barrier to trade. Article 30 of the Treaty of Rome prohibits measures which are equivalent to quantitative restrictions on imports; and case law relating to Article 30 has reduced the attempts to use national intellectual property rights as a means to restrict imports. However, it is still advisable for companies to obtain patent or trade mark coverage in all the Member States where their products are marketed; which is an expensive and repetitive task.

In December 1988 the Directive to approximate the laws of Member States on trade marks was adopted: this will apply to all registered national trade marks for goods and services, and whether individual, collective or guarantee trade marks. The Directive gives a standard definition of trade mark signs, and a list of the grounds for refusal or invalidity. A further proposal is to introduce a Community trade mark, which would be valid throughout the Community. Adoption is still awaited of the regulation to implement the Community trade mark, and there are also proposals on the rules of procedure for the Boards of

Appeal, on fees, and on the site and working language of the Community Trade Marks Office.

A separate proposed Directive outlines the legal protection of biotechnological inventions, which will be relevant to food additives, plant breeding and seeds as well as other sectors not related to food, and which should come into effect on 30 September 1990.

The Community Patent Convention (the Luxembourg Convention), signed in 1975 by the then nine Member States, is still under discussion and only slow progress towards implementation has been made. The objective is to agree a text which can come into operation on 31 December 1992 as the working procedures for the granting of a single Community patent which would be recognised in all of the Member States. The major outstanding problems which stand in the way of a Community patent are the criteria for allocating expenditure and procedures to amend them, and the working languages. An intergovernmental conference in December 1988 was set up to try to resolve these difficulties.

The Community Patent Convention would, when agreed, extend the patent protection afforded by the existing European Patent Convention of 1973 (the Munich Convention). This grants a European patent from its office in Munich, and this gives patent rights in the states which are contracting to the Convention through a single application. These contracting states are not the same as the Community Member States: they include Switzerland, Sweden and Austria, but not the EC States Ireland, Denmark or Portugal. The European patent is considered as a group of national patents, and legal disputes are resolved by the national law courts of participating states.

In contrast, the Community patent will be a single instrument valid in all Member States. It will be necessary for the Convention to establish a legal mechanism for disputes on patent infringement. An existing proposal has been made for the establishment of a Community Patents Appeal Court (COPAC), and each Member State will assign some of its courts to be responsible for litigation on Community patents; the rulings to be binding throughout the Community.

PRODUCT LIABILITY

Council Directive 85/374/EEC concerning liability for defective products required the Member States to incorporate its provisions into national law by 30 July 1988. The Directive provides that all persons injured by a defective product will be able to claim compensation from the seller. The claimant is only required to prove that injury resulted from a defective product. The UK implemented the Directive in the Consumer Protection Act of 1987. Prior to this, the position in the UK was that only the buyer of defective goods was protected under the Sale of Goods Act 1979.

The Directive provides a defence of "development risks": a seller will not be liable if the defect could not be discovered according to the state of scientific and technical knowledge at the time when the product was put on the market. Furthermore, the Directive is not applicable to primary agricultural products.

The implications of the 1985 Directive for the food industry are significant. Manufacturers will need to reassess both their product liability insurance policies, and procedures for the recall of defective products.

Only Greece, Italy and the UK implemented the Directive by the deadline of 30 June 1988. Towards the end of 1988 the Commission began infringement proceedings against the nine Member States which had failed to comply with the Directive. Separate infringement proceedings were brought against Italy and the UK for failure to conform to the specific requirements of the Directive.

COMMUNITY RESEARCH AND DEVELOPMENT PROGRAMMES

The Single European Act specifically points out the Community's intention to strengthen the scientific and technological basis of industry in Europe. It aims to do this by promoting international competition and research intended to complement that of individual Member States.

Collaborative European research relevant to the food industry has been organised under several programmes operating since 1978: the COST 90 and COST 91 programmes on the effects of processing on the physical properties of foodstuffs, and the effects of thermal processing and distribution on the quality and nutritive value of food. (COST is the European initiative for cooperation in the field of scientific and technological research; which includes Norway, Sweden, Finland, Switzerland, Austria, Yugoslavia and Turkey as well as the EC Member States.) There have also been Community research programmes to coordinate agricultural research, principally on the quality of agricultural produce in relation to production techniques. The medical health research programme (1987-1991) includes nutrition, and the R&D programme on applied metrology and chemical analysis (1987-1992) covers nutritional labelling, dietetic foods, bacterial contamination and additives.

There are two proposed programmes for the future relating to food science and technology within the current framework programme for 1987-1991. These are FLAIR - Food-Linked Agro-Industrial Research, and ECLAIR - European Collaborative Linkage of Agriculture and Industry through Research.

ECLAIR

The ECLAIR programme provides for collaborative research conducted in agreement between research institutes and universities with one or more industrial organisations; in the development of agricultural products and techniques, development of pesticides, fertilisers and disease control systems, and improvement of waste management.

The proposal was intended to be adopted in time for it to start operating on 1 July 1988, for a five-year period. At the time of writing (January 1989) the proposal has not yet been adopted, but an advance call for proposed projects to be supported by ECLAIR has been made, and was published in OJ C324 of 17 December 1988.

FLAIR

FLAIR is much more closely related to the major part of the food production and processing industry. The aim of the programme is to contribute to the competitiveness of the European food industry. It has three sectors for collaborative pre-competitive projects, which are the assessment and enhancement of food quality; food hygiene, safety and toxicology; and nutrition and wholesomeness. It is intended that universities will collaborate with industrial companies, and all projects must include participants from more than one Member State. The proposal for FLAIR was published in OJ C306 of 1 December 1988. The programme was intended to operate from January 1989 until mid 1993. A Community budget of ECU 25m (£16.1m) is proposed, and this is not to exceed 50% of the total cost: the remainder should be provided mainly by industry.

5. THE FOOD INDUSTRY - TOWARDS 1992

BACKGROUND

European Community legislation affecting the food industry has implications for the production, processing, packaging and marketing of all foodstuffs sold in the Community.

The objective of Community law has been the removal of all barriers to the free movement of goods. The main barriers to an internal European market for the food and drink industry are:

- physical barriers - in particular border controls, customs formalities, transportation restrictions and divergent national hygiene requirements for fresh meat and dairy products;

- technical barriers - in particular differing national regulations on labelling, materials in contact with food, additives, and foodstuffs with special nutritional uses;

- fiscal barriers - differing rates of VAT and excise duties.

The Commission has sought to establish a common set of rules relating to these areas. However, in practice the harmonisation of the national laws of the Member States has been a complex issue. Attempts to protect the health and safety of consumers has led each country to develop its own regulations governing the manufacture and sale of food and drink. Furthermore, with the exception of Ireland and the UK, Member States have detailed rules to determine the composition of almost all foods, together with general requirements for the sale of foodstuffs.

In theory, completion of an internal market for food and drink has the potential to benefit both manufacturers, by opening up new product markets, and consumers, by improving choice and reducing costs. In practice, the Commission has had only limited success in achieving this goal. In order to understand fully the issues at stake in current attempts to harmonise food law it is important to understand the extent of problems which have been encountered, and in particular the legal context within which the Commission's internal market programme was conceived.

1969 HARMONISATION PROGRAMME

Progress towards the goal of harmonised Community food law began in 1960 with the establishment of a "Legislation on Foodstuffs" working group. Legislation which was adopted in the early 1960s had the objective of restricting the use of substances to those which had been approved at the European level. In this context the first directive on colourings was adopted in 1962.

Elsewhere, since non-processed foodstuffs fell under the remit of the Common Agricultural Policy, initial progress was more prominent in the field of harmonising regulatory health controls concerning live animals, meat, plants and plant products.

A more coherent plan for the harmonisation of national food law was achieved in May 1969 when the Council adopted a general programme for 42 proposed directives in the foodstuffs sector. The legislative progress of specified directives was to be achieved within five time periods: the first four groups were to be adopted by 1 July 1969, 1 October 1969, 1 January 1970 and 1 July 1970; the final group was to be proposed by the Commission by 1 July 1970.

The 1969 programme introduced the concept of mutual recognition of national regulations; the regulatory practices of the Member States were to be regarded as equivalent in the case of products covered by these directives.

The 1969 programme also provided for a new procedure for amending directives. Previously it had been the case that where technical amendments to a directive were necessary, this could be done by means of a Commission Directive, but only after prior consultation with the Council. In order to accelerate the legislative process, a new consultation procedure was introduced. This enabled the Commission to amend directives on the basis of the opinion of a new Standing Committee for Foodstuffs, a body composed of experts representing each Member State and voting by an agreed procedure. The function of the Committee was augmented by a Scientific Committee on Foodstuffs, which was given a permanent function as an advisory body in 1973, and by the Consultative Committee on Food, created in 1975.

The first of the directives in the 1969 programme, determining the composition of cocoa and chocolate products, was adopted in 1973. However, despite the objectives of the programme, after four years only three directives had been adopted. The timetable set by the 1969 programme had proved unrealistic, and consequently it was abandoned.

1973 HARMONISATION PROGRAMME

Slippage in the timetable for the 1969 programme led to agreement on a revised plan for the harmonisation of Community food law. Fresh momentum was sought for the new proposals by incorporating them within the 1973 Industrial Policy Programme, a general plan to remove barriers to trade initiated in the wake of Community enlargement to include Denmark, Ireland and the UK.

Of the 42 directives proposed by the 1973 programme, all except six were vertical directives, determining the composition of specific foodstuffs. Adoption of the directives was anticipated over a timescale between July 1974 and January 1978.

By 1976 a number of the proposed vertical directives had already been withdrawn from the programme. Working within a fixed timetable had again proved an unsuitable basis for the adoption of complex legislation which aimed to determine the permitted composition of foodstuffs. Deadlines for completion of the 1973 programme were formally abandoned in December 1976, when the Commission also withdrew plans to propose several vertical directives.

Although the Commission had expressed its intention only to harmonise national laws which it considered necessary for the removal of obstacles to intra-Community trade in foodstuffs, proposals for vertical compositional directives seemed at odds with this objective. Instead the pursuit of agreement on the composition of specified foodstuffs clogged up the legislative process, a problem exacerbated by the requirement of the Member States to reach a unanimous decision in the Council on all matters.

Failure of the 1973 legislative programme led to a shift in Commission policy in 1975. Two directives were proposed which, although vertical in the sense that they were applicable to specific products (bread and mayonnaise), were also optional in the sense that while applicable to intra-Community trade, national standards would continue to be applied in the country where products are manufactured. Despite this attempt to remove the constraints imposed by compositional directives, both these proposals were later withdrawn.

From 1977 onwards the Commission, while accepting the impracticability of the timescale proposed, continued its work on directives within the 1973 programme. This work was supplemented by the addition of new initiatives in a number of other areas. Yet despite persevering with proposals for vertical directives, plans for seven directives on the composition of specific foodstuffs were abandoned in 1979. It is perhaps an indication of the failure of the vertical directive approach that the labelling directive adopted in 1979 moved away from this trend and was applicable horizontally to all foodstuffs on the market.

By 1985 there appeared to be a marked imbalance between the successes achieved in adopting horizontally applicable directives on matters such as labelling and additives, and a failure to reach agreement on vertical measures applicable to specific foodstuffs.

1985 WHITE PAPER PROPOSALS

The Commission's White Paper proposals of 14 June 1985 for the removal of all technical, physical and fiscal barriers to trade in the Community by 1992 were particularly applicable to the removal of barriers to trade in the food industry. Consequently, on 8 November 1985 the Commission supplemented its White Paper proposals with a communication on completion of the internal market in foodstuffs, COM(85)603. The importance of the Commission's communication lay in the distinction drawn between food law which must continue to be subject to Community legislation in order to remove barriers to trade, and those matters on which legislation is not considered necessary.

The Commission's rationale for its proposals for the food sector were based on the Treaty of Rome, which prohibits Member States from preventing the marketing of a product lawfully produced and marketed in another Member State. This requirement had been reinforced by the decision of the Cassis de Dijon case in 1978, which established the "principle of proportionality" for determining whether national legal measures are necessary to achieve a desired objective. As a result, Community legislation on foodstuffs since 1985 has been based on the criteria that legislation must be justified by the need to:

- protect public health;

- provide consumers with information and protection on matters other than health;

- ensure fair trading;

- provide for the necessary public controls.

Public health

Justification for additional national legislation on grounds of protection of public health is recognised as an acceptable objective for Member States. However, national laws relating to public health may be deemed to be excessive and constitute a barrier to intra-Community trade.

Despite differences in national laws and systems for inspection, the Commission recognised that since a common objective lay behind public health provisions, mutual recognition of national standards should be accorded by Member States.

Complete recognition of public health provisions would clearly remove barriers to trade. However, the Commission felt that problems will remain due to the lack of a clear position as to whether a barrier is justified or excessive. Clearly Member States with particularly stringent national rules relating to public health will seek to maintain these rules.

The Commission's view was that the principle of mutual recognition was only applicable in cases where barriers to trade were justifiable. In all other cases, harmonisation of national laws is necessary on grounds of:

- industrial policy;

- consumer protection;

- intra-Community trade.

The Commission's White Paper highlighted a number of areas in which further harmonisation of laws is necessary. Seven "framework" measures were proposed in these areas:

- labelling;

- nutritional labelling;

- contact materials;

- additives;

- foodstuffs with particular nutritional uses;

- inspection of foodstuffs;

- irradiation.

Consumer protection

The development of EC food law has been based on consumer protection on two levels:

- regulations on the composition of specific foodstuffs;

- provision of adequate information on the composition of foodstuffs, considered sufficient for the protection of public health.

The Commission's White Paper advocated the adoption of Community law based on the second route, considering detailed regulations on the composition of foodstuffs an unnecessary burden on the EC legislative process and on manufacturers in the Member States.

While the compositional "recipe" laws established prior to 1985 have remained in place, and have been amended when necessary, the emphasis is now very much upon providing the consumer with sufficient information on the labelling, presentation and advertising of foodstuffs. No further compositional laws have been adopted since 1985, despite fears voiced by manufacturers in the Member States that the absence of compositional directives would lead to a reduction in the quality of foodstuffs.

The general principle established by the White Paper is that consumers must be correctly and adequately informed, whilst producers must be protected against unfair competition. Provided these conditions are met, the Commission does not consider that an examination of the "fair trading" principle is necessary. In industry there is some difficulty in comprehending how this policy will work in practice, since there will be differences between what Member States consider to be sufficiently precise information to adequately inform the consumer.

Official inspection

The Commission's intention in the White Paper was that Member States should carry out inspections not only on foodstuffs intended for domestic consumption, but also to the inspection of foodstuffs intended for use in other Member States.

Retail inspection alone was considered to be inappropriate as a means of verifying the quality of mass produced foodstuffs. Therefore, an increase in inspection at the manufacturing level was proposed.

European Agricultural Guidance and Guarantee Fund

With the adoption of the Commission's White Paper proposals in the Single European Act, provision was made to reduce adverse economic and social consequences of the internal market programme for the agricultural sector by increasing the budget of the EAGGF - commonly known by its French acronym, FEOGA.

The Guidance Section of FEOGA takes the form of measures for increasing agricultural productivity and improving agricultural structures. The Processing and Marketing regulation is particularly applicable to the agricultural food industry. The scheme provides grants to assist primary producers in improving the processing or marketing of products.

Full details of this scheme are published in Council Regulation (EEC) 355/77, see OJL 81, 23.2.77; as amended by Regulation (EEC) 1932/84.

Simplified procedure

To achieve the aims of the White Paper for the foodstuffs sector the Commission proposed simplified procedures in order to avoid the legislative backlog experienced during the 1969 and 1973 programmes. The Commission proposed that, whilst the Council would continue to set the basic framework of directives, detailed and technical aspects of legislation would be drawn up by the Commission, advised by experts in a standardised committee procedure.

In practice, for example in respect of Community law on additives, this means that the Council will establish the basic provisions of the framework directive and will then pass to the Commission the task of deciding upon amendments to lists of approved substances. The Commission then consults with experts from the Member States within the Standing Committee for Food. However, it should be noted that the requirement for the Commission to seek advice from the Committee is only compulsory where matters of public health are at stake.

In order to facilitate completion of the internal market in foodstuffs by 1992, the Single European Act implemented the Commission's strategy for accelerating the adoption of EC food law by giving formal recognition to three types of Committees to be used for the new legislation and matters relating to completion of the internal market:

- the Advisory Committee;

- the Management Committee;

- the Regulatory Committee.

It will be for the Council to decide which Committee the Commission is required to consult before adopting legislation.

The Advisory Committee Procedure

The Advisory Committee will be the principal consultative body on matters relating to completion of the internal market. The Committee may reach a common opinion by majority voting, although no vote will necessarily be taken. The opinions communicated to the Commission are more important.

Within this procedure, the Advisory Committee on Foodstuffs is consulted on all draft food law. The Committee consists of experts from the Member States representing the interests of agriculture, industry, commerce and consumers.

The Management Committee Procedure

The Commission must consult the Management Committee when instructed to do so by the Council, but may adopt its own proposal regardless of the opinion delivered.

The Regulatory Committee Procedure

The Commission must consult with the Regulatory Committee when instructed to do so and cannot adopt legislation until the Committee has agreed with the proposal. Therefore the Commission is required to act in accordance with the opinion of the Regulatory Committee at all times. The Standing Committee on Foodstuffs has performed the function of a Regulatory Committee since 1969.

CASE LAW OF THE EUROPEAN COURT

Article 100 of the Treaty of Rome lays down the goal of harmonised food laws in the Community in order to remove barriers to trade and to protect the consumer from fraud and ensure health and safety. Barriers to intra-Community trade in foodstuffs can be caused by both tariff constraints and import quotas ("quantitative restrictions") and non-tariff measures, where Member States are required to comply with national regulations.

During the development of the EC quantitative restrictions in the form of tariff quotas have been successfully removed from intra-Community trade. Barriers to trade which remain have tended to be non-tariff barriers which nonetheless amount to "measures having equivalent effect" to quantitative restrictions.

Despite being prohibited by Articles 30 to 34 of the Treaty of Rome, non-tariff barriers to trade have proved difficult to remove where national regulations act as a technical barrier to exclude goods purchased in another Member State. Article 30 states that:

"Qualitative restrictions on imports and all measures having equivalent effect shall, without prejudice to the following provisions, be prohibited between Member States."

Similarly, Article 34 prohibits quantitative restrictions and measures having equivalent effect in respect of goods exported to another Member State.

The term "measures having equivalent effect" is particularly important in the context of interpreting the scope of Articles 30 to 36 since, as the European Court ruled in Case 82/77: Openbarr Ministerie of the Netherlands v. Van Tiggle (1978), the term is applicable to all national rules which are capable of hindering intra-Community trade.

This principle was reinforced by the Court ruling in Case 124/81: Commission v. UK (1983). In this instance the UK had required that all milk marketed within its territory had to be packed on premises authorised for use by an inspector. However, the jurisdiction of inspectors was limited to the geographical area of that local authority. Despite the fact that the rule had originated as part of the UK's milk hygiene controls, its application effectively excluded imports of all milk into the UK. The UK argued that it was acting in accordance with the exception to Article 36, which provides that trade may be prohibited on grounds of the protection of health and life. Article 36 states that:

"The provisions of Articles 30 to 34 shall not preclude prohibitions or restrictions on imports, exports or goods in transit justified on grounds of public morality, public policy or public security; the protection of health and life of humans, animals or plants; the protection of national treasures possessing artistic, historic or archaeological value; or the protection of industrial and commercial property. Such prohibitions or restrictions shall not, however, constitute a means of arbitrary discrimination or a disguised restriction on trade between Member States."

Despite accepting that exceptions to Article 30 were permitted on grounds of protecting human or animal health, the European Court ruled that a total ban on imported milk was excessive since the measure was not "proportionate" for the purpose intended.

Interpretation of the phrase "all measures having equivalent effect" has been a frequent issue of Community case law, where Article 36 has been used as a defence for maintaining non-tariff barriers to trade. However, while Article 36 provides Member States with a justifiable defence for restricting trade for reasons of a non-economic nature, the derogations which it provides from Article 30 are applicable only to the extent that they can be justified.

In Case 8/74: Procureur de Roi v. Dassonville (1974), where Belgian law required a certificate to be supplied by an officially recognised body, the European Court ruled that:

"All trading rules enacted by Member States which are capable of hindering, directly or indirectly, actually or potentially, intra-Community trade are to be considered as measures having an effect equivalent to quantitative restrictions."

The position of Article 36 was clarified by Case 120/78: Rewe-Zentral AG v. Bundesmonopolverwaltung fur Branntwein (1978) - the "Cassis de Dijon" case - where the European Court stipulated that although Article 30 prohibits all possible restrictions on intra-Community trade, some obstacles remain justified. A German company was refused a licence to import Cassis de Dijon, a low-alcohol liqueur manufactured in France, on the grounds that German law requires a liqueur to have a minimum alcohol content of 32%. The German government argued that it was entitled to refuse a licence to permit entry on grounds of public health and consumer protection.

The European Court ruled that the German legislation amounted to a "measure having equivalent effect". Article 36 therefore provided no defence, and the restriction was prohibited by Article 30. The Court went beyond the decision of the Dassonville case and established the principle that a product lawfully manufactured and marketed in one Member State must be allowed to compete elsewhere in the Community.

The Cassis de Dijon case highlighted the fact that restrictions on the free movement of goods based on a defence of Article 36 will only be justified in specific circumstances. The "principle of proportionality" is therefore the key to interpreting the scope of Article 36; restrictions to trade must go no further than is necessary to protect the health and life of humans, animals or plants. Where justification for restrictive measures cannot be found under Article 36, the principle of "mutual recognition " of national product standards will apply in order to ensure the free movement of goods.

The Cassis de Dijon case illustrates a basic difficulty faced by national administrations and industry - there are no rules to determine whether a barrier is excessive or can be justified. Each instance must be considered separately. In most cases this will be done without a European Court ruling, but on several occasions the Court has been required to intervene when a Member State has strongly defended its national regulations. Subsequent case law has confirmed the principle established by the Cassis de Dijon case.

In Case 788/79: Gilli and Andres (1980), Italian law prohibiting the sale of certain vinegar in Italy was held to be contrary to Article 30.

In Case 130/80: Kelderman (1980), Dutch law stipulating the dry matter content required in bread was held to be unnecessary in order to fulfil any mandatory requirement and was therefore contrary to Article 30.

In Case 27/80: Fietje (1980), Dutch law prohibiting the sale of certain beverages which did not meet national labelling requirements was held to be contrary to Article 30 and not justified on grounds of consumer protection since information could be given by product labelling.

In Case 178/84: Commission v. Federal Republic of Germany, the European Court questioned the validity of the German Reinheitsgebot of 1516, which limited the constituents of beer to the use of malted barley, hops, yeast and water. Since beers produced in other Member States are produced with additional ingredients, imports of these products was prohibited by German national law. The European Court ruled that since the restriction did not fall within the meaning of Article 36, it was not proportional to the declared objective. Adequate labelling was instead considered sufficient protection for the German consumer.

In Case 302/86: <u>Commission v. Kingdom of Denmark</u>, the European Court appeared to set an important new precedent in September 1988 which may have implications for future cases brought for contravention of Article 30. The Commission had claimed that, by imposing a ban on all imports of drinks in non-returnable bottles, Denmark had unfairly restricted the free movement of goods. The European Court upheld the Danish decision to restrict imports for environmental reasons, but ruled that foreign drink manufacturers should not be required to obtain certification of bottles as environmentally sound. This was the first time that trade restrictions had been successfully justified on environmental grounds.

Similarly, in Case 407/85: <u>Drei Glocken GmbH and Gertraud Kritzinger v. USL Centro-Sud and Provincia Autonoma di Bolzano</u>, the European Court ruled in July 1988 that the Italian authorities could not prohibit the marketing of West German pasta within its territory. The Court ruled that the sale in Italy of West German pasta, made from a mixture of common wheat and durum wheat, could not be considered a hazard to human health, nor was it likely to mislead the consumer provided that adequate information was given on labelling. The restriction was not justifiable on grounds of Article 36.

It is important to stress that Articles 30 to 36 of the Treaty of Rome are applicable only to goods moved across frontiers. Goods produced, marketed and consumed within the territory of a Member State may still be subject to more stringent national laws than those imposed on imported products. This requirement may place an unnecessary restriction on home producers.

IMPLICATIONS FOR THE FOOD AND DRINK INDUSTRY

The Commission has sought to establish both horizontal measures, applying to a wide range of foodstuffs, and vertical measures, applying to specific foods. In the 1970s progress in the implementation of vertical directives was extremely slow due to the problems involved in reaching agreement on the detailed composition of foodstuffs. Similarly, national derogations, claiming a defence of Article 36, limited the impact of the little progress achieved.

In the early 1980s, developments in Community case law provided the Commission with the stimulus to develop a new approach to the creation of an internal market for food and drink. The Cassis de Dijon case reinforced the Commission's interpretation of Articles 30 to 36 by insisting that a Member State must permit the marketing in its territory of all products manufactured and sold legally in another Member State, even where this is done on the basis of different technical specifications.

The aim of the Commission's internal market programme is the elimination of all barriers to intra-Community trade by 31 December 1992. This was embodied in the 1985 White Paper proposals to:

- remove remaining barriers to the free movement of goods;

- increase use of the "mutual recognition" principle, underpinned by safeguards which Articles 30 to 36 provides for human and animal health, fair trading and the environment;

- improve enforcement by implementing Community methods of sampling and analysis.

Until the aim of an internal market is achieved, the food and drink industry will continue to focus on national rather than European markets.

While opportunity to operate on a European scale has always existed in principle, in practice national regulations on imported goods continue to discourage and hinder such attempts. The intention is that the Commission's legislative programme for removing barriers to intra-Community trade, coupled with stringent enforcement of the Treaties by the Commission and the European Court, will minimise the misuse of Article 36.

A more problematic barrier to the creation of an internal market for foodstuffs may be found in the form of differing regional and national tastes, high distribution costs and the short product-life of many foodstuffs. It is certainly the case that only a few food products are at present marketed throughout the Community, indicating the problems which lie ahead in attempts to achieve a pan-European market for food and drink.

6. REMOVAL OF PHYSICAL BARRIERS

BACKGROUND

The harmonisation of Community health and hygiene standards is considered by the Commission to be a prerequisite for creating an internal market in agricultural products: fruit, vegetables and cereals, meat, dairy products and fish.

The regulation of quantitative restrictions within the Common Agricultural Policy has been a cornerstone of Community activity since the early 1960s. However, more recent attempts to create an internal market for food have focused on measures designed to facilitate the convergence of national product standards with the aim of removing all remaining physical barriers to intra-Community trade.

The Commission's White Paper contained a large number of proposed Directives which have the aim of achieving this objective within the 1992 deadline. The high level of legislative activity reflects the complexity of the issues involved. Detailed national legislation already exists in each Member State for the purpose of safeguarding both human and animal health within its own territory. The Commission intends to remove all physical barriers to trade by achieving the highest possible level of health and hygiene standards throughout the Community and ensuring free access to the markets of other Member States.

Fruit, vegetables and cereals

The Commission's White Paper proposals concerning fruit and vegetable are consistent with the overall goal of harmonising health and hygiene standards. Legislation already exists in a number of areas.

The 1967 Directive on the use of preservatives for the surface treatment of citrus fruit was followed by three directives with similar objectives: the 1976 Directive on pesticide residues for fruit and vegetables; the 1977 Directive protecting against harmful plant organisms; and the 1979 Directive on plant protection products. In 1986 a further Directive was introduced to control the level of pesticide residues in and on cereals.

More proposals are expected within the internal market programme which will complete Community-wide standardisation of health and hygiene conditions for plant products, however many of these proposals have yet to be tabled by the Commission.

Meat and meat products

Initial progress towards the harmonisation of health and hygiene standards for fresh meat was achieved prior to the internal market programme. By 1972, three Directives had already been adopted which were intended to improve conditions for intra-Community trade in fresh meat and poultrymeat. Two further Directives in 1977 and 1980 extended the scope of Community-wide health standards to cover trade in fresh meat products.

In order to extend the scope of Community action to all meat marketed within the twelve Member States, parallel action was taken between 1972 and 1986 to regulate the quality of all fresh meat originating from non-member countries. Further directives to control the importation of meat from third countries are anticipated.

Other products

The Commission envisages future legislation which will harmonise health and hygiene conditions for fish, shellfish and eggs.

Proposals of a more general nature are expected between 1991 and 1992 which will complete the EC legislative framework for agricultural products by harmonising all remaining national supervisory requirements.

FRUIT, VEGETABLES AND CEREALS - EXISTING LEGISLATION

Council Directive 67/427/EEC of 27 June 1967 on the use of certain preservatives for the surface treatment of citrus fruit and on the control measures to be used for the qualitative and quantitative analysis of preservatives in and on citrus fruit.

Summary

The Council Directive of 5 November 1963 on the approximation of the laws of the Member States concerning the preservatives authorised for use in foodstuffs intended for human consumption stipulated that national provisions relating to the surface treatment of citrus fruit with biphenyl (diphenyl), orthophenylphenol and sodium orthophenylphenate could be retained until 30 June 1967.

This Directive lays down provisions relating to the use of these substances as preservatives for the surface treatment of citrus fruit after 30 June 1967.

Timetable

Member States were required to comply with the Directive by 1 July 1968.

The full text was published in OJL 148, 11.7.67.

Council Directive 76/895/EEC of 23 November 1976 relating to the fixing of maximum levels for pesticide residues in and on fruit and vegetables.

As amended by:
Commission Directive 80/428/EEC, see OJL 102, 19.4.80
Council Directive 81/36/EEC, see OJL 46, 19.2.81
Council Directive 82/528/EEC, see OJL 234, 9.8.82
Council Directive 88/298/EEC, see OJL 126, 20.5.88

Sampling methods:
Council Directive 79/700/EEC, see OJL 207, 15.8.79

Summary

The Directive relating to the fixing of maximum levels for pesticide residues in and on fruit and vegetables requires that Member States may ~~hibit~~ or impede the sale of products listed in Annex I of

Directive on grounds that they contain pesticide residues in quantities not exceeding those laid down in Annex II of the Directive.

National derogations

A Member State may permit the circulation of products which contain a higher level of pesticide residues than those laid down in Annex II in cases where this is considered justified.

Where a Member State has reasonable grounds for establishing that the maximum levels fixed in Annex II might endanger human health or animal health, the Member States may temporarily reduce the permitted level within its own territory. The Commission will take appropriate measures on the basis of consultation with the Standing Committee on Plant Health.

The Directive is not applicable in the case of products where at least one appropriate element of proof can be brought that they are intended for export to third countries.

Timetable

Member States were required to comply with the Directive by 1 May 1980.

The full text was published in OJL 340, 9.12.76.

Council Directive 77/93/EEC of 21 December 1976 on protective measures against the introduction into the Member States of harmful organisms of plants or plant products.

As amended by:
Council Directive 80/392/EEC, see OJL 100, 17.4.80
Council Directive 80/393/EEC, see OJL 100, 17.4.80
Council Directive 84/378/EEC, see OJL 207, 2.8.84
Commission Decision 85/634/EEC, see OJL 379, 31.12.85
Council Directive 85/574/EEC, see OJL 372, 31.12.85
Commission Directive 86/545/EEC, see OJL 323, 18.11.86
Commission Directive 86/546/EEC, see OJL 323, 18.11.86
Commission Directive 86/547/EEC, see OJL 323, 18.11.86
Council Directive 86/651/EEC, see OJL 382, 31.12.87
Council Directive 87/278/EEC, see OJL 151, 11.6.87
Commission Directive 88/271/EEC, see OJL 116, 4.5.88

Commission Directive 88/272/EEC, see OJL 116, 4.5.88
Commission Directive 88/430/EEC, see OJL 208, 2.8.88

Summary

The Directive requires Member States to prohibit the introduction into their territory of harmful organisms, or plants and plant products contaminated by harmful organisms, which are listed in the Annexes of the Directive.

Member States are required to prohibit the introduction of plants or plant products listed in Annex III of the Directive where these products originate from certain specified countries. The Directive lays down a list of additional plants, plant products and other objects which a Member State may prevent from entering its territory.

Special requirements

Annex IV of the Directive lays down a list of special requirements which must be met. A Member State is required to prohibit the entry into its territory of plants, plant products and other objects which fail to meet the special requirements. Annex IV provides a list of additional requirements which a Member State may impose on products imported from non-member countries.

Official inspection

A Member State must require that products and their packaging are officially examined, at least in respect of the introduction into another Member State. Where necessary, vehicles transporting these products must also be officially examined.

Phytosanitary certificate

Where, as a result of official inspection, it is considered that the conditions laid down in the Directive have been fulfilled, a phytosanitary certificate must be issued in accordance with the specimen set out in Annex VIII of the Directive.

Member States are required to prohibit the introduction into another Member State of plants, plant products and other objects listed in Annex V, unless these products are accompanied by a phytosanitary certificate. This certificate must be made out within 14 days before transit.

Re-forwarding phytosanitary certificate

Where plants, plant products and other objects from a Member State have been split up or have been stored or re-packaged in a second Member State before being introduced into a third Member State, the second Member State need not re-inspect the goods if it has been officially established that no change has occurred in the products which would result in non-compliance with the conditions laid down in the Directive. A re-forwarding phytosanitary certificate must be then be issued.

The re-forwarding certificate will be attached to the original phytosanitary certificate (or a copy of the certificate) and entitled "phytosanitary certificate for re-export". The re-forwarding phytosanitary certificate must be made out within 14 days before transit.

Requirements for a re-forwarding phytosanitary certificate must also apply to goods introduced successively into several Member States. In such cases, products must be accompanied by:

- the latest phytosanitary certificate, or a copy of this document;

- the latest re-forwarding phytosanitary certificate;

- previous re-forwarding phytosanitary certificates, or copies of these documents.

Member States may extend the requirement for a reforwarding phytosanitary certificate to consignments from non-member countries.

Prohibitions and restrictions

Member States may subject products, their packaging and vehicles transporting them to an inspection on entry into their territory. A Member State may prohibit entry into its territory of plants, plant products or other objects where:

- appropriate phytosanitary certificates and re-forwarding phytosanitary certificates are not produced;

- products are not introduced at a prescribed entry-point;

- products are not submitted to official inspection.

Prohibitions or restrictions imposed by a Member State must be in accordance with the procedure established by the Commission on the basis of consultation with the Standing Committee on Plant Health.

Verification

A Member State may not require a statement in addition to the phytosanitary certificate. In the case of fruit and vegetables and potatoes other than seed potatoes, a Member State must not supplement the official inspection and check on identity except where:

- there is reason to believe that one of the provisions laid down in the Directive has not been complied with;

- plants originate in a non-member country and examination has not been carried out in another Member State.

In other cases, official inspection of fruit and vegetables and potatoes other than seed potatoes must be by sampling only. Sampling must constitute no more than one third of the consignment introduced from a Member State and are evenly spread over time and over all products.

Member States must require an official entry stamp on the phytosanitary certificates of all products introduced into its territory.

Products from non-member countries

In the case of products coming from non-member countries, a Member State must require that plants, plant products, other objects and their packaging are officially inspected either in their entirety or by sampling. Where necessary, vehicles transporting these products must also be officially inspected.

This requirement does not apply in the case of products imported into a Member State via another Member State which has previously carried out the official inspection.

National derogations

A Member State is required to inform other Member States and the Commission of any derogations which it permits within its territory in accordance with the provisions of the Directive.

Where a Member State has reasonable grounds for establishing that there is a danger of the spread of harmful organisms in its territory, the Member State may take additional protective measures. The Commission will take appropriate action on the basis of consultation with the Standing Committee on Plant Health.

Timetable

Member States were required to comply with the Directive by 1 May 1980.

The full text was published in OJL 26, 31.1.77.

Council Directive 79/117/EEC of 21 December 1978 prohibiting the placing on the market and use of plant protection products containing certain active substances.

As amended by:
Council Directive 83/131/EEC, see OJL 91, 9.4.83
Council Directive 85/298/EEC, see OJL 154, 13.6.85
Council Directive 86/214/EEC, see OJL 152, 6.6.86
Council Directive 86/355/EEC, see OJL 212, 2.8.86
Council Directive 87/181/EEC, see OJL 71, 14.3.87
Council Directive 87/477/EEC, see OJL 273, 26.9.87

Summary

The Directive requires Member States to prohibit the use of plant protection products containing one or more of the active substances listed in the Annex.

The Annex of the Directive lays down a list of cases in which placing on the market is permitted in the case of:

- mercury compounds;

- persistent organo-chlorine compounds.

An active substance must be included in the list of prohibited substances if, when used for the purpose intended, it gives rise to:

- harmful effects on human or animal health;

- unreasonable adverse effects on the environment.

The Directive is not applicable to:

- plant protection products which contain negligible impurities because of the nature of their manufacturing processes (provided that they have no harmful effects on human beings, animals or the environment);

- plant protection products intended for research and analysis;

- plant protection products intended for export to third countries.

Scientific Committee on Pesticides

The Commission is required to adopt any amendments to the lists of prohibited substances, or permitted uses for the substances, on the basis of consultations with the Scientific Committee on Pesticides.

Where a derogation provided for in the Annex is to be cancelled, prior consultation of the Scientific Committee will not be necessary if all Member States have informed the Commission that they no longer intend to use the derogation.

The Commission is required to examine the status of permitted uses of mercury compounds and persistent organo-chlorine compounds at least every two years. All amendments must be made on the basis of developments in scientific and technical knowledge.

National derogations

A Member State may temporarily permit the use within its territory of plant protection products containing certain active substances listed in the Annex of the Directive. The Member State must inform other Member States and the Commission of the temporary derogation, and provide details of the extent to which active substances are used.

In the case of an unforeseeable danger threatening plant production which cannot be contained by other means, a Member State may permit the use of a plant protection product containing certain active substances listed for a maximum period of 120 days. The Commission is required to take appropriate action on the basis of consultation with the Standing Committee on Plant Health.

Timetable

Member States were required to comply with the Directive no later than 1 January 1981.

The full text was published in OJL 33, 8.2.79.

Council Directive 86/362/EEC of 24 July 1986 on the fixing of maximum levels for pesticide residues in and on cereals.

As amended by:
Council Directive 88/298/EEC, see OJL 126, 20.5.88

Summary

The Directive on the fixing of maximum levels for pesticide residues in and on cereals requires Member States to ensure that products listed in Annex I of the Directive do not present a danger to human health as a result of the presence of residues of pesticides listed in Annex II of the Directive.

The Directive applies to cereals which fall within the categories of:

- wheat;

- rye;

- barley;

- oats;

- maize;

- paddy rice;

- buckwheat, millet, grain, sorghum, triticale and other cereals.

The Directive does not apply to products intended for:

- export to third countries;

- the manufacture of products other than foodstuffs;

- sowing.

Maximum prescribed levels of pesticide residues are specified for the substances listed in Annex II of the Directive.

Member States are required to permit the free circulation of cereals in which the quantity of such residues does not exceed maximum levels specified in the Annex of the Directive.

Verification

Methods of sampling and analysis must be carried out by the Member States in accordance with the procedure established on the basis of consultation within the Standing Committee on Plant Health. Member States are required to report to the Commission annually on the results of official checks.

Amendments to maximum permitted levels may be adopted by the Council on the basis of developments in scientific or technical knowledge.

Products imported from third countries or intended for other Member States may continue to be subject to existing national systems of checking.

National derogations

Member States may allow the presence of pesticide residues in or on cereals in greater quantities than those specified provided that these products are not made available for consumption until the residues no longer exceed the maximum levels.

Where the maximum permitted level of pesticide residue is regarded by a Member State as being a danger to human health, that State may temporarily reduce the permitted level in its territory, prior to consultation with the Standing Committee on Plant Health.

Timetable

Member States were required to comply with the Directive no later than 30 June 1988. On the basis of a Commission report, the Council will re-examine the effectiveness of these measures no later than 30 June 1991. The full text was published in OJL 221, 7.8.86.

FRUIT, VEGETABLES AND CEREALS - PROPOSED LEGISLATION

COM(88) 798. Proposal for a Council Regulation on the fixing of maximum levels for pesticide residues in and on certain products of plant origin, including fruit and vegetables, and amending the procedural rules of Directive 76/895/EEC relating to the fixing of maximum levels of pesticide residues in and on fruit and vegetables.

Summary

The proposal for a Regulation is applicable to those groups of products laid down in the Annex. The list of permitted pesticide residues and maximum levels for their use will be determined in accordance with the procedure involving the Standing Committee on Plant Health. Pesticide residues will not be included in the list for as long as a maximum level is fixed for it by Directive 76/895/EEC.

The Regulation does not affect the status of:

- the provisions of Directive 64/54/EEC relating to biphenyl (diphenyl), orthophenylphenol, sodium orthophenyl phenate and 2-(4-thiazolyl)-benzimidazole (thiabendazole), which will continue to regulate the use of those substances until maximum levels are included in the list determined in accordance with the procedure involving the Standing Committee on Plant.

- the provisions of Directive 74/63/EEC;

- the provisions of Directive 76/895/EEC, with the exception of alterations to certain alterations to procedural rules;

- the provisions of Directive 86/362/EEC.

The Regulation is not applicable to the products on the approved list where they are intended for:

- export to third countries;

- the manufacture of products other than foodstuffs;

- sowing or planting.

From the time they are put into circulation, products must not contain levels of pesticide residues greater than those specified in the list.

Member States are required to ensure compliance with the maximum levels stipulated.

Member States must not prohibit the putting into circulation of the products authorised by the list on the grounds that they contain pesticide residues, if the quantity of such residues in the product does not exceed the maximum permitted levels.

Post-harvest treatment

Fruit and vegetables may contain pesticide residues resulting from post-harvest treatment to protect them until sale to the ultimate consumer. Products which have undergone such treatment must be accompanied by the words "treated with....." followed by the common name or the chemical name of the pesticide used. This indication must be made:

- in the wholesale trade, on invoices and on one external surface of the packaging;

- in the retail trade, by a visible indication giving the consumer clear information.

Verification

In the case of fruit and vegetables, the sampling methods laid down in Directive 79/700/EEC will be used to ensure compliance with the Regulation.

In the case of products other than fruit and vegetables, the sampling methods will be determined in accordance with the Standing Committee procedure.

The existence of Community sampling methods will not prevent Member States from using other recognised methods, provided that this does not hinder the free movement of products. If this produces different interpretations of results from the Community method, the latter shall apply.

National derogations

Where a Member State has detailed evidence that a maximum pesticide residue level endangers human or animal health, that Member State may temporarily reduce the level in its own territory. The Member State must immediately inform the Commission and other Member States of its reasons for doing so. The Commission will take appropriate action after consultation with the Standing Committee on Plant Health.

Timetable

At the time of writing the full text was not published in the OJC series.

FRUIT, VEGETABLES AND CEREALS - LEGISLATION NOT YET PROPOSED

Proposal for the placing of plant protection products on the market. Delay vis-a-vis White Paper.

Proposal for a system of certification of reproductive materials in fruit plants. Proposal expected 1989. Adoption expected 1990. Delay vis-a-vis White Paper.

Establishment of certain rules on liability in respect of plant health. Proposal expected 1989. Adoption expected 1990. Delay vis-a-vis White Paper.

Amendments to Directive 77/93/EEC on entry into Member States of organisms harmful to plants or plant products. Proposal expected 1988. Delay vis-a-vis White Paper.

Simplification of Annexes in Directive 77/93/EEC. Proposal expected 1990. Adoption expected 1992. Delay vis-a-vis White Paper.

Alignment of national standards in plant health. Proposal expected 1990. Adoption expected 1991. Delay vis-a-vis White Paper.

Reinforcement of controls of harmful organisms, especially in seed potatoes and in fruit plant reproductive material. Proposal expected 1989. Adoption expected 1990. Delay vis-a-vis White Paper.

Guidelines for checking requirements in connection with the approval of plant protection production. Proposal expected 1989. Adoption expected 1990. Delay vis-a-vis White Paper.

Proposal for criterion of a European law on plant breeders. Proposal expected 1989. Adoption expected 1990. Delay vis-a-vis White Paper.

Suppression of plant health certificates. Proposal expected 1991. Adoption expected 1992.

Proposal on organic production of foodstuffs and marketing of organically produced foodstuffs. Proposal expected 1988. Adoption expected 1989. Delay vis-a-vis White Paper.

MEAT AND MEAT PRODUCTS - EXISTING LEGISLATION

Council Directive 64/433/EEC of 26 June 1964 on health problems affecting intra-Community trade in fresh meat.

As amended by:
Council Directive 83/90/EEC, see OJL 59, 5.3.83
Council Decision 85/446/EEC, see OJL 260, 2.10.85
Council Directive 85/323/EEC, see OJL 168, 28.6.85
Council Directive 85/325/EEC, see OJL 168, 28.6.85
Council Directive 86/587/EEC, see OJL 339, 2.12.86
Council Decision 87/562/EEC, see OJL 341, 3.12.87
Council Decision 88/235/EEC, see OJL 105, 26.4.88
Council Directive 88/288/EEC, see OJL 124, 18.5.88
Council Directive 89/136/EEC, see OJL 49, 21.2.89

Summary

The Directive on health problems affecting intra-Community trade in fresh meat requires Member States to ensure that only fresh meat which complies with the provisions of the Directive may be sent to another Member State. The Directive is applicable to fresh meat from the following species:

- bovine animals (including buffalo);

- swine;

- sheep and goats;

- domestic solipeds (horses, asses and hinnies).

The Directive is not applicable to meat intended for personal consumption which forms part of travellers' personal luggage, meat sent as small packages to private persons, or meat for consumption by the crew and passengers on board means of transport operating commercially between the Member States.

Carcases, half carcases or half carcases, cut into no more than three wholesale cuts, and quarters must:

- have been obtained in an officially approved slaughterhouse;

- come from a slaughtered animal inspected ante mortem by an official veterinarian and passed fit for slaughter for intra-Community trade in fresh meat;

- have been treated under satisfactory hygiene conditions;

- have been inspected post mortem by an official veterinarian and have not shown changes except for traumatic lesions which occurred shortly before slaughter or localised malformations or changes, provided that these do not render the carcase and offal unfit for human consumption;

- bear an official health mark;

- be accompanied by a health certificate during transportation to the country of destination;

- be stored under satisfactory hygiene conditions in approved establishment after post mortem inspection;

- be transported under satisfactory hygiene conditions to the country of destination.

Smaller cuts or pieces, or boned meat must:

- have been boned or cut in an approved cutting plant and officially supervised;

- have been obtained from fresh meat from animals coming from the Member State and complying with the requirements set out in the Directive, or coming from fresh meat coming from another Member State and meeting the requirements set out in the Directive, or coming from fresh meat imported from a third country in accordance with Community provisions;

- have been stored under conditions laid down in the Directive in approved establishments and officially supervised;

- have been supervised by an official veterinarian;

- comply with the packaging requirements of the Directive;

- have been treated under satisfactory hygiene conditions;

- bear an official health mark;

- be accompanied by a health certificate during transportation to the country of destination;

- be transported under satisfactory hygiene conditions to the country of destination.

Offal must come from an approved slaughterhouse or cutting plant in the exporting country.

Fresh meat which has been stored in an approved cold store of a Member State and has not undergone any handling in connection with storage must:

- have been treated under satisfactory hygiene conditions;

- bear an official health mark;

- be stored under satisfactory hygiene conditions in an approved establishment after post mortem inspection;

- be transported under satisfactory hygiene conditions to the country of destination;

- be accompanied by a certificate which corresponds to the model laid down in the Directive during transportation to the country of destination.

Exemptions

The above animal health requirements are not applicable to:

- fresh meat brought in with the authorisation of the country of destination for uses other than human consumption;

- fresh meat intended for exhibition, special studies or analysis, provided that official control ensures that the meat is not used for human consumption;

- fresh meat brought in with the authorisation of the country of destination and intended exclusively as supplies for international organisations and military forces.

Obligations on the country of export

In addition to the general provisions for the intra-Community trade in fresh meat laid down by the Directive, each Member State must ensure that the following requirements are met by fresh meat sent to another Member State:

- fresh pig meat must have undergone an examination for trichinosis;

- animals or meat must have undergone a sampling examination for residues in accordance with recognised methods.

Meat which shows traces of residues in prohibited quantities must be excluded from intra-Community trade.

The following meat must not be sent from the territory of a Member State to that of another Member State:

- fresh meat from male pigs used for breeding, cryptorchid and hermaphrodite pigs, or uncastrated male pigs with a carcase weight exceeding a specified limit, unless fresh meat of these types are intended to undergo one of the treatments provided for in Directive 77/99/EEC and carry a special mark;

- minced meat, meat cut up in a similar manner or mechanically recovered meat;

- fresh meat which has been treated with stilbenes or stilbene derivatives, their salts or esters or thyrostatic substances and containing residues of these substances, or containing residues of other substances having a hormonal action, antibiotics, antimony, arsenic, pesticides, or other substances which are may be harmful to human health;

- fresh meat from animals which have been administered with substances which may be harmful to human health and on which the Scientific Veterinary Committee has expressed an opinion;

- fresh meat treated with ionizing or ultra-violet radiation or which has been marked with colourants other than those permitted in accordance with the Directive;

- fresh meat from animals which have been found to have a form of tuberculosis or fresh meat found to be carrying cysticerci bovis or cysticerci cellulosae or, in the case of swine, have trichinae;

- fresh meat from animals slaughtered too young;

- parts of the carcase of offal with traumatic lesions, malformations or contamination;

- heads of bovine animals, parts of the muscular or other tissues of the head, excluding tongues and brains;

- meat from animals to which tenderisers have been administered;

- blood which has not been removed under specified conditions of hygiene;

- fresh meat in pieces weighing less than 100 grams.

Obligations on the country of import

A Member State receiving fresh meat may grant general authorisations, or authorisations restricted to specific cases, to one or more exporting Member State in the case of:

- fresh pigmeat which has not undergone an examination for trichinosis;

- fresh meat from male pigs used for breeding, cryptorchid and hermaphrodite pigs, or uncastrated male pigs with a carcase weight exceeding a specified limit, unless fresh meat of these types are intended to undergo one of the treatments provided for in Directive 77/99/EEC and carry a special mark;

- other fresh meat listed above which may not normally be sent between the territories of Member States.

Approved establishments

Member States are required to draw up a list of establishments approved by it and give a veterinary approval number to each approved establishment. Approved establishments must comply with the provisions of the Directive. Inspection and supervision must be carried out under the responsibility of the official veterinarian.

The operator or proprietor of the establishment must regularly check the general hygiene of the establishment. This obligation extends to the hygiene of utensils, fittings and machinery at all stages of production and the products themselves.

Where a Member State considers that an establishment in another Member State is not fulfilling the provisions governing approval, it must inform the central authority of the latter State accordingly. The two Member States must together seek a remedy to the situation. Where no remedy can be reached, the Commission will instruct one or more veterinary experts to give an opinion. On the basis of the opinion of veterinary experts, Member States may prohibit provisionally the introduction into their territory of fresh meat from that establishment.

Verification

In order to verify compliance with the Directive, veterinarian experts from the Commission are empowered to make on-the-spot checks.

Inspection of imports

Where irregularities are suspected, the country of destination may carry out non-discriminatory inspections.

Where, as the result of an inspection, meat is found not to comply with the Directive, the competent authority in the country of destination may give the consignor the opportunity of turning back the consignment or using the meat for other purposes, provided that health considerations permit this. Precautions must be taken to prevent improper use of such meat.

Inspection of personnel

Persons employed to work with or handle fresh meat must show, by means of a medical certificate, that there is no impediment to employment. Unless a recognised medical check-up scheme is provided, medical certificates must be renewed annually. Any person who is a possible source of contamination, particularly through pathogenic agents, will be prohibited from working with meat products.

National derogations

The Directive does not affect channels of appeal available in the Member States, provided that decisions are taken by competent authorities and provided for in the Directive.

Timetable

Member States were required to comply with the provisions of the Directive by 29 June 1965.

The full text was published in OJL 121, 29.7.64.

Council Directive 71/118/EEC of 15 February 1971 on health problems affecting trade in fresh poultrymeat.

As amended by:
Council Directive 75/431/EEC, see OJL 192, 24.7.75
Council Directive 78/50/EEC, see OJL 15, 19.1.78
Council Directive 80/216/EEC, see OJL 47, 21.2.80
Council Directive 85/324/EEC, see OJL 168, 28.6.85
Council Directive 85/326/EEC, see OJL 168, 28.6.85

Summary

The Directive on health problems affecting trade in fresh poultrymeat lays down provisions concerning both intra-Community trade and trade within Member States. The Directive is applicable to fresh meat from:

- hens;

- turkeys;

- guinea-fowls;

- ducks;

- geese.

For the purposes of the Directive, all poultrymeat which has not undergone any preserving process will be considered as fresh meat, together with chilled and frozen poultrymeat.

Intra-community trade and trade within Member States

In the case of carcases and offal, Member States are required to ensure that trade is allowed only in fresh meat which:

- has been obtained from an approved slaughterhouse. Birds intended for the production of "foie gras" may be stunned, bled and plucked on the fattening farm, provided this is carried out in a separate room and that uneviscerated carcases are transported immediately to the approved cutting plant where they must be eviscerated within 24 hours;

- comes from an animal inspected ante mortem by an official veterinarian and is considered suitable for slaughter for trade in fresh poultrymeat;

- has been treated under satisfactory hygiene conditions;

- has been inspected post mortem by an official veterinarian and found to be fit for human consumption;

- bears a health marking in accordance with the Annex of the Directive;

- has been stored after post mortem inspection under satisfactory hygiene conditions;

- has been suitably packed in accordance with the provisions of the Directive;

- has been transported in accordance with the Directive.

In the case of parts of carcases or boned meat, Member States are required to ensure that trade is allowed only in fresh meat which:

- has been cut in approved cutting premises and cut in accordance with the provisions of the Directive;

- comes from fresh meat from animals slaughtered in the Member State and complying with the Directive, or fresh meat introduced from another Member State and complying with the Directive, or fresh meat imported from third countries in accordance with Community provisions;

- has been stored under conditions complying with the Directive;

- has been subject to control by an official veterinarian.

Exclusions

Trade in the following products is prohibited:

- fresh poultrymeat treated with hydrogen peroxide, other bleaching substances or with natural or artificial colouring matters;

- fresh poultrymeat treated with antibiotics, preservatives or tenderisers.

Where a Member State of destination allows, conditions laid down for carcases and offal and for parts of carcases or boned meat need not be satisfied in the case of meat intended for uses other than human consumption.

Conditions laid down for carcases and offal are not applicable to fresh poultrymeat which is supplied by the producer direct to the final consumer for his own consumption otherwise than by itinerant sale, sale by mail order or sale on a market.

Storage conditions laid down for fresh poultrymeat are not applicable to storage operations carried out within premises in which carcases and cut or boned poultrymeat are supplied directly to the final consumer.

Packaging requirements of the Directive are not applicable to carcases not packed individually which are brought into premises referred to above.

Conditions laid down for parts of carcases or boned meat are not applicable to fresh poultrymeat where cutting or boning operations are carried out in the premises where meat is sold or used in adjacent premises for the purpose of supplying the final consumer directly otherwise than by itinerant sale, sale by mail order or sale on a market.

Authorised establishments

Approved slaughterhouses and cutting premises must be registered on separate lists and each establishment must have a veterinary approval number. An establishment must be approved by a Member State and must comply with the Directive.

Where a Member State considers that an establishment in another Member State is not fulfilling the provisions governing approval, it must inform the central authority of the latter State accordingly. The two Member States must together seek a remedy to the situation. Where no remedy can be reached, the Commission will instruct one or more veterinary experts to give an opinion. On the basis of the opinion of veterinary experts and in accordance with the procedure involving the Standing Veterinary Committee, Member States may prohibit the introduction into their territory of fresh meat from that establishment.

This authorisation may be withdrawn where the findings of a later inspection warrant a withdrawal.

Verification

Veterinary experts from the Member States and the Commission are required to make regular on-the-spot checks to verify compliance with the Directive.

Cold stores located outside a slaughterhouse or cutting premises will remain under the supervision of an official veterinarian.

National derogations

The Directive does not affect more stringent national provisions relating to:

- conditions for the approval of cold stores;

- the treatment of poultry with substances likely to make the product dangerous to human health, and the absorption by poultry of substances such as antibiotics, oestrogens, thyrostats, tenderisers, pesticides, herbicides or substances containing arsenic or antimony;

- the addition of foreign substances to fresh poultrymeat and its treatment by ionising and ultraviolet radiation.

Intra-community trade

Member States are required to ensure that fresh meat sent to another Member State is accompanied during transportation by a health certificate conforming to the Directive.

A Member State may prohibit the marketing in its territory of fresh poultrymeat from another Member State if it is found that:

- such meat is unfit for human consumption, or

- the provisions of the Directive have not been complied with.

Where a product is prohibited from entering a Member State, the reasons for this decision must be communicated to the consignor or his representative, together with an indication of what appeals are open to him. Consignors have the right to obtain the opinion of a veterinary expert. Where decisions are based on the diagnosis of a contagious or infectious disease, a deterioration dangerous to human health or a serious infringement of the provisions of the Directive, the decisions must be communicated to the competent authority in the exporting Member State.

Where there is a danger that animal diseases may be spread by the introduction into its territory of fresh poultrymeat from another Member State, a Member State may:

- in the event of an outbreak of an epizootic disease in another Member State, temporarily prohibit or restrict the introduction of fresh poultrymeat from the affected areas of a Member State;

- in the case of a widespread epizootic disease or an outbreak of another serious animal disease, temporarily prohibit or restrict the introduction of fresh poultrymeat from the entire territory of a Member State.

A Member State is required to inform other Member States and the Commission of the outbreak in its territory of any such disease.

Decisions to repeal or amend prohibitive measures will be taken on the basis of consultation with the Standing Veterinary Committee.

Timetable

Member States were required to comply with the Directive by August 1982 in respect of intra-Community trade and by 1 January 1977 in respect of fresh poultrymeat produced and marketed in their territory.

The full text was published in OJL 55, 8.3.71.

Council Directive 72/471/EEC of 12 December 1972 on health problems affecting intra-Community trade in fresh meat.

As supplemented by:
Council Directive 80/213/EEC, see OJL 47, 21.2.80
Council Directive 87/64/EEC, see OJL 34, 5.2.87

As amended by:
Council Directive 85/322/EEC, see OJL 168, 28.6.85
Council Directive 87/489/EEC, see OJL 280, 3.10.87

Summary

The Directive on health problems affecting intra-Community trade in fresh meat requires Member States to ensure that no meat suspected to be contaminated forms part of intra-Community trade. The Directive is applicable to trade in fresh meat from:

- domestic bovine animals;

- swine;

- sheep and goats;

- solipeds.

All meat which has not undergone any preserving process will be considered to be fresh meat, together with chilled and frozen meat.

Fresh meat sent from one Member State to another Member State must fulfil the following requirements:

- in the case of meat from sheep, goats or solipeds, meat must come from animals which have stayed in the territory of the Community for at least twenty-one days prior to slaughter or from birth in the case of animals less than twenty-one days old;

- meat must not have been obtained from animals which have come from a holding area or are subject to prohibition subject to Directive 64/433/EEC;

- meat must not be obtained from slaughterhouses in which cases of foot and mouth disease, swine fever or contagious swine paralysis have been recorded;

- in the case of swine, sheep or goats, meat must not come from holdings which are subject to prohibition as a result of an outbreak of porcine, ovine or caprine brucellosis.

Fresh meat which does not meet the requirements outlined above must not be given the health mark laid down by Directive 64/433/EEC.

Where the country of destination prohibits the introduction into its territory of fresh meat on the grounds that the requirements of the Directive have not been met, that Member State must allow the return of the fresh meat, provided that this is not contrary to health provisions. Where the return of fresh meat to the country of origin is not authorised, the country of origin may order the consignment to be destroyed.

Exemptions

General authorisations may be granted by a country of destination to an exporting country in the case of fresh meat from animals which have not stayed at least twenty-one days in the territory of the Community immediately prior to slaughter. A corresponding authorisation must be obtained from the countries of transit.

Prohibitive measures

Where there is a danger that animal diseases may be spread by the introduction into its territory of fresh meat from another Member State, the following measures may be taken:

- in the case of an outbreak of epizootic disease in another Member State, a Member State may temporarily prohibit the introduction into its territory of fresh meat from affected areas;

- where an epizootic disease becomes more widespread, or in the case of an outbreak of another infectious animal disease, it may temporarily prohibit or restrict the introduction of meat from the whole territory of that Member State.

A Member State is required to notify the Commission and other Member States of any such outbreak of disease and of the measures taken to control it. Notification must also be given of the disappearance of the disease. On the basis of consultations within the Standing Veterinary Committee, a Member State may be required to amend these measures.

Measures relating to swine fever

A Member State in whose territory African swine fever has been recorded in the last 12 months must not export fresh pigmeat to the territory of another Member State. However, in the basis of consultations within the Standing Veterinary Committee, one or more parts of the territory of that Member State may be exempt from the prohibition.

Timetable

Member States were required to comply with the Directive by 1 January 1974.

The full text was published in OJL 302, 31.12.72.

Council Directive 72/462/EEC of 12 December 1972 on health and veterinary inspection problems upon importation of bovine animals and swine and fresh meat from third countries.

As amended by:
Council Directive 77/96/EEC, see OJL 26, 31.1.77
Council Directive 83/91/EEC, see OJL 59, 5.3.83
Council Directive 88/289/EEC, see OJL 124, 18.5.88

As implemented by:
Commission Decision 78/685/EEC, see OJL 227, 18.8.78

As supplemented by:
Council Directive 86/469/EEC, see OJL 275, 26.9.86
Council Directive 87/64/EEC, see OJL 34, 5.2.87

Summary

The Directive applies to imports of:

- domestic bovine animals and swine for breeding, production or slaughter;

- fresh meat from domestic animals of bovine animals, swine, sheep and goats and from domestic solipeds;

- fresh meat of cloven-hoofed wild animals and wild solipeds from certain third countries of origin.

The Directive is not applicable to:

- animals intended exclusively for grazing or draught purposes in the vicinity of Community frontiers on a temporary basis;

- meat forming part of travellers' personal luggage and intended for their personal consumption, in so far as the quantity does not exceed one kilogram per person;

- meat sent as small packages to private persons, provided that such meat is not imported by way of trade, in so far as the quantity does not exceed one kilogram;

- meat for consumption by the crew and passengers on board means of transport operating internationally.

Where meat of this kind or kitchen waste is unloaded, it must be destroyed. It is not necessary to destroy meat when it is transferred from one means of transport to another.

Authorised list

The Council, acting on a proposal from the Commission, is required to draw up a list of the third countries from which the Member States will authorise importation of bovine animals, swine and fresh meat. The list may be amended in accordance with the consultation procedure with the Standing Veterinary Committee.

In deciding whether a third country may appear on the list, account must be take of:

- the state of health of the livestock, other domestic animals and wildlife in the third country;

- the regularity of information supplied by the third country relating to the existence of contagious diseases in its territory;

- the country's rules on animal disease prevention and control;

- the structure of the veterinary services in the country and their powers;

- the organisation and implementation of measures to prevent and control infectious and contagious animal diseases;

- that country's legislation on the use of substances, in particular legislation concerning the prohibition or authorisation of substances, their distribution, release on to the market and their rulings covering administration and inspection.

Approved establishments

In accordance with the procedure involving the Standing Veterinary Committee, lists are to be drawn up of establishments from which Member States may authorise importation of fresh meat.

In deciding whether a slaughterhouse, cutting plant or store outside a slaughterhouse or plant may appear on the list of approved establishments, particular account must be taken of:

- guarantees which the third country can offer with regard to compliance with the Directive;

- the third country's regulations with regard to the administration to animals of any substances which might affect the wholesomeness of meat;

- in each particular case, compliance with the Directive and with Directive 64/433/EEC;

- organisation of the meat inspection service of the third country.

Verification

Inspection must be carried out on the spot by veterinary experts of the Member States and the Commission.

Where inspection brings to light serious facts as against an approved establishment, the Commission must inform the Member States and provisionally suspend the approval. A final decision must be taken according to the consultation procedure with the Standing Veterinary Committee.

Importation of fresh meat

Fresh meat must come from animals which have remained in the territory of a third country on the approved list for at least three months before slaughter, or since birth if the animals in question are less than three months old.

Member States must not authorise the importation of fresh meat unless it comes from third countries:

- which have been free from the following diseases for at least twelve months: cattle plague, exotic foot-and-mouth disease, African swine fever, contagious porcine paralysis (Teschen disease). It may be decided in accordance with the procedure involving the Standing Veterinary Committee that this provision is applicable only to part of the territory of a third country;

- in which no vaccinations have been carried out for the previous twelve months against the diseases listed above to which the animals from which meat has come are susceptible. It may be decided in accordance with the procedure involving the Standing Veterinary Committee that importation of fresh meat may be permitted from a third country or part of the territory of a third country where vaccinations have been carried out.

Member States must not authorise importation of fresh meat from a third country unless meat complies with the public health and animal health requirements adopted for the importation of fresh meat from that country.

Until 31 December 1996 Member States may authorise imports of glands and organs, including blood, as raw materials for the pharmaceutical processing industry, coming from third countries which appear on the authorised list and are not subject to a ban.

In accordance with the consultation procedure with the Standing Veterinary Committee, Member States may be authorised to import the raw materials from countries which do not appear on the authorised list, under conditions which take account of the specific health situation of the third countries concerned.

Member States must not authorise importation of fresh meat in the form of carcases, including half-carcases in the case of swine, and halves or quarters in the case of bovine animals or solipeds, unless it is possible to reconstruct the entire carcase of each animal.

In the case of such importation, fresh meat must:

- have been obtained in a slaughterhouse included in the approved list;

- come from an animal which has successfully undergone ante mortem inspection in accordance with Directive 64/433/EEC. Additional requirements may be decided on with regard to specific situations of countries where certain diseases are likely to endanger human health;

- have been treated in conditions of hygiene in accordance with Directive 64/433/EEC;

- have undergone a post mortem inspection carried out under the control of an official veterinarian in accordance with Directive 64/433/EEC and have shown no change except for traumatic lesions incurred shortly before slaughter, or localised malformations or changes, provided that it is established that these do not render the carcase and offal unfit for human consumption or dangerous to human health;

- bear an official health mark;

- have been stored in satisfactory hygienic conditions in accordance with Directive 64/433/EEC after post-mortem inspection;

- have been transported in accordance with Directive 64/433/EEC and undergone handling and satisfactory hygiene conditions.

<u>Derogations</u>

By way of derogation, Member States may permit the importation of:

- half-carcases, half-carcases cut into no more that three wholesale cuts, quarters or offal complying with the conditions set out in the Directive;

- cuts smaller than quarters or boned meat or offal or sliced livers from approved cutting plants. Such meat must have been cut and obtained in compliance with Directive 64/433/EEC, inspected by an official veterinarian, packaged in accordance with Directive 64/433/EEC, and the fresh meat of solipeds must undergo inspection by the country of destination with a view to possible restrictions on the use of such meat.

Member States may authorise the importation into their territories of masseter muscles and brains provided that they comply with the provisions of the Directive.

The Directive is not applicable to:

- fresh meat imported with the authorisation of the country of destination for uses other than human consumption;

- fresh meat intended for exhibition, special studies or analyses, provided that administrative supervision makes it possible to ensure that meat is not used for human consumption and provided that when its use has ceased it is withdrawn from the Community or destroyed;

- fresh meat intended for the supply of international organisations, subject to approval by the Standing Veterinary Committee, provided that meat comes from a third country on the approved list and provided that animal health requirements are complied with.

Prohibited products

Member States must prohibit the importation of:

- fresh meat from boars or cryptorchid pigs;

- fresh meat from animals to which hormonal substances prohibited under Directives 81/602/EEC and 88/146/EEC have been administered; or containing residues of hormonal substances authorised in accordance with the exceptions provided for in Directive 81/602/EEC and Directive 85/649/EEC, residues of antibiotics, pesticides, or of other substances likely to make the consumption of fresh meat dangerous to human health, in so far as residues exceed the permitted level;

- fresh meat treated with ionizing or ultraviolet radiation, and fresh meat from animals to which tenderisers or products likely to adversely affect the meat's composition or organoleptic characteristics having been administered;

- fresh meat to which substances other than those provided for in Directive 64/433/EEC have been added for the purpose of health marking;

- fresh meat from animals which have been found to have any form of tuberculosis, or fresh meat from animals which have been found after slaughter to have any form of tuberculosis or to be carrying cycisterci bovis or cycterci cellulosae, or in the case of swine to have trichinae;

- fresh meat from animals slaughtered too young;

- parts of the carcase or offal with traumatic lesions incurred shortly before slaughter or malformations or changes;

- blood;

- minced meat, meat cut up in a similar manner and mechanically recovered meat;

- fresh meat in pieces of less than 100 grams;

- heads of cattle, parts of the muscular and other tissues of the head, except for the tongue and the brain.

Veterinary certificate

Member States must not authorise fresh meat to be imported without an animal health certificate and a public health certificate drawn up by an official veterinarian of the exporting third country.

Certificates must:

- be drawn up in at least one of the official languages of the country of destination and the Member State in which the import inspections are carried out;

- accompany the fresh meat in the original;

- consist of a single sheet of paper;

- be made out for a single consignee.

Verification

Upon arrival in the territory of the Community, Member States must ensure that fresh meat is subjected without delay to an animal health inspection carried out by the competent authority .

Member States must ensure that importation is prohibited if inspection reveals that:

- meat does not come from the territory of a third country included on the approved list;

- meat comes from a third country from which imports are prohibited;

- the animal health certificate which accompanies the meat does not comply with the conditions laid down by the Directive.

Member States may authorise fresh meat from one third country to be transported to another provided that:

- the party concerned supplies proof that the first third country to which the meat is being sent will not reject or send back the meat to the Community;

- such transport has been previously authorised by the competent authorities of the Member State in the territory of which the inspection is carried out;

- such transport is carried out without the goods being unloaded on Community territory and under the supervision of the competent authorities, in containers sealed by the competent authorities.

Member States must ensure that each consignment of fresh meat undergoes a public health inspection before being released in the Community. The public health inspection must be carried out by random sampling. The purpose of inspection will be to verify:

- the public health certificate, compliance with the stipulation on the certificate, the health marking;

- the state of preservation, presence of dirt or pathogenic agents;

- the presence of residues of substances referred to in the Directive;

- whether slaughter and cutting have been carried out in establishments approved for that purpose;

- conditions of transport.

Member States must prohibit the marketing of fresh meat if inspections have shown that:

- fresh meat is not suitable for human consumption;

- conditions laid down in the Directive and Directive 64/433/EEC have not been fulfilled;

- one of the certificates which accompany each consignment does not comply with the requirements of the Directive.

If fresh meat cannot be imported it must be returned or destroyed in the territory of the Member State in which the inspections have taken place.

Distribution certificate

When forwarded to the country of destination, each consignment of fresh authorised for circulation in the Community must be accompanied by a certificate. The certificate must:

- be drawn up by the official veterinarian at the inspection post or place of storage;

- be issued on the day of loading for dispatch of the fresh meat to the country of destination;

- be drawn up in at least one of the official languages of the country of destination;

- accompany the consignment of fresh meat in the original.

Inspection posts

Member States must draw up and communicate to the Commission lists of:

- frontier inspection posts for the importation of bovine animals and swine;

- inspection posts for importation of fresh meat.

Outbreak of disease

Where an infectious animal disease breaks out or spreads in a third country and the disease can be carried by fresh meat and is likely to endanger public health or livestock, a Member State must prohibit the importation of that meat (whether imported directly or indirectly) from either the whole of the third country or part of its territory.

The resumption of importation from the third country will be authorised in accordance with the procedure involving the Standing Veterinary Committee.

Timetable

Member States were required to comply with the Directive by 1 January 1976.

The full text was published in OJL 302, 31.12.72.

Council Directive 77/99/EEC of 21 December 1976 on health problems affecting intra-Community trade in meat products.

As amended by:
Council Directive 80/214/EEC, see OJL 47, 21.2.80
Commission Directive 83/201/EEC, see OJL 112, 28.4.83
Council Directive 85/327/EEC, see OJL 168, 28.6.85
Council Directive 85/328/EEC, see OJL 168, 28.6.85

Summary

The Directive on health problems affecting intra-Community trade in meat products requires Member States to comply with the following general conditions when products are sent from its territory to the territory of another Member State:

- they must have been prepared in an establishment approved and inspected in accordance with the provisions of the Directive;

- they must have been prepared, stored and transported in accordance with the provisions of the Directive;

- they must be prepared from fresh meat as defined in the Directive. Meat may originate in the Member State in which the preparation is carried out; or in any other Member State, or in a third country, being imported either directly or by another Member State; or in a third country in so far as products obtained from meat fulfil the requirements of the Directive, the health marking laid down in the Directive is not carried out on these products, and intra-Community trade remains subject to national provisions. They must have been prepared from a meat product which complies with the requirements of the Directive;

- they must have been prepared by heating, salting or drying. These processes may be combined with smoking or maturing;

- they must be prepared from fresh meat handled in accordance with the Directive;

- they must have undergone an inspection carried out by the competent authority;

- they must meet the standards laid down in the Directive;

- they must be wrapped and packaged in accordance with the Directive;

- they must bear the health marking in accordance with the Directive;

- they must be accompanied by a health certificate during transport to the country of destination;

- they must be stored and transported to the country of destination under satisfactory health conditions in accordance with the Directive.

Meat products must not have been subjected to ionizing radiation unless this is justified on medical grounds and unless such procedure is clearly indicated on the product and on the health certificate.

Storage temperature

Meat products which have undergone complete treatment in accordance with the Directive may be stored and transported at normal ambient temperatures.

Where meat products have undergone incomplete treatment, the producer is required to ensure that the packaging of meat products bears a clear and legible indication of the temperature at which products must be transported and stored.

Derogations

The requirements laid down above are not applicable to meat products which are imported with the authorisation of the country of destination for uses other than human consumption. The country of destination must ensure that these products are used only for the purposes for which they were dispatched to that country.

Approved establishments

Each Member State is required to draw up a list of the establishments approved by it and having a veterinary approval number.

Personnel

Persons employed to work with or handle these products must show, by means of a medical certificate, that there is no impediment to employment. Medical certificates are to be renewed annually unless a recognised equivalent medical check-up scheme is provided. Any person who is a possible source of contamination, particularly through pathogenic agents, must be prohibited from working with the products in question.

National derogations

In accordance with the consultation procedure with the Standing Veterinary Committee, it may be decided that certain provisions of the Directive will not apply to certain products which contain other foodstuffs and only a small percentage of meat or meat product. Such derogations must relate only to:

- conditions of approval;

- inspection requirements;

- health marking and health certificate requirements.

Prohibited products

Where, in the course of a health inspection, a Member State has established that:

- meat products imported from another Member State are unfit for human consumption;

- the Directive has not been complied with;

the marketing of such products must be prohibited.

If reconsignment of the products is not possible, the products must be destroyed. However, the Member State may authorise the entry of such products into their territory for use other than for human consumption, to the extent that there is no danger to human or animal health.

Right of appeal

The Directive does not affect channels of appeal open under national legislation.

Each Member State must grant the consignors of meat products which have been prohibited the right to obtain the opinion of an expert.

Imports from third countries

In the case of imports of meat products from third countries, Member States must apply provisions not more favourable than those governing intra-Community trade.

Timetable

Member States were required to comply with the Directive no later than 1 July 1979.

The full text was published in OJL 26, 31.1.77.

Council Decision 79/542/EEC of 21 December 1976 drawing up a list of third countries from which the Member States authorise imports of bovine animals, swine and fresh meat.

As supplemented by:
Council Decision 85/473/EEC, see OJL 278, 18.10.85

As amended by:
Council Decision 85/575/EEC, see OJL 372, 31.12.85
Council Decision 86/425/EEC, see OJL 243, 28.8.86

Summary

The system established by Directive 72/462/EEC is based on the establishment of a list of third countries from which imports of bovine animals and swine and imports of fresh meat from bovine animals, swine, sheep, goats and domestic solipeds are authorised.

This Decision requires Member States to authorise imports of animals and fresh meat in accordance with the list laid down in the Annex.

Timetable

Member States were required to comply with the Decision by June 1981.

The full text was published in OJL 146, 14.6.79.

Council Directive 80/215/EEC of 22 January 1980 on animal health problems affecting intra-Community trade in meat products.

As amended by:
Council Directive 80/1100/EEC, see OJL 225, 1.12.80
Council Directive 85/321/EEC, see OJL 168, 28.6.85
Council Directive 87/491/EEC, see OJL 279, 2.10.87

Summary

The Directive on health problems affecting intra-Community trade in meat products requires Member States to ensure that meat products intended for intra-Community trade are prepared from or with:

- fresh meat as defined in Directive 64/433/EEC and fulfilling the animal health requirements of Directive 72/461/EEC;

- fresh meat as defined in Directive 72/462/EEC and complying with the animal health requirements of that Directive.

Meat products which are prepared in whole or in part from fresh meat as defined in Directive 64/433/EEC and which fulfil the requirements of Directive 72/461/EEC may enter intra-Community trade if:

- heat treatment has been carried out in a hermetically sealed container;

- products are prepared under the supervision of an official veterinarian;

- products are prepared exclusively from or with pigmeat from farms or areas not subject to banning orders on health policy grounds.

Where the existence of African swine fever has been established:

- meat must be fully boned and the main lymphatic glands removed;

- the piece of meat to be treated must weigh no more than five kilograms;

- before heating, each piece of meat must be enclosed in a hermetically sealed container;

- heat treatment must involve subjection to a temperature of at least 60 degrees centigrade for a minimum of four hours during which the temperature must be at least 70 degrees centigrade for a minimum of 30 minutes. The temperature must be monitored constantly;

- the conditions of Directive 72/461/EEC must be fulfilled;

- after treatment, a public health mark must be put on each of the containers in accordance with Directive 77/99/EEC;

- Member States which make use of the heat treatment provided for must notify the Commission and the other Member States accordingly.

Member States must ensure that fresh meat referred to above is:

- transported and stored separately from other meat products;

- used in such a way as to avoid it being introduced into meat products intended for intra-Community trade;

- marked with the stamp provided for in Directive 72/461/EEC.

The health certificate specified in Directive 77/99/EEC must contain under the entry "Nature of products" the words "Treated in accordance with Article 4(1)(a) of Directive 80/215/EEC" or "Treated in accordance with Article 4(1)(b) of Directive 80/215/EEC".

Country of destination

Where it has been established that the provisions of the Directive have not been complied with, the country of destination may prohibit entry into its territory of such meat products.

At the request of the consignor or his representative, the country of destination must authorise the return of the whole consignment, provided that this is not contrary to animal health considerations.

Where the country of export or transit does not authorise return of the consignment, the competent authority of the country of destination may order the consignment to be destroyed.

At the request of the consignor or his representative, the grounds on which these decisions have been taken must be communicated in writing with an indication of the remedies for which provision is given, and the time limits applicable.

Member States must grant consignors the right to obtain the opinion of a veterinary expert.

A Member State may take measures necessary if there is a danger that animal diseases may spread by the introduction of meat products from another Member State into its territory:

- in the case of an outbreak of classical foot and mouth disease, classical swine fever, swine vesicular disease or Teschen disease in the other Member States, the introduction of products prepared from the meat of animals which are susceptible to the diseases, other than products which have undergone one of the treatments may be temporarily prohibited or restricted from those parts of the territory of the Member State in which the disease has appeared;

- in the case of a widespread outbreak of a serious animal disease, the introduction of products prepared from the meat of animals which are susceptible to these diseases may be temporarily prohibited or restricted.

Member States must notify the other Member States and the Commission of the outbreak of any such disease.

Swine fever

Where an outbreak of African swine fever has been recorded within the previous 12 months, a Member State must not export pigmeat products other than those having undergone heat treatment in a hermetically sealed container, according to the provisions of the Directive. Where the disease has not been recorded for at least 12 months in a Member State, such measures will apply exclusively to a part of the territory concerned.

Decisions to lift these measures must be taken in accordance with the consultation procedure with the Standing Veterinary Committee.

In the case of swine fever, Member States which have availed themselves of the authorisation laid down in Directive 80/218/EEC and which are officially swine fever free must not oppose the introduction into their territory of meat products which have been prepared from fresh pigmeat which satisfies the requirements of Directive 72/461/EEC, or from fresh pigmeat obtained from pigs vaccinated against swine fever more than three months before slaughter.

Timetable

Member States were required to comply with the Directive by 31 December 1980.

The full text was published in OJL 47, 21.2.80.

Commission Directive 80/879/EEC of 3 September 1980 on health marking of large packagings of fresh poultrymeat.

Summary

This Commission Directive lays down that the health marking of carcases, parts of carcases or offal required by Directive 71/118/EEC will not be necessary in specified cases.

Consignments of carcases, including those which have had parts removed within the meaning of Directive 71/118/EEC, must be dispatched from an approved slaughterhouse to approved cutting premises for cutting, subject to the conditions that:

- the packaging containing the fresh poultrymeat bears a health mark in accordance with Directive 71/118/EEC;

- the dispatch office maintains a record of the amount, type and destination of consignments dispatched in accordance with the Directive;

- the recipient cutting premises maintains a record of the amount, type and origin of consignments received in accordance with the Directive;

- the health mark on large packaging is destroyed only under the supervision of the official veterinarian when the large packaging is opened;

- the destination and intended use of the consignment is clearly indicated on the external surface of the package in accordance with the Directive.

Consignments of carcases, including those which have had parts removed in accordance with Directive 71/118/EEC, parts of carcases and the following offals, hearts, livers and gizzards must be dispatched from an approved slaughterhouse or cutting premises to a meat product establishment for treatment subject to the conditions that:

- the large packaging containing the fresh poultrymeat bears the health mark in accordance with Directive 71/118/EEC;

- the dispatch office maintains a record of the amount, type and destination of consignments dispatched;

- the recipient establishment maintains a record of the amount, type and origin of consignments received;

- where the fresh poultrymeat is intended for use in meat products for intra-Community trade, the health mark of large packaging is destroyed only under the supervision of the competent authority when the package is opened;

- the destination and intended use of the consignment is clearly indicated on the external surface of the large package.

Member States may authorise the dispatch of consignments of carcases, including those which have had parts removed in accordance with Directive 71/118/EEC, from an approved slaughterhouse or cutting premises to restaurants, canteens and institutions for direct supply to the final consumer, subject to the conditions that:

- the packaging containing the fresh poultrymeat bears the health mark in accordance with Directive 71/118/EEC;

- the dispatch office maintains a record of the amount, type and destination of consignments dispatched;

- the recipient outlet maintains a record of the amount, type and origin of consignments received;

- outlets are subjected to control by a competent authority, which must be given access to the records kept;

- the destination and intended use of the consignment is clearly indicated on the external surface of the large packaging.

Timetable

Member States were required to comply with the Directive by 1 January 1981.

The full text was published in OJL 251, 24.9.80.

Council Directive 81/602/EEC of 31 July 1981 concerning the prohibition of certain substances having a hormonal action and of any substances having a thyrostatic action.

As supplemented by:
Council Directive 85/358/EEC, see OJL 191, 23.7.85

Summary

The Directive concerning the prohibition of certain substances having a hormonal action and of any substances having a thyrostatic action requires Member States to prohibit:

- the administering to a farm animal of substances having a thyrostatic action or substances having an oestrogenic, androgenic or gestagenic action;

- the placing on the market or placing on the market of farm animals which have been treated with such substances;

- the placing on the market of meat treated with such substances;

- processing of the meat treated with such substances and the placing on the market of meat products prepared from or with such meat;

- the placing on the market of stilbenes, stilbene derivatives, their salts and esters and thyrostatic substances for administering to animals of all species.

<u>Veterinary medicinal products</u>

Member States are permitted to authorise the administering to farm animals of substances with oestrogenic, androgenic or gestagenic action (other than stilbenes, stilbene derivatives, their salts and esters and thyrostatic substances) approved in accordance with the Directives on veterinary medicinal products for therapeutic use, synchronisation of oestrus, termination of unwanted gestation, the improvement of fertility and the preparation of donors and recipients for the implantation of embryos.

Substances authorised for use in accordance with the Directives on veterinary medicinal products must be administered by a veterinarian. Member States are permitted to allow the synchronization of oestrus and the preparation of donors and recipients for the implantation of embryos to be effected not by the veterinarian but under his direct responsibility.

<u>Verification</u>

Council Directive 85/358/EEC supplements Directive 81/602/EEC by placing an obligation on Member States to ensure that on-the-spot random checks are made on animals and their meat in order to detect the presence of substances prohibited by Directive 81/602/EEC. Where there is a justified suspicion of an infringement, competent national authorities are required to make:

- random checks on animals on farms of origin;

- an official check for the presence of prohibited substances on farms where the animals are reared, kept or fattened.

Checking for the presence of prohibited substances must take the form of samples taken from either:

- live animals;

- carcases after slaughter;

- animals and meat.

The analysis of samples must be in accordance with methods laid down by the Standing Veterinary Committee.

Where analysis detects the presence of a prohibited substance, the competent national authorities must ensure that:

- an investigation is made at the farm of origin;

- an investigation is made to determine the source of the prohibited substance.

- animals containing the substance are marked and withheld from sale on the market for human or animal consumption;

- the slaughter of animals intended for human consumption is prevented until the residue of the substance no longer exceeds prohibited limits;

- animals are not disposed of to other persons during the period of analysis unless under the supervision of the official veterinarian.

At least once a year Member States are required to inform the Commission of control measures which have been adopted in order to comply with this Directive. On the basis of this information, the Commission is required to ensure the uniform application of control measures.

Timetable

Member States were required to comply with Directive 81/602/EEC by August 1982.

The full text was published in OJL 222, 7.8.81.

Council Directive 85/73/EEC of 29 January 1985 on the financing of health inspections and controls of fresh meat and poultrymeat.

Summary

The Directive lays down provisions in accordance with the requirements of Directive 71/118/EEC on health problems affecting trade in fresh poultrymeat.

The Directive is applicable to domestic animals of the following species:

- bovine;
- swine;
- sheep and goats;
  - domestic solipeds and hens;
- turkeys;
- guinea-fowl;
- ducks;
- geese.

Member States are required to ensure that:

- fees are collected when animals are slaughtered for the costs occasioned by health inspections and controls;

- in order to ensure the equivalence of treatment and to cover costs, provision is made for the collection of a fee on meat imported from third countries;

- any direct or indirect refund is prohibited.

Timetable

Member States were required to comply with the Directive by 1 January 1986.

The full text was published in OJL 32, 5.2.85.

Council Directive 86/363/EEC of 24 July 1986 on the fixing of maximum levels for pesticide residues in and on foodstuffs of animal origin.

Summary

The Directive requires the Member States to ensure that products referred to do not present a danger to human health as a result of the presence of pesticide residues. Member States may not prohibit or impede the putting into circulation within their territories of such products on the grounds that they contain pesticide residues if the quantity of such residues does not exceed the maximum levels specified in the Directive.

The Directive specifies the following categories for foodstuffs of animal origin:

- meat and edible offals of horses, asses, mules, hinnies, bovine animals, swine, sheep and goats, whether fresh, chilled or frozen;

- dead poultry and edible offals, whether fresh, chilled or frozen;

- poultry liver, whether fresh, chilled, frozen or in brine;

- meat or edible offals of domestic pigeons, domestic rabbits and game;

- pig fat and poultry fat, whether fresh, chilled, frozen, salted, in brine, dried or smoked;

- meat and edible meat offals (except poultry liver) whether salted, in brine, dried or smoked;

- milk and cream when fresh - not concentrated or sweetened;

- milk and cream, whether preserved, concentrated or sweetened;

- butter;

- cheese and curd;

- eggs;

- meat sausages and similar products;

- other prepared or preserved meat or meat offal.

The Directive does not apply to foodstuffs of animal origin which are intended for export to third countries.

Maximum prescribed levels

Without prejudice to Community or national provisions concerning dietary or children's food, the Directive lays down maximum prescribed levels of the following pesticide residues which may be permitted in the foodstuffs of animal origin specified above:

- aldrin;

- dieldrin (HEOD);

- chlordane;

- DDT;

- endrin;

- heptachlor;

- hexachlorobenzene (HCB);

- hexachlorocyclohexane (HCH);

Member States are required to permit the free circulation of foodstuffs of animal origin in which the quantity of such residues does not exceed maximum levels specified in the Directive.

Verification and national derogations

Methods of verification and permitted national derogations are in accordance with the procedure outlined in Directive 86/362/EEC.

Timetable

Member States were required to comply with the Directive by 30 June 1988. On the basis of a Commission report, the Council will re-examine the effectiveness of these measures no later than 30 June 1991.

The full text was published in OJL 221, 7.8.86.

Commission Decision 86/474/EEC of 11 September 1986 on the implementation of the on-the-spot inspections to be carried out in respect of the importation of bovine animals and swine and fresh meat from non-member countries.

Summary

The Commission Decision on the implementation of the on-the-spot inspections to be carried out in respect of the importation of bovine animals and swine and fresh meat from non-member countries provides that veterinary experts from the Member States and the Commission must carry out on-the-spot inspections to verify compliance with the provisions of Directive 72/462/EEC. Inspections must be carried out every three years in each country appearing on the list drawn up in accordance with Directive 72/462/EEC.

The Commission may postpone or advance inspections, or carry out additional inspections, where reasons of animal health so warrant and after consultation with the Standing Veterinary Committee.

Amending the list of approved establishments

Before a Decision to supplement the list drawn up in accordance with Directive 72/462/EEC is submitted to the Standing Veterinary Committee, veterinary experts from the Member States and the Commission must carry out an inspection in the country concerned.

Veterinary experts from the Member States and the Commission may carry out a veterinary inspection in the country concerned before submitting a proposal for a Decision to:

- amend the list drawn up in accordance with Directive 72/462/EEC;

- authorise the resumption of imports of animals or fresh meat in accordance with Directive 72/462/EEC;

- concerning the measures to be taken if observations, made during the veterinary inspection upon importation of bovine animals or swine or of fresh meat indicate that the provisions of Directive 72/462/EEC are not being complied with.

Verification

Veterinary experts from the Member States and the Commission must carry out on-the-spot health inspections to verify whether the provisions of Directive 72/462/EEC and Directive 77/96/EEC are being applied in practice. Inspections must be carried out at least once a year in all slaughterhouses, cutting plants and cold stores situated outside a slaughterhouse or cutting plant, that appear on the lists drawn up in accordance with Directive 72/462/EEC or Directive 77/96/EEC.

On grounds of health the Commission may:

- postpone or advance certain inspections or carry out additional inspections;

- replace these systematic inspections by sample inspections.

Veterinary experts from the Member States and the Commission must subject the establishment concerned to on-the-spot health inspection before a proposal for a Decision to supplement one of the lists drawn up in accordance with Directive 72/462/EEC or Directive 77/96/EEC is submitted to the Standing Veterinary Committee.

At the request of a Member State, veterinary experts from the Member States and the Commission may, under the direction of the Commission, subject the establishment concerned to on-the-spot health inspection before submitting to the Standing Veterinary Committee a proposal for a Decision:

- amending one of the lists drawn up in accordance with Directive 77/96/EEC;

- concerning the measures to be taken if observations made during the health inspection upon importation indicate that the provisions of Directives 72/462/EEC and 77/96/EEC are not being complied with.

Veterinary experts

The Commission is required to determine the number and qualifications of the veterinary experts whom it appoints to carry out the inspections. The Commission must inform the Member States of the results of the inspections by written reports within the Standing Veterinary Committee.

The Decision will be reviewed before 1 January 1992.

The full text was published in OJL 279, 30.9.86.

Commission Decision 87/410/EEC of 14 July 1987 laying down the methods to be used for detecting residues of substances having a thyrostatic action.

Summary

The Commission Decision laying down the methods to be used for detecting residues of substances having a thyrostatic action requires use of the following analytical procedures:

- immunoassay (IA);

- thin layer chromatography (TLC);

- high performance liquid chromotography (HPLC);

- gas chromotography (GC);

- mass spectrometry (MS);

- spectrometry (SP).

Samples must be drawn according to the rules that:

- size of the sample must be sufficient to allow adequate analysis and to allow a repeat analysis and confirmatory tests;

- samples must be marked in such a way that identification remains possible at all stages of the procedure;

- packaging, preservation and transport of samples must be such as to maintain their integrity and not prejudice to result of the examination.

The Decision will be re-examined before 1 January 1991.

The full text was published in OJL 223, 11.8.87.

Council Directive 88/146/EEC of 7 March 1988 prohibiting the use in livestock farming of certain substances having a hormonal action.

Summary

The Directive prohibiting the use in livestock farming of certain substances having a hormonal action replaces Directive 85/649/EEC, which was annulled for infringement of a procedural requirement by the European Court of Justice. The content of the Directive is identical to the text of the Directive of 31 December 1985.

The Directive requires Member States to prevent authorisation of any derogation from the requirements of Directive 81/602/EEC concerning the prohibition of certain substances having a hormonal action and of substances having a thyrostatic action. As a result, Member States must prohibit:

- the administering to a farm animal of substances having a thyrostatic action or substances having an oestrogenic, androgenic or gestagenic action;

- the placing on the market or slaughtering of farm animals to which such substances have been administered;

- the placing on the market of meat of farm animals to which such substances have been administered;

- processing of the meat of farm animals to which such substances have been administered and the placing on the market of meat products prepared from or with such meat.

Derogations

By way of derogation from the above requirement, Member States may authorise the administering to farm animals for therapeutic purposes of oestradiol -17-B, testosterone and progesterone and those derivatives which readily yield the parent compound on hydrolysis after absorption at the site of application.

Implementation

For the purposes of implementation of the Directive:

- there must be established a list of products containing the active substances referred to above and satisfying the relevant criteria of Directives 81/851/EEC and 81/852/EEC; the conditions of use of these products; the means of identification of animals;

- products used for therapeutic treatment may be administered only by a veterinarian in the form of an injection to farm animals which have been clearly identified;

- any decision on the possible inclusion of a new substance to the group of substances referred to above must be taken by the Council, acting on a proposal from the Commission.

Production of substances

Member States are required to prescribe that undertakings having a thyrostatic, androgenic or gestagenic action and those authorised to market those substances, and undertakings producing pharmaceutical and veterinary products based on those substances, must keep a register detailing quantities produced or acquired and those sold or used for the production of pharmaceutical and veterinary products.

Export

Member States are required to ensure that no animals are dispatched from their territory to that of another Member State which have had this type of hormones administered to them, and that no meat from such animals is dispatched. The Community stamp must be reserved for the meat of untreated animals.

Import

Member States are required to prohibit the importation from third countries of animals and meat from animals to which have been administered substances of a thyrostatic, oestrogenic, androgenic or gestagenic action.

Member States are required to ensure that imported fresh meat coming from approved slaughterhouses in third countries is circulated in accordance with Directive 72/462/EEC.

Member States are required to ensure that imports from third countries do not receive more favourable treatment than Community products. In accordance with consultations within the Standing Veterinary Committee, the Commission must establish the frequency of routine inspections on imports from each third country, taking account of the guarantees offered by the inspection regulations of third countries.

Reproductive animals

Council Directive 88/299/EEC provides certain derogations in respect of trade in animals intended for reproduction and reproductive animals at the end of their career which have been treated under the provisions of Directive 81/602/EEC, and in respect of meat from these animals, taking into account the guarantees offered.

Timetable

Member States were required to comply with the Directive by 1 January 1988.

The full text was published in OJ L70, 16.3.88.

Council Directive 88/299/EEC of 17 May 1988 on trade in animals treated with certain substances having hormonal action and their meat, as referred to in Article 7 of Directive 88/146/EEC.

Summary

The Directive on trade in animals treated with certain substances having a hormonal action and their meat lays down the conditions for applying derogations provided for in Article 7 of Directive 88/146/EEC.

The Directive requires Member States to authorise trade in animals intended for reproduction and reproductive animals at the end of their career which have undergone treatment referred to in Directive 81/602/EEC. Member States may authorise the use of the Community stamp on meat from such animals, provided that the requirements of the Directive are met.

Only one of the following substances may be administered to animals:

- for therapeutic treatment: oestradiol-17-B, testosterone and progesterone, and derivatives (approved in accordance with Directive 88/146/EEC) which readily yield the parent compound on hydrolysis after absorption at the site of application;

- for synchronisation of oestrus, termination of unwanted gestation, the improvement of fertility and the preparation of donors and recipients for the implantation of embryos: substances mentioned in Directive 81/602/EEC, provided that conditions of use, the necessary waiting period, detailed provisions concerning the monitoring of those conditions for use and means of identification of animals are established in accordance with the procedure involving the Standing Veterinary Committee. The Committee's decision will be reached after opinions have been received from the Committee for Veterinary Medicinal Products. Until such decisions have been reached, Member States must monitor the use of substances which have been subject to national authorisation; on the basis of these findings the Commission will draw up a provisional list of approved substances. Provisional lists will be valid until 31 December 1991.

Approved substances

In establishing lists of substances which may be administered to animals intended for intra-Community trade, account must be taken of:

- the possibility of monitoring use of the substance;

- the need to exclude sustained-release products or salts or esters with long half-life, where the therapeutic objective could be achieved by using products with a shorter half-life;

- the need to exclude products with a waiting period exceeding 15 days after the end of the treatment;

- the availability of reagents and materials required for the methods of analysis for detecting the presence of residues exceeding permitted limits.

The veterinarian responsible for administering the substances must keep a register of:

- nature of the treatment;

- nature of the products authorised;

- date of the treatment;

- identity of the animals treated.

<u>Export</u>

Member States must ensure that animals are sent to the territory of another Member State only if:

- the conditions laid down in the Directive and the waiting period specified in Directive 88/146/EEC have been complied with;

- in the case of reproductive animals at the end of their career, no treatment referred to in Directive 81/602/EEC has been administered.

Member States must ensure that meat of animals intended for reproduction or reproductive animals at the end of their career comply with the above provisions.

The Community stamp may be affixed to meat only if the waiting time has ended before animals are slaughtered.

Imports from third countries

By way of derogation from Directive 88/146/EEC and for the purposes of complying with Directive 86/469/EEC, imports from third countries of animals intended for reproduction and reproductive animals at the end of their career, or the meat of such animals must satisfy requirements at least equivalent to those laid down in this Directive.

Timetable

Member States were required to comply with the Directive by 31 December 1988.

The full text was published in OJ L128, 21.5.88.

Commission Decision 89/15/EEC of 15 December 1988 on the importation of live animals and fresh meat from certain third countries.

As amended by:
Commission Decision 89/17/EEC, see OJL 8, 11.1.89
Commission Decision 89/137/EEC, see OJL 49, 21.2.89

Summary

This Commission Decision requires Member States to continue to authorise imports of fresh meat and live animals from those countries which comply with the Annex of Directive 86/469/EEC and which provide guarantees concerning substances having a thyrostatic, oestrogenic, androgenic or gestagenic effect.

As regards substances other than those mentioned above, the third countries on the list provided for in Directive 72/462/EEC must continue to appear on that list.

Timetable

The Decision entered into force on 1 January 1989.

The full text was published in OJL 8, 11.1.89.

MEAT AND MEAT PRODUCTS - PROPOSED LEGISLATION

COM(85) 678. Proposal for a Council Directive amending Directive 77/99/EEC on health problems affecting intra-Community trade in meat products.

Summary

The proposal for a Directive on health problems affecting intra-Community trade in meat products will amend Directive 77/99/EEC as set out below.

The amended Directive is not applicable to meat products which:

- form part of travellers' personal luggage, on the condition that they are not subsequently used for commercial purposes;

- are sent as small packages to private persons, in so far as no commercial operation is involved;

- are intended for consumption aboard transport operating commercially between Member States.

Member States are required to ensure that meat products sent from its territory to the territory of another Member State comply with the following general conditions:

- they must have been prepared in an establishment approved and inspected in accordance with the amended Directive;

- they must have been prepared, stored and transported in accordance with the Annex of the amended Directive;

- they must have been prepared from fresh meat. The meat may originate:

    - in accordance with Directive 64/433/EEC and 71/118/EEC in the Member State in which the preparation is carried out or in any other Member State;

    - in accordance with Directive 72/461/EEC, in the Member State in which the preparation is carried out;

- in accordance with Directive 72/462/EEC, in the third country, where the product is imported directly or by way of another Member State;

- in accordance with Directive 71/118/EEC, in a third country. The product must fulfil the conditions of the amended Directive, bear the health mark laid down in the Annex and remain subject to the national provisions of each Member State;

- they must have been prepared from a meat product which meets the requirements of the Directive;

- they must have been prepared from mechanically recovered meat obtained in accordance with the provisions of the Directive;

- they must have been prepared by heating, salting or drying. The process may be combined with smoking or maturing, possibly under microclimatic conditions; or they must have been prepared from meat with the addition of other foodstuffs, additives or condiments;

- they must have been prepared from fresh meat handled in accordance with the Annex of the amended Directive;

- they must have undergone inspection in accordance with the Annex of the amended Directive;

- they must meet the standards laid down in the Annex of the amended Directive;

- where necessary, they must have been wrapped and packaged in accordance with the Annex of the amended Directive;

- they must bear the health mark laid down in the Annex of the amended Directive;

- during transport to the country of destination, they must be accompanied by the health certificate laid down in the Annex of the amended Directive. Transport must be under satisfactory health conditions.

Storage temperature

Meat products which have undergone treatment in accordance with the Annex of the amended Directive may be stored and transported at normal ambient temperatures.

Where meat products have undergone incomplete treatment, the producer is required to ensure that the packaging of meat products bears a clear and legible indication of the temperature at which products must be transported and stored.

Approved establishments

Each Member State is required to draw up a list of approved establishments. Each establishment will be issued with a veterinary approval number.

An approved establishment must comply with this Directive.

Verification

Inspection of approved establishments will be carried out by the competent authority.

The Member State will take account of the results of checks made in accordance with the amended Directive. Any withdrawal of approval must be communicated to the Commission and other Member States.

National derogations

A country of destination may check that all consignments of meat products are accompanied by the official health certificate.

If irregularities are suspected, the country of destination may carry out non-discriminatory inspections to check compliance with the provisions of the Directive.

Checks and inspections will normally be carried out at the place of destination of goods. Checks and inspections may be carried out at another place provided that this interferes as little as possible with the movement of goods.

If, during inspection, it is found that meat products do not comply with the amended Directive, the competent authority of the country of destination may give the consignor or his representative the choice between re-consignment of the meat products, their use for other purposes where health considerations permit this, or their destruction. Any measures taken must prevent improper use of such meat products.

The proposal was adopted by the Council on 20.12.88.

The full text was published in OJC 349, 1985.

COM(86) 658. Amended proposal for a Council Directive on public health and animal health problems affecting importation of meat products from third countries.

Summary

The original proposal for a Council Directive, COM(84) 530, intended to lay down provisions relating to public health and animal health applicable to the importation of meat products from third countries, with the exception of those applicable to the importation of meat products which are prepared wholly or partly from fresh poultrymeat or from meat products containing poultrymeat. This amended proposal introduces new regulatory committee and advisory committee procedures.

The proposed Directive is not applicable to:

- meat products forming part of a travellers' personal luggage and intended for their personal consumption, in quantities less than 1 kilogram per person and provided that the meat products are not prohibited by the Directive;

- meat products sent as small packages to private persons, provided that such meat products are not imported by way of trade, that the quantity does not exceed 1 kilogram and that the meat products come from a third country which importation is not prohibited by the Directive;

- meat products for consumption by the crew and passengers carried on means of transport operating internationally.

Meat products

Meat products must be produced wholly or partly from meat:

- satisfying the requirements of Directive 72/462/EEC;

- originating in a Member State and satisfying the requirements of Directive 72/461/EEC.

However, Member States may authorise the importation of meat products from which imports of fresh meat are not authorised under Directive 72/462/EEC where such products satisfy the requirements of the Directive and originate in authorised parts of third countries.

Meat products must satisfy the following requirements:

- the meat product must have been produced wholly or partly from fresh meat referred to in the Directive or from fresh meat not in accordance with the requirements of the Directive, originating in a third country and bearing the mark provided for;

- to prevent any risk of transmission of contagious diseases of animals, the meat product must have undergone a heat treatment in a hermetically sealed container with an Fc value or 3.00 or more. Other treatments may be accepted in accordance with the consultation procedure involving the Standing Veterinary Committee.

Contagious diseases

If a contagious animal disease breaks out or spreads in a third country for which a list of establishments has been drawn up, and where the disease can be carried by meat products and is likely to endanger public health or the health of livestock, the Member State concerned or the Commission may prohibit the importation of those products coming directly or indirectly either from the third country as a whole or from part of its territory.

Resumption of importation from the third country may be authorised in accordance with the procedure involving the Standing Veterinary Committee.

Public health

Fresh meat used for the production of meat products intended for export or intended for the production of other meat products must:

- have been obtained in an establishment appearing on one of the lists drawn up pursuant to Directive 72/462/EEC or Directive 64/433/EEC, or in an establishment situated in a third country or a part of a third country appearing on the authorised list established by this Directive;

- have been obtained in accordance with the conditions of Directive 72/462/EEC or Directive 64/433/EEC;

- fulfil the conditions laid down in Directive 77/99/EEC.

Meat products intended for the production of other meat products must have been obtained in an establishment appearing on the approved list or one of the lists laid down on the basis of Directive 77/99/EEC.

Meat products imported from third countries will be subject to the following conditions:

- they must have been obtained from an establishment appearing on the approved list;

- the establishment must comply with the provisions of Directive 77/99/EEC;

- they must have been processed in conditions of hygiene complying with Directive 77/99/EEC;

- they must have undergone one of the treatments or a combination of the treatments provided for in Directive 77/99//EEC;

- they must have undergone an official veterinary inspection in accordance with Directive 77/99/EEC;

- they must satisfy the standards laid down in Directive 77/99/EEC;

- where meat products have been wrapped and packaged, this must have been done in accordance with Directive 77/99/EEC;

Irradiation

Meat products must not have been subjected to ionising radiation except where justified for medical reasons and where that operation is mentioned clearly on the product and on the public health certificate.

Authorised establishments

After consultations with the Standing Veterinary Committee, the Commission will draw up one or more lists of establishments authorised for the importation of meat products and one or more lists of establishments in third countries authorised to export meat products.

An establishment will be included on the authorised list on the basis of:

- assurances which the third country can offer with regard to compliance with this Directive or Directive 72/462/EEC;

- compliance with the provisions of this Directive or Directive 77/99/EEC;

- organisation of the meat product inspection service or services of the third country or part of that country, the powers of such service and the supervision to which it is subject.

An establishment may not appear on the approved list unless it is situated in one of the third countries which meet the requirements of the Directive and has been officially approved by the competent authorities of the third country for exporting to the Community. Approval of an establishment will be subject to:

- compliance with Directive 77/99/EEC or Directive 64/433/EEC;

- constant supervision by an official veterinarian of the third country.

Verification

On-the-spot inspections will be carried out by veterinary experts of the Member States and the Commission. Where an inspection reveals serious deficiencies concerning an authorised establishment, the Commission will immediately inform the Member States and adopt a decision provisionally suspending the authorisation.

Member States are required to ensure that each consignment of meat products undergoes a physical inspection relating to both public and animal health aspects before being released for consumption within the Community.

Member States must prohibit the release for consumption of meat products if inspections have revealed that:

- meat products are not suitable for human consumption;

- conditions laid down in the Directive have not been fulfilled.

Where the importation of meat products is prohibited, they must be returned, unless this is contrary to animal or public health considerations.

Where the return of such meat products is not permitted, they must be destroyed in the territory of the Member State in which inspections have taken place.

However, if the importer or his representative so requests, the Member State carrying out the animal and public health inspections may authorise the entry of the meat products for uses other than human consumption provided that there is no danger for humans or for animals.

Certification

The importation of meat products will be subject to submission of an animal health certificate and a public health certificate drawn up by an official veterinarian of the exporting third country.

Health certificates must:

- be drawn up in the official language of the country of destination and in the language of the Member State in which import inspections are carried out;

- accompany the meat products in the original;

- consist of a single sheet of paper;

- be made out for a single consignee.

Animal health certificates must certify that meat products comply with animal health requirements of the Directive and with requirements laid down with respect to the importation meat products from the third country.

Public health certificates must correspond in presentation and content to the specimen laid down in the Directive and be issued on the day on which the meat products are loaded with a view to consignment to the country of destination.

Importation will be prohibited if inspection reveals that:

- meat products are not obtained in an approved establishment;

- fresh meat or meat products from which meat products were manufactured in whole or in part were not obtained from an approved establishment;

- meat products coming from an authorised third country, but have not undergone processing provided for;

- certificates do not fulfil the requirements of the Directive.

Member States must authorise the transportation of meat products from one third country to another where:

- the person concerned supplies proof that the first third country to which the meat products are being sent undertakes under no circumstances to send back to the Community meat products of which it has authorised the importation;

- transportation has been previously authorised by the competent authorities of the Member State in the territory of which the animal health inspection on import is carried out;

- transportation is carried out, without goods being unloaded on Community territory, under the supervision of the competent authorities in vehicles or containers sealed by the competent authorities. The only handling authorised during transit will be carried out at the point of entry or exit from Community territory for direct transhipment from ship or aircraft to any other means of transport or vice versa.

Meat products of each consignment authorised for circulation in the Community by a Member State before being forwarded to the country of destination must be covered by a certificate. This certificate must:

- be drawn up by the official veterinarian at the inspection post or at the place of storage;

- be issued on the day of loading for consignment of the meat products to the country of destination;

- be drawn up in the official language of the country of destination;

- accompany the consignment of meat products in the original form.

The full text of the original proposal, COM(84) 530, was published in OJC 286, 1984.

COM(87) 207. Proposal for a Council Decision on a system for health control imports from third countries at frontier inspection posts (SHIFT Project).

Summary

The proposal for a Council Decision on a system for health control imports for third countries at frontier inspection posts lays down that the Commission will be responsible for the coordination of the development of computerisation of veterinary importation procedures (SHIFT Project) by the Member States and itself until 31 December 1991.

The SHIFT Project will be undertaken as part of the CADDIA programme. The long term objectives of the SHIFT Project will be to provide the necessary organisational infrastructure and data processing facilities to enable the Commission and Member States to obtain access to and process the information needed to achieve the objectives of such Regulations and Directives made in the field of harmonisation of animal and public health rules relating to the importation of animals and animal products from third countries.

In order to achieve the objectives of the SHIFT Project, the Commission, in accordance with the consultation procedure with the Standing Veterinary Committee and the CADDIA Steering Committee, will:

- establish a programme for the development and application of systems designed to achieve the objectives of the Decision;

- coordinate the action to be taken by Member States;

- adopt appropriate standards for the interchange of data and rules governing the security of the data exchanged.

The full text was published in OJC 153, 11.6.87.

COM(87) 658. Proposal for a Council Directive on health problems affecting the production, placing on the market of the Community and importation from third countries of minced meat and meat in pieces of less than one hundred grams.

Summary

The proposed Directive on health problems affecting the production, placing on the market of the Community and importation from third countries of minced meat and meat in pieces less than one hundred grams is not applicable to:

- minced meat and meat in pieces of less than one hundred grams prepared on the spot for the consumer;

- intra-Community trade in minced meat and meat in pieces of less than one hundred grams:

    - contained in travellers' personal luggage, provided that it is not used for commercial purposes;

    - sent in small packages to private persons, provided that consignments are not of a commercial nature;

    - intended for consumption on board means of transport operating commercially between Member States.

Trade in meat defined in the Directive will be subject to animal health rules governing trade in fresh meat.

Intra-Community trade

Products must have been prepared from fresh meat which:

- complies with the provisions of Directive 464/433/EEC and comes from the territory of a Member State;

- complies with the provisions of Directive 72/462/EEC and comes from a third country either directly or via another Member State.

Products must have been prepared either:

- in a cutting plant approved and supervised in accordance with Directive 64/433/EEC; or

- in an establishment approved and supervised in accordance with Directive 77/99/EEC.

An establishment used for the production of minced meat and meat in pieces of less than one hundred grams must operate with:

- a room for cutting, mincing and wrapping, equipped with a recording thermometer or recording telethermometer. The temperature must not exceed 12 degrees centigrade. Where minced meat is not obtained by means of a mechanical process which is continuous and closed until wrapping, room temperature must not exceed 7 degrees centigrade;

- a room for packaging, except where the conditions of Directive 64/433/EEC are fulfilled;

- a room for storing seasonings;

- refrigeration equipment enabling compliance with mandatory temperatures.

The provisions of Directive 64/433/EEC are applicable to the hygiene of staff, premises and equipment.

Approved establishments will be subject to supervision by the official service, which will be responsible for:

- supervision of the entry of fresh meat;

- supervision of the exit of meat products;

- supervision of the hygiene of premises, facilities and instruments;

- sampling in accordance with the microbiological tests referred to in the Annex of the Directive.

Production of meat in pieces of less than one hundred grams

Meat in pieces of less than one hundred grams must be prepared, packaged and stored under the following conditions:

- before cutting, the meat must be examined to detect any contamination. All contaminated parts must be removed before the meat is cut up;

- the meat must not be obtained from waste or trimmings;

- all operations from the time at which the meat enters the room for examination to the time when the finished product undergoes chilling or freezing must take place within one hour;

- after cutting, the meat must be stored at temperatures of not more than 3 degrees centigrade in the case of chilled meat and not more than -18 degrees centigrade in the case of frozen meat;

- immediately after production the meat must be hygienically wrapped or packaged.

Production of minced meat

Minced meat must be prepared, stored and packaged under the following conditions:

- before cutting, the meat must be examined to detect any contamination. All contaminated parts must be removed before the meat is cut up;

- minced meat must not be obtained from waste or trimmings;

- all operations from the time at which the meat enters the room for examination to the time when the finished product undergoes chilling or freezing must take place within one hour. During mincing, meat must be kept at a temperature not exceeding 4 degrees centigrade;

- immediately after production, minced meat must be stored at a temperature of not more than -18 degrees centigrade. Minced meat may be stored at a higher temperature by a decision of the official service;

- immediately after production the minced meat must be hygienically wrapped or packaged.

Microbiological testing of minced meat must be carried out daily. Samples must be examined every day for aerobic mesophile bacteria and every week for salmonella, staphylococci, Escherichia coil and sulphite reducing anaerobes. Guidelines for interpreting the results of tests are laid down in the Annex. Analysis methods will be adopted in accordance with the consultation procedure involving the Standing Veterinary Committee.

Labelling

Minced meat and meat in pieces of less than one hundred grams which has been produced in the cutting plants referred to must be marked on the packaging with the health mark of the establishment laid down in the Annex.

The following information must also be given on the packaging:

- the species from which the meat was obtained;

- the date of preparation;

- the list of seasonings.

Where meat is wrapped in commercial portions intended for direct sale to the consumer a printed reproduction of the official stamp must appear on the label or the wrapping. The stamp will include the establishment's approval number.

Transport

Minced meat and meat in pieces less than one hundred grams during transport must be equipped in such a way as to ensure that maximum permitted temperatures are not exceeded.

During transportation to the country of destination, products must be accompanied by the health certificate laid down in the Annex.

Imports from third countries

Minced meat and meat in pieces of less than one hundred grams must comply with the health and animal health conditions adopted by the Commission in accordance with the consultation procedure involving the Standing Veterinary Committee.

The provisions of Directive 72/462/EEC will be applicable to all mechanically separated meat.

The proposal was adopted by the Council on 20.12.88.

The full text was published in OJC 18, 23,1,88.

COM(88) 720. Proposal for a Council Decision fixing the powers and conditions of operation of the Community reference laboratories for residue testing.

Summary

Council Directive 86/469/EEC concerning the examination of animals and fresh meat for the presence of residues required that the Council will determine the powers and conditions of operation of the Community reference laboratories for residue testing.

This proposal for a Council Decision intends that the functions of Community reference laboratories will be:

- to monitor the application of the rules designed to promote good laboratory practice within the national reference laboratories;

- to provide national reference laboratories with the necessary details on methods of analysis and the comparative tests to be carried out, and the results of such tests;

- to provide technical advice in connection with the field of analysis for which they have been designated for Community testing;

- to store and distribute reference standards for the substances to be tested and their metabolites;

- to organise comparative tests between national laboratories at least once every two years;

- to inform national reference laboratories of advances in analytical apparatus and techniques;

- to identify and determine the concentration of residues in cases where the results of an analysis give rise to a disagreement between Member States;

- to conduct initial and further training courses in residue analysis for experts;

- to provide the Community authorities with support in the form of advice and analytical and technical backup;

- to compile an annual report on work.

In order to carry out its functions adequately, Community reference laboratories must:

- possess qualified staff;

- possess the necessary equipment, substances and materials;

- possess the necessary administrative infrastructure;

- have sufficient data-processing capacity to produce statistics based on their findings and to enable rapid communication of information;

- preserve the confidentiality of specific issues, results or communications;

- have sufficient knowledge of international rules applying to the methods they use.

At the time of writing the full text was not published in the OJC series.

MEAT AND MEAT PRODUCTS - LEGISLATION NOT YET PROPOSED

Formulation of directives concerning animal health problems relating to trade in live poultry, meat and hatching eggs. Proposal expected 1988. Adoption expected 1989.

Harmonising health and hygiene conditions for production and trade in game meat, products and preparations. Proposal expected 1988. Adoption expected 1990.

Harmonised health conditions for production and trade in food products of animal origin not covered by existing legislation. Proposal expected 1990. Adoption expected 1992. Proposal partially approved by Commission: eggs COM(88) 646.

Second revision of the safeguard clause concerning the veterinary sector, requiring the exporting Member State to take appropriate measures in order to avoid specific obstacles to intra-Community trade. Proposal expected 1991. Adoption expected 1992.

Suppression of veterinary certificates for animal products and simplification of certificates for live animals. Proposal expected 1991. Adoption expected 1992.

Poultry products: proposed amendments to Directive 71/118/EEC to provide for inspection and certification at the place of production and re-inspection, in the case of suspicion of fraud at the place of destination. Proposal expected 1988. Adoption expected 1989. Delay vis-a-vis White Paper.

OTHER PRODUCTS - EXISTING AND PROPOSED LEGISLATION

Council Directive 85/397/EEC of 5 August 1985 on health and animal-health problems affecting intra-Community trade in heat-treated milk.

Summary

The Directive on health and animal-health problems in heat treated milk aims to approximate the health requirements of Member States in order to facilitate the functioning of the common market in milk. The general principle of the Directive is that milk must come from cattle which are free from diseases which may endanger human health. In order to achieve this, a Community-wide code of hygiene for the production, storage and transportation of milk is established by the Directive.

The Directive provides rules for trade only in products derived from heat-treated milk, or for concentrated, pasteurised milk imported into a Member State and intended for sale without further processing. Principal obligations to impose the common code of hygiene are placed on those Member States exporting milk. Those countries importing milk are permitted to carry out checks and inspections of a non-discriminatory nature.

Obligations of the exporting Member State

Member States are required to ensure that milk products covered by the scope of this Directive carry no residues of substances having a pharmacological or hormonal action, or residues of antibiotics, pesticides, detergents and other substances which are harmful or which may alter the organoleptic characteristics of milk or make its consumption harmful to human health.

The Directive imposes specific obligations on Member States exporting heat-treated milk within the Community with regard to:

- ensuring that nothing has been removed from or added to the milk, except as a consequence of fat-content standardisation;

- checking that milk originates from cows fulfilling the conditions of the Directive;

- imposing general hygiene conditions at production holdings;

- ensuring that cows and production holdings are checked at regular intervals;

- maintaining standards of hygiene during milking, handling and transportation;

- checking cows and production holdings at regular intervals;

- checking milk;

- examining milk treatment establishments;

- checking subsequent packaging;

- checking methods of storage;

- providing a standardised health certificate during transportation;

- checking conditions of transportation

- ensuring that pasteurised milk has undergone only one pasteurisation process.

The Directive further requires that heat-treated milk intended for direct human consumption must weigh no less than 1,030 grammes per litre established from milk at 15 degrees centigrade or the equivalent from totally fat-free milk at 20 degrees centigrade and contains a minimum of 28 grammes of protein per litre and a fat-free dry matter content of not less than 8.5%. Stricter requirements may not be set for milk intended for industry.

Transportation

Member States are required to ensure that tankers are used exclusively for the transportation of milk, milk products and potable water, and that premises, instillations and working equipment are used only for the production of milk. However, Member States may allow tankers and working equipment to come into contact with other liquid foodstuffs so long as appropriate measures are taken to prevent the subsequent contamination or deterioration of heat-treated milk products.

Inspection

Member States are required to designate approved milk-treatment establishments. Regular inspection of approved establishments must then be carried out by national supervisory authorities.

In cooperation with Member States, veterinary experts from the Commission may make on-the-spot checks in order to ensure uniform application of the Directive. Member States must take all measures necessary to comply with the results of such an investigation.

A Member State importing heat-treated milk may check that all consignments are accompanied by the prescribed health certificate. Such checks would normally be carried out at the place of destination, or at another suitable place which interferes as little as possible with the transportation or sale of the goods. If milk is found not to comply with the Directive, the consignor may be given the option of returning the milk to its place of origin, using it for other purposes or destroying it.

The establishment of a modified method of analysis is required which enables a distinction to be made between sterilised milk and UHT milk. This is to be established in accordance with the consultation procedure with the Scientific Veterinary Committee.

National derogations

Member States may take the following measures by way of derogation from the Directive:

- where there is an outbreak of foot-and-mouth disease in another territory, a Member State may temporarily prohibit or restrict the introduction of pasteurised milk from the affected area;

- if foot-and-mouth disease becomes widespread or if there is a further outbreak of infectious animal disease, a Member State may temporarily prohibit or restrict the introduction of pasteurized milk and UHT milk from the whole territory.

National legislation which provides for appeal against the decisions of supervisory authorities are not affected by this Directive.

Timetable

Member States are required to provide methods of analysis and testing adopted in compliance with the consultation procedure involving the Scientific Veterinary Committee by 1 January 1989. Pending these decisions, Member States are required to use methods of analysis which are internationally acceptable.

The introduction of measures considered necessary to facilitate the standardisation of heat-treated milk must be achieved by Member States by 1 April 1990. The standards laid down in the Directive must be applicable to all intra-Community trade in heat-treated milk by 1 January 1993.

Member States were required to comply with the Directive by 1 January 1989.

The full text was published in OJL 226, 24.8.85.

COM(88) 646. Amended proposal for a Council Directive on health problems affecting the production and the placing on the market of egg products.

Summary

The proposal for a Directive on health problems affecting the production and the placing on the market of egg products, COM(87) 46, laid down general requirements which must be complied with. This amended proposal takes account of the opinion of the European Parliament.

Member States are required to ensure that only egg products which meet the following requirements are produced as foodstuffs and used for the manufacture of foodstuffs:

- they must have been treated or prepared in an establishment which has been approved in accordance with the Directive;

- they must have been prepared under hygiene conditions meeting the requirements of the Directive, with eggs meeting the requirements laid down in the Annex of the Directive;

- they must have undergone treatment in accordance with the provisions laid down in accordance with the Directive;

- they must comply with the end-product specifications of the Directive;

- they must have undergone a health check in accordance with the Directive;

- they must have been packed in accordance with the Directive;

- they must be stored and transported in accordance with the Directive;

- they must bear the mark of wholesomeness provided for in the Directive.

Competent authorities of the Member States must ensure that:

- samples for laboratory examination are taken in order to check that end-product specifications have been observed;

- temperatures at which the egg products must be transported and stored and the period during which their preservation is assured have been established;

- the results of checks and tests are recorded and kept for presentation to the competent authority for a period of two years;

- the date of treatment of each batch is indicated.

Member States must ensure that random checks are carried out on eggs and egg products to detect residues of substances having a pharmacological or hormonal effect, and residues of antibiotics, pesticides, detergents or other substances which are harmful or liable to render their consumption dangerous or harmful to human health.

Where egg products show traces of residues in excess of the permitted levels, they must not be placed on the market as foodstuffs.

The Commission, in accordance with the consultation procedure involving the Standing Veterinary Committee, will establish:

- detailed arrangements for checks and tests;

- permitted levels for residues;

- intervals at which samples are to be taken;

- reference methods for evaluating the results of the tests for residues;

- lists of reference laboratories in the Community.

Approved establishments

Inspection and monitoring of establishments must be carried out regularly on the responsibility of the competent authority, which will have free access to all parts of the establishment.

In co-operation with the competent authorities of the Member States, experts from the Commission may make on-the-spot checks in order to ensure the uniform application of the Directive.

Prohibited products

Where there are serious grounds for suspecting that there are irregularities, the country of destination may carry out non-discriminatory inspections of egg products which are subject to intra-Community trade in order to check that the consignment meets the requirements of the Directive.

Inspections must be carried out at the place of destination of the goods or at another suitable place, provided that this interferes as little as possible with the routeing of the goods. Inspections may not be carried out at or because of the crossing of internal frontiers.

Inspections must not delay unduly the placing of egg products on the market, or cause delays which may impair quality.

Where egg products are found not to comply with the Directive, the competent authority may give the consignor or his representative the choice of withdrawing the consignment from the market in order that it may undergo further treatment or of using it for other purposes if this is permissible on health grounds. If this is not possible, destruction of the eggs must be offered.

Decisions and the grounds for taking them must be communicated to the consignor or his representative. If decisions are based on the existence of a serious risk to human health, they must be communicated to the Commission or the competent authority of the Member State of dispatch. Appropriate measures may then be taken in accordance with the consultation procedure involving the Standing Veterinary Committee.

Right of appeal

Where egg products may not be placed on the market, Member States must grant consignors the right to obtain expert opinion. The expert must be a national of a Member State other than the country of destination.

Disputes

Where a Member State considers that the provisions of the Directive are no longer being fulfilled in an establishment in another Member State, it must inform the central authority of that Member State accordingly.

Where the Member States are unable to reach agreement, the matter must be referred to the Commission, which will instruct experts to deliver an opinion.

On the basis of that opinion or the result of checks, Member States may temporarily deny access to their territory for egg products coming from that establishment.

Third country products

National provisions for eggs imported from third countries must not be more favourable than those governing intra-Community trade.
Pending adoption of Community measures relating to third countries, on-the-spot inspections will be carried out by experts from the Member States and the Commission.

Additives

The use of additives in egg products will continue to be subject to national law.

At the time of writing the full text was not available in the OJC series.

The full text of the original proposal, COM(87) 46, was published in OJC 67, 14.3.87.

COM(88) 47. Proposal for a Council Regulation laying down health conditions for the marketing of fish and fish products concerning nematodes.

Summary

The proposal for a Council Regulation laying down health conditions for the marketing of fish and fish products concerning nematodes requires fresh fish and fish products to comply with the conditions laid down in the Annex of the Regulation.

Treatment

Fresh fish intended to be consumed raw and fish products which have undergone an incomplete treatment and are liable to be consumed in this state may only be marketed after they have been subjected to the treatment laid down in the Annex of the Regulation. Treatment will no longer be necessary if the raw material from which they have been prepared has already undergone such treatment.

Approved establishments

Establishments carrying out a complete treatment of fish must be approved by the competent authority of the Member State in which they are situated.

Persons responsible for each establishment must keep a register of each production load which has undergone a complete treatment, together with charts recording heat or cold treatment and results of the analyses of brine and marinating solutions.

Establishments must be subjected to a regular control by the competent authorities. Controls will include a check on the content of the register and the taking of samples in order to verify that the criteria laid down has been complied with.

Verification

Where there are serious grounds for suspecting that irregularities exist, the country of destination may carry out non-discriminatory inspections of fish and fish products which are subject to intra-Community trade. Inspections will be carried out at the place of destination of the goods, and must not unduly delay the marketing of fresh fish and fish products or cause delays which would adversely affect their quality.

Where inspection reveals that fish and fish products do not comply with the Regulation, the competent authority may give the consignor or his representative the choice of withdrawing the consignment from the market for further treatment or of using it for other purposes permitted on health grounds. If not, one of the choices offered must be the destruction of the fish and fish products. In any event, precautionary measures will be taken to prevent improper use of such fish or fish products.

Decisions and the grounds for taking them must be notified to the consignor, the consignee or their representative. If such decisions are based on the existence of a particularly serious risk to human health, these reasons must be communicated to the Commission or the competent authority of the Member State of dispatch.

Appropriate measures may be taken in accordance with the consultation procedure involving the Standing Veterinary Committee, particularly for the purpose of coordinating measures taken in other Member States with regard to the products concerned.

Where fish or fish products are prohibited from being placed on the market, Member States may grant consignors the right to obtain an expert's opinion.

The full text was published in OJC 66, 11.3.88.

OTHER PRODUCTS - LEGISLATION NOT YET PROPOSED

Formulation of directives concerning animal health problems relating to trade in live poultry, meat and hatching eggs. Proposal expected 1988. Adoption expected 1989.

Proposal for directives on animal health problems relating to trade in fish and fish products. Proposal expected 1988. Adoption expected 1989.

Harmonised health and hygiene conditions for production and trade in shellfish and crustacea preparation. Proposal expected 1989. Adoption expected 1990. Delay vis-a-vis White Paper.

Harmonised health conditions for production and trade in food products of animal origin not covered by existing legislation. Proposal expected 1990. Adoption expected 1992. Proposal partially approved by Commission: eggs COM(88) 646.

Application of health standards to national products. Proposal expected 1991. Adoption expected 1992.

7. REMOVAL OF TECHNICAL BARRIERS

BACKGROUND

The Commission's White Paper proposals to remove all technical barriers to trade by the end of 1992 marked a change in emphasis away from proposals designed to determine the composition of foodstuffs, and towards the establishment of seven framework Directives, outside the scope of which differing national laws would remain in force.

The White Paper proposed that while a Member State may retain national legislation relating to foodstuffs, products originating in another Member State must be allowed free access to the domestic market even if they do not comply with more stringent national rules. Proposals for Community legislation in the foodstuffs sector are now restricted to those measures considered necessary to provide adequate consumer information (labelling, food for special nutritional needs), or for the protection of the health and safety of humans (materials in contact with food, flavourings and additives).

The Compositional Directives adopted before 1985 will remain in force and will be updated when necessary, but no new Directives on the specific composition of foodstuffs will now be proposed.

Since 1985, mutual recognition of divergent national regulations has provided the key to understanding the Commission's legislative proposals. The rationale behind the Commission's dual strategy of harmonisation and mutual recognition is explained in detail in Chapter 5, while the implications of the proposed framework Directives are discussed in Chapter 9.

LABELLING - EXISTING LEGISLATION

Council Directive 79/112/EEC of 18 December 1978 on the approximation of the laws of the Member States relating to the labelling, presentation and advertising of foodstuffs for sale to the ultimate consumer.

Summary

The objective of the Directive on the approximation of the laws of the Member States relating to the labelling, presentation and advertising of foodstuffs for sale to the ultimate consumer is to establish general rules, applicable horizontally to all foodstuffs put on the market, which would contribute to the functioning of the common market. The Directive sets out to approximate the laws of Member States relating to the labelling, presentation and advertising of consumer foodstuffs by:

- requiring that adequate labelling information is provided and prohibiting the use of information that would mislead the purchaser;

- removing differences in national labelling regulations which could impede the free movement of goods.

The Directive is applicable to the labelling of foodstuffs sold to the ultimate consumer and to certain aspects of the presentation and advertising of these foodstuffs. Member States may also decide to apply the Directive to foodstuffs intended for supply to restaurants or other mass caterers.

Products for processing or preparation

Rules applicable to the labelling of products intended for subsequent processing or preparation will be fixed by subsequent directives, although in specific circumstances this Directive does refer to the labelling of foodstuffs sold in bulk.

Labelling

Labelling, presentation and advertising of foodstuffs must not mislead the consumer:

- as to the characteristics of the foodstuff, particularly its nature, identity, properties, composition, quantity, durability, origin or provenance, method of manufacture or production;

- by attributing effects or properties to the food which it does not possess;

- by attributing to the food special characteristics which are in fact common to all similar products;

- by attributing to any foodstuff medicinal properties, except in the case of particular nutritional uses.

Without prejudicing the more precise extent of provisions regarding weights and measures, the Directive makes compulsory provision of the following information:

- the name of the product;

- the list of ingredients;

- the net quantity (for prepackaged food);

- the minimum period of durability;

- special conditions for storage or usage;

- the name and address of the manufacturer, packager or seller within the Community (in the case of butter in indication of the manufacturer is considered sufficient);

- details of the place of origin or provenance in cases where failure to give such information might mislead the consumer;

- where necessary, appropriate instructions for the use of the foodstuff.

The name under which the foodstuff is sold should be sufficiently precise as to inform the purchaser of its true nature and enable it to be distinguished from other products. This name may not be substituted by a trade mark, brand name or fancy name. The name of the foodstuff should be accompanied by details of its physical condition and of any specific treatment which it has undergone, in cases where the omission of these details could confuse the purchaser.

Ingredients

The Directive defines as an ingredient any substance, including additives, used in the production of a foodstuff which is still present in the finished item, even if in an altered form. In the case of a compound ingredient which is the product of several ingredients, the latter shall all be regarded as ingredients for the purposes of labelling. If national regulations require that compound ingredients are listed, this must be immediately followed by a list of the items which constitute the compound ingredient. This list shall not be compulsory in the case of compound ingredients constituting less than 25% of the foodstuff (except in the case of additives), or in cases where the listing of ingredients constituting a compound ingredient is not required under Community law.

The following foodstuffs are not required to provide details of ingredients:

- fresh fruit and vegetables;
- carbonated water;
- fermentation vinegars, where no other ingredient has been added:
- cheese;
- butter;
- fermented milk and cream;
- products consisting of a single ingredient.

In addition, the following shall not be regarded as ingredients for the purposes of labelling:

- the constituents of an ingredient which have been temporarily separated and later reintroduced in amounts not in excess of their original proportions;
- additives, the presence of which is solely due to the fact that they were contained in one or more ingredients, provided that they serve no technological function in the finished product;
- additives used as processing aids;
- substances used in quantities necessary to act as solvents or media for additives or flavouring.

The list of ingredients should be recorded in descending order of weight at the time of manufacture, subject to the following exceptions:

- concentrated and dehydrated ingredients may be listed in order of their weight before this process has been undertaken;
- where a mixture of fruit or vegetables varies in its precise constitution, these ingredients may be listed in an order not

relating to their weight, provided that this fact is specified on labelling.

Added water and volatile products should be recorded according to their weight in the finished product. Water content need not be specified where it is used during manufacture solely for the purpose of reconstituting an ingredient from its concentrated or dehydrated form, or if the amount is less than 5% of the weight of the finished product.

<u>Identification of ingredients</u>

Ingredients should be designated by their specific name, where applicable; however the following categories of ingredient may be designated by their general name rather than their specific name where they are constituents of another foodstuff:

- oil;
- fat;
- starch;
- fish;
- poultrymeat;
- cheese;
- spices or mixed spices;
- herbs or mixed herbs;
- gum base;
- crumbs or rusks;
- sugar;
- dextrose;
- caseinates;
- cocoa butter;

- crystallised fruit.

Community provisions or, where appropriate national provisions, may provide for additional categories. Ingredients belonging to the following categories must be designated by the name of that category, followed by their specific name or EEC number:

- colour;

- preservative;

- antioxidant;

- emulsifier;

- thickener;

- gelling agent;

- stabiliser;

- flavour enhancer;

- acid;

- acidity regulator;

- anticaking agent;

- modified starches;

- artificial sweetener;

- raising agent;

- antifoaming agent;

- glazing agent;

- emulsifying salts;

- flour improvers.

Flavourings should be described in accordance with national provisions until Community provisions enter into force.

Where the labelling of a foodstuff emphasises the presence or low content of particular ingredients, the minimum or maximum percentage should be stated. This provision will not apply if labelling is intended to characterise a foodstuff by providing a name which distinguishes it from similar products, or if ingredients are used in small quantities only as ingredients.

Prepackaged foodstuffs

In the case of prepackaged foodstuffs, net quantity shall be expressed in terms of:

- units of volume in the case of liquids;

- units of mass in the case of other products;

using the litre, centilitre, millilitre, kilogram or gram as appropriate.

Certain derogations to this provision of the Directive may be permitted.

Where the indication of a certain type of quantity is required (for example the minimum or average quantity) this will be regarded as being the net quantity, unless other indications of quantity are required. Where a solid foodstuff is presented in liquid form, the drained net weight should be indicated. An indication of the net quantity will not be required in the following cases:

- foodstuffs sold by number, provided that the number of items may be seen and counted from outside the packaging;

- foodstuffs subject to considerable losses in volume or mass and sold by number or weight in the presence of the purchaser;

- foodstuffs of a net quantity less than 5g or 5ml, except in the case of herbs and spices.

Durability

The date of minimum durability is the date until which a foodstuff retains its specific properties when stored. The date shown should consist of the day, month and year and be preceded by "best before" or "best before end". Highly perishable foodstuffs may be required to display a "use before" date. An indication of the minimum date of durability will not be required in the case of the following foodstuffs:

- fresh fruit and vegetables;

- wines;

- beverages containing 10% or more by volume of alcohol;

- bakers' or pastry-cooks' wares;

- vinegar;

- cooking salt;

- solid sugar;

- confectionery products consisting of flavoured and/or coloured sugars.

Instructions for use

Instructions for use of a foodstuff should be indicated so as to enable appropriate use of the product.

Member States must ensure that labelling appears in a language easily understood by purchasers, except where other measures have been taken to inform the purchaser.

National derogations

Member States are permitted to retain national provisions which require additional indication of the factory or packaging centre for the product originating in the home market.

Member States may authorise that all or some of the labelling requirements of this Directive be given only in the relevant trade documents when the product is prepackaged and marketed prior to sale to the ultimate consumer.

Member States may not prevent the sale of foodstuffs which comply with this Directive except on the grounds of:

- protection of public health;

- prevention of fraud;

- protection of industrial or commercial property rights.

A Member State which maintains national laws shall inform the Commission and other Member States within two years. If a Member State intends to adopt new legislation on the labelling of foodstuffs, it shall communicate to the Commission and other Member States its reasons for doing so.

In either of these cases, the Commission may reject the reasons given by a Member State, the matter then being referred to the Standing Committee on Foodstuffs. The Commission shall submit to the Committee a draft of measures to be taken. If the Committee rejects the measures proposed by the Commission, the matter is submitted to the Council for decision.

The Directive does not apply to products intended for export outside the Community.

Timetable

Member States were required to permit trade in products complying with the Directive by 8 February 1981 and to prohibit trade in products not complying with the Directive by 8 February 1983.

The full text was published in OJL 33, 8.2.79.

Commission Directive 83/463/EEC of 22 July 1983 introducing temporary measures for the designation of certain ingredients in the labelling of foodstuffs for sale to the ultimate consumer.

Summary

Directive 79/112/EEC introduced general rules applicable to the labelling, presentation and advertising of foodstuffs for sale to the ultimate consumer. Specifically, Directive 79/112/EEC provided that listed ingredients must be designated by a category name followed by their specific name or EEC number. Directive 83/463/EEC lays down a temporary numbering system for ingredients which belong to the categories listed in Directive 79/112/EEC but which are yet to receive an EEC number, pending the adoption of new provisions.

Timetable

Member States were required to allow the numbers listed in this Directive to be used in place of the specific name of an ingredient for the purposes of labelling, presentation or advertising of foodstuffs for sale to the ultimate consumer by 1 July 1984.

The full text was published in OJL 255, 15.9.83.

Council Directive 86/197/EEC of 26 May 1986 amending Directive 79/112/EEC on the approximation of the laws of the Member States relating to the labelling, presentation and advertising of foodstuffs for sale to the ultimate consumer.

Summary

Directive 79/112/EEC established general rules applicable horizontally to the labelling, presentation and advertising of all foodstuffs put on the market. In line with provisions for the compulsory wording of labels laid down by that Directive, Directive 86/197/EEC requires an indication of the alcoholic strength of beverages in order to ensure that consumers are provided with adequate information.

The Directive makes compulsory an indication of actual alcoholic strength by volume on the labelling of beverages containing more than 1.2% by volume of alcohol.

Where products are covered by tariff heading Nos 22.04 and 22.05, rules concerning an indication of alcoholic strength by volume will be laid down by specific Directives applicable to such products.

Rules concerning the alcoholic strength by volume of other beverages which contain more than 1.2% by volume of alcohol will be adopted by the Commission following consultation with the Standing Committee on Foodstuffs.

Timetable

Member States were required to permit trade in products complying with this Directive by 1 May 1988 and prohibit trade in products which do not comply with the Directive by 1 May 1989. Trade in beverages which do not comply with this Directive but are labelled before 1 May 1989 may continue until stocks are exhausted.

The full text was published in OJL 144, 29.5.86.

Commission Directive 87/250/EEC of 15 April 1987 on the indication of alcoholic strength by volume in the labelling of alcoholic beverages for sale to the ultimate consumer.

Summary

Directive 79/112/EEC on the approximation of the laws of the Member States relating to the labelling, presentation and advertising of foodstuffs for sale to the ultimate consumer, as amended by Directive 86/197/EEC, laid down the requirement to indicate actual alcoholic strength by volume in the labelling of beverages containing more than 1.2% by volume of alcohol. This Directive supplements Directive 79/112/EEC by stipulating an indication of alcoholic strength by volume of alcohol for beverages other than those classified under tariff Nos. 22.04 and 22.05.

Positive and negative tolerances allowed in respect of the indication of the alcoholic strength by volume shall be:

- 0.3% vol. for beverages not specified below;

- 0.5% vol. for beers having an alcoholic strength not exceeding 5.5% vol., or beverages classified under tariff heading 22.07 B II and made from grapes;

- 1.0% for beers having an alcoholic strength exceeding 5.5% vol.; beverages classified under tariff No. 22.07 B I and made from grapes; ciders, perries, fruit wines and similar products obtained from fruits other than grapes, whether semi-sparkling or sparkling; or beverages based on fermented honey;

- 1.5% vol. for beverages containing macerated fruit or parts of plants.

These tolerances apply without prejudice to tolerances deriving from the method of analysis used for determining alcoholic strength.

Timetable

Member States are required to permit trade in products which comply with this Directive by 1 May 1988 and prohibit trade in products which do not comply by 1 May 1989. Trade in beverages which do not comply with the Directive but are labelled before 1 May 1989 will be permitted until stocks are exhausted.

The full text was published in OJL 113, 30.4.87.

LABELLING - PROPOSED LEGISLATION

COM(87) 242. **Amended proposal for a Council Directive amending Directive 79/112/EEC on the approximation of the laws of the Member States relating to the labelling, presentation and advertising of foodstuffs for sale to the ultimate consumer.**

Summary

Directive 79/112/EEC established general rules requiring adequate labelling information to be provided for all foodstuffs sold to the ultimate consumer, prohibiting the use of information that would mislead the purchaser and removing national regulations which could impede the free movement of goods. Following the Opinion issued by the European Parliament the original Commission proposal, COM(86) 89, has been amended. The proposed Directive aims to eliminate certain derogations provided for by Directive 79/112/EEC and clarify the procedure to be followed where a matter is referred to the Standing Committee on Foodstuffs.

Ingredients

The Commission proposes the removal of a Member State's option to retain national provisions for flavouring matter and the option to create additional categories of ingredients which may be designated by name of category only on labelling. As an alternative, it is proposed that Member States may add further categories of ingredients to the list of substances laid down by Directive 79/112/EEC, which may be designated by the category name rather than the specific name, in accordance with the consultation procedure involving the Standing Committee on Foodstuffs. It is specifically proposed that aromatisers (flavourings) be added to the list.

Prepackaged foodstuffs

Where national provisions derogate from Community rules concerning the labelling, presentation and advertising of the net quantity of prepackaged foodstuffs, it is proposed that the procedure laid down for consultation with the Standing Committee on Foodstuffs would apply.

Where Directive 79/112/EEC required that the particulars stipulated in the Directive be provided in the labelling of all prepackaged foodstuffs, it is proposed that this need not apply to milk or milk bottles intended for reuse. Other derogations may be permitted subject to consultation with the Standing Committee on Foodstuffs.

Labelling

The proposal takes account of Directive 80/777/EEC, relating to natural mineral waters, by making the rules governing labelling, presentation and advertising of a foodstuff subject to that Directive. The amended proposal extends the obligation to inform consumers to include foodstuffs for sale to the ultimate consumer which have been exposed to ionizing radiation.

Directive 79/112/EEC required that labelling particulars need only appear on commercial documents referring to foodstuffs if this is prior to their sale to the ultimate consumer. The amended proposal stipulates that guarantees must be given that these documents, together with adequate labelling information accompany the foodstuff to which they refer.

Directive 79/112/EEC required that the net quantity of spices and herbs be indicated on packaging, even when less than 5g. It is proposed that this requirement now be deleted.

Durability

Directive 79/112/EEC allowed Member States to replace the date of minimum durability (best before) with an expiry date (use before) in the case of perishable foodstuffs. The deletion of this derogation clause is proposed on the grounds that it is not necessary for the provision of information to the ultimate consumer. Where a foodstuff is considered highly perishable and its durability does not exceed seven days, the amended proposal replaces the date of minimum durability with the date of last consumption.

The amended proposal also requires the date of minimum durability to be followed by a description of the storage conditions which must be observed.

Where the Directive provided that Member States need not require an indication of the date of minimum durability, it is proposed that this list be extended. An indication of minimum durability would not be required for:

- fresh fruit and vegetables;

- wines;

- beverages containing 10% or more by volume of alcohol;

- bakers' and pastry cooks' wares;

- vinegar;

- cooking salt;

- solid sugar;

- confectionery products consisting of flavoured and/or coloured sugars;

- chewing gums and similar chewing products;

- edible ices put up in individual portions for immediate consumption after sale;

- fermented cheeses intended to fully or partially mature in prepackaging.

Instructions for use

Where no Community provisions apply, the Directive stipulates that national provisions may specify the way in which instructions for use are indicated on certain foodstuffs. It is proposed that in these cases the consultation procedure with the Standing Committee on Foodstuffs should be used to ascertain whether national provisions will apply.

Standing Committee on Foodstuffs

In order to introduce a simplified procedure for adopting alterations to the rules governing the labelling, presentation and advertising of foodstuffs, the proposal amends the procedure established by Directive 79/112/EEC. According to the revised procedure, the Committee would discuss matters on which the Commission had requested an opinion within the time limit set. No vote would be taken, but any member of the Committee would be able to demand that his views be set down in the minutes of the opinion submitted to the Commission.

The proposal was adopted by the Council on 14.10.88.

The full text was published in OJC 154, 12.6.87.

The full text of the original proposal, COM(86) 89, was published in OJC 124, 1986.

COM(87) 501. Proposal for a Council Regulation on indications or marks identifying the lot to which a foodstuff belongs.

Summary

The proposal for a Council Regulation on indications or marks identifying the lot to which a foodstuff belongs requires that a foodstuff may not be marketed unless it is accompanied by an indication or mark laid down in the Regulation.

The Regulation is not applicable to:

- agricultural products sold or delivered by the producer to temporary storage, preparation or packaging stations or transported from the holding to producers' organisations;

- foodstuffs which, at the time of sale to the ultimate consumer, are not prepackaged, are prepackaged at the request of the purchaser or are prepackaged for immediate sale.

Indications or marks will be determined and affixed under the responsibility of the producer, manufacturer or packager of the foodstuff, or the first seller within the Community.

Indications or marks will be preceded by the letter "L", except in cases where they are clearly distinguishable from the other indications or marks on the labels. They must appear on the packaging or label in a conspicuous place and be clearly legible and indelible.

Where the date of minimum durability appears on the label, indications or marks need not appear on the foodstuff, provided that the date clearly consists at least of the indication of the day and month in that order.

The full text was published in OJC 310, 20.11.87.

COM(88) 489. Proposal for a Council Directive on the introduction of compulsory nutrition labelling of foodstuffs intended for sale to the ultimate consumer.
AND
Proposal for a Council Directive on nutrition labelling rules for foodstuffs intended for sale to the ultimate consumer.

Summary

The proposal for a Council Directive on the introduction of compulsory nutrition labelling of foodstuffs intended for sale to the ultimate consumer lays down the requirement for compulsory nutritional labelling, on the basis of consultations between the Commission and the Standing Committee on Foodstuffs.

Compulsory nutritional labelling will be required where a Member State can prove that there is:

- epidemiological evidence linking the intake of certain foods or nutrients by the population or by substantial groups thereof to specific diseases;

- a need to improve the nutrition status of the population or substantial groups thereof.

The proposal for a Council Directive on nutrition labelling rules for foodstuffs intended for sale to the ultimate consumer lays down that where a nutrition claim has been made in labelling or advertising, compulsory nutritional labelling will be required. In all other cases, nutritional labelling would be optional.

The proposal also applies to the nutrition labelling of foodstuffs intended for supply to restaurants, hospitals, canteens and similar mass caterers.

Compulsory nutritional labelling

Where nutritional labelling is required, the following information must be provided:

- the energy value;
- the amounts of protein, carbohydrate, sugars, fat, dietary fibre and sodium.

Optional nutritional labelling

Labelling may also indicate amounts of the following:

- starch;
- sugar alcohols;
- saturates;
- monosaturates;
- polyunsaturates;

Optional nutritional labelling may indicate amounts of the following vitamins or minerals, where these are present in significant amounts as defined in the proposal:

- vitamin A;
- vitamin D;
- vitamin E;
- vitamin C;
- thiamin;
- riboflavin;
- niacin;
- vitamin B6;

- folacin;
- vitamin B12;
- biotin;
- pantothenic acid;
- calcium;
- phosphorus;
- iron;
- magnesium;
- zinc;
- iodine.

Calculation of energy value

The proposal lays down the method of calculation of energy value and stipulates the units by which energy value and nutrient content may be declared.

Calculation of nutritional value

Figures declared will be derived average values based on one of the following:

- the manufacturer's analysis of the food;
- calculations based on the actual or average values of the ingredients used;
- calculations based on generally acceptable data.

Labelling

Information relating to the nutritional content of a foodstuff must appear in tabular form in one place and, if space permits, with the numbers aligned. Where space does not permit, information must appear in linear form.

The full text was published in OJC 282, 5.11.88.

PACKAGING - EXISTING LEGISLATION

Council Directive 75/106/EEC of 19 December 1974 on the approximation of the laws of the Member States relating to the making-up by volume of certain prepackaged liquids.

As amended by:
Commission Directive 78/891/EEC, see OJL 311, 4.11.78
Council Directive 79/1005/EEC, see OJL 308, 4.12.79
Council Directive 85/10/EEC, see OJL 4, 5.1.85
Council Directive 88/316/EEC, see OJL 143, 10.6.88

Summary

The Directive relating to the making-up by volume of certain prepackaged liquids is applicable to the following categories of products, measured by volume for the purpose of sale in individual quantities of between 5 ml and 10 litres:

- wine of fresh grapes;

- "yellow" wines entitled to use the following designations of origin: "Cotes du Jura", "L'Etile" and "Chateau-Chanlon";

- other non-sparkling fermented beverages;

- vermouths and other wines of fresh grapes flavoured with aromatic extracts and liqueur wines;

- sparkling wines;

- wine in bottles with "mushroom" stoppers held in place by ties or fastenings, and wine otherwise put up with an excess pressure of not less than one bar but less than three bar, measured at a temperature of 20 degrees centigrade;

- other fermented sparkling beverages;

- beer made from malt, except acid beers;

- acid beers, gueuze;

- spirits, liqueurs, other spirituous beverages and compound alcoholic beverages for the manufacture of beverages;

- vinegar and substitutes of vinegar;

- olive oils;

- fresh milk, not concentrated or sweetened, excluding yogurt, kephir, curdled milk, whey and fermented or acidified milk;

- milk-based beverages;

- waters, including spa waters and aerated waters;

- lemonades, flavoured spa waters and flavoured aerated waters and other non-alcoholic beverages not containing milk or milkfats, excluding fruit and vegetable juices falling within CCT heading No. 22.07 and concentrates;

- beverages labelled as alcohol-free aperitifs;

- unfermented fruit juices or vegetable juices not containing spirit falling within CCT subheading 20.07 B, fruit nectar and similar products.

The Directive defines a "prepacked" product as a product which is placed in a package of whatever nature without the purchaser being present and the quantity of product contained in the package has a predetermined value and cannot be altered without the package either being opened or undergoing a perceptible modification. The prepackages which may be marketed with the EEC mark are those which comply with the Annex of the Directive.

All prepackaged liquids which fall within the scope of the Directive must bear an indication of the "nominal volume of the contents" which they are required to contain.

The following prepackaged products may only be marketed if they have the nominal values set out in the Annex:

- wine of fresh grapes;

- other non-sparkling fermented beverages.

National derogations

Member States which on 31 December 1973 allowed nominal volumes in the case of the volumes of 0.375 litre and 0.75 litre for the products listed in the Annex may continue to do so until 31 December 1991.

The Directive will not be an impediment to national laws governing on environmental grounds the use of packaging with regard to its recycling.

Timetable

Member States were required to comply with the Directive by 15 August 1977.

The full text was published in OJL 42, 15.2.75.

Council Directive 76/211/EEC of 20 January 1976 on the approximation of the laws of the Member States relating to the making-up by weight or by volume of certain prepackaged products.

As amended by:
Commission Directive 78//891/EEC, see OJL 311, 4.11.78

Summary

The Directive relating to the making-up by weight or by volume of certain prepackaged products is applicable to prepackages containing products intended for sale in nominal quantities which are:

- equal to values predetermined by the packer;

- expressed in units of weight or volume;

- not less than 5g and not more than 10 kg or 10 l.

The Directive is not applicable to those prepackaged products referred to in Directive 75/106/EEC.

The Directive defines a "prepackaged product" as a product which has been prepackaged without the purchaser being present and the quantity contained in the package has a predetermined value and cannot be altered without the package being opened or undergoing a perceptible modification.

Prepackaged products which fall within the scope of the Directive must bear the EEC sign specified in the Annex, together with an indication of the nominal weight or nominal volume which they are required to contain.

Prepackaged liquid products must bear an indication of the nominal volume. Prepackages containing other products must bear an indication of the nominal weight. Where trade practice or national regulations require otherwise, this provision need not be met. However, all prepackages must bear an indication of the metrological information corresponding to the requirements of the country of destination.

Timetable

Member States were required to comply with the Directive by 21 August 1978.

The full text was published in OJL 46, 21.2.76.

Council Directive 76/893/EEC of 23 November 1976 on the approximation of the laws of the Member States relating to materials and articles intended to come into contact with foodstuffs.

Summary

Council Directive 76/893/EEC on the approximation of the laws of the Member States relating to materials and articles intended to come into contact with foodstuffs establishes the principle that any material or article intended to come into direct or indirect contact with foodstuffs must be sufficiently stable so as not to transfer substances to foodstuffs in quantities which could endanger human health or bring about an unacceptable change in the composition of the foodstuff. This principle provides the general horizontal framework for subsequent vertical Directives to approximate the laws of Member States relating to specific materials and articles intended to come into contact with foodstuffs.

The Directive applies to materials and articles which in their finished state are intended to come into contact with foodstuffs. This includes those materials and articles which are in contact with water intended for human consumption, but does not apply to fixed public or private water supply equipment.

Materials and articles must not transfer their constituents to foodstuffs in quantities which could:

- endanger human health;

- bring about an unacceptable change in the composition of the food.

Specific provisions

The Directive requires the adoption of special provisions applicable to certain groups of materials and articles in the form of specific Directives which may include:

- a list of substances authorised for use;

- purity standards for these substances;

- special conditions for the use of these substances and/or the materials and articles in which they are to be used;

- specific limits on the migration of certain constituents or groups of constituents into or onto foodstuffs;

- an overall limit on the migration of constituents into or onto foodstuffs;

- provisions aimed at protecting human health against hazards which might arise through oral contact with these materials and articles;

- rules to ensure compliance;

- rules deemed necessary for checking compliance.

National derogations

A Member State may permit the use of a substance not included on the list of substances authorised for use only if the following conditions are met:

- authorisation must be limited to a maximum period of three years;

- Member States must carry out an official check of materials and articles manufactured from that substance;

- materials and articles manufactured from that substance must bear a distinctive indication, to be determined by the authorisation.

Within two months of authorising the use of a substance not listed in the specific Directive, the Member State must notify the Commission and other Member States. Within three years the Member State may request that the Commission include the substance on the authorised list. The Commission should reach a decision on the basis of consultation with the Scientific Committee for Food and the Standing Committee for Foodstuffs.

If the decision of the Committee requires a Member State to revoke authorisation, this decision shall apply also to any other national authorisation for that substance. This procedure applies in all instances where a Member State proposes alterations to a list of substances authorised by a specific Directive.

Where a Member State has detailed grounds for establishing that the use of a material or article composed of authorised substances endangers human health, that Member State may temporarily suspend or restrict authorisation for the substance in question within its territory. The withdrawal of authorisation may be justified by a Member State only on grounds of:

- protection of public health;

- prevention of fraud;

- protection of industrial or commercial property.

The Commission and other Member States must immediately be informed of any withdrawal of authorisation by a Member State on these grounds. The Commission would then be required to take appropriate measures on the basis of consultations with the Standing Committee for Foodstuffs.

Labelling

Except where specific Directives provide otherwise, materials and articles not already in contact with foodstuffs must be accompanied by the following information when placed on the market:

- "food for use", or a specific indication of their use, or a recognised symbol;

- where appropriate, any special conditions to be observed during use;

- the name or trade name and address or registered office, or the trade mark of the manufacturer or processor, or of a seller established within the Community.

These details must be indicated clearly, legibly and indelibly, either at the retail stage or at marketing stages other than the retail stage. At the retail stage details must be shown:

- on the materials and articles or on the packaging; or

- on labels affixed to the materials and articles or their packaging; or

- on a sign in the immediate vicinity of the materials and articles and clearly visible to purchasers.

If provided at a marketing stage other than the retail stage, this information must appear either:

- on the accompanying documents; or

- on the labels or packaging; or

- on the materials and articles themselves.

This information must appear in the national or official language of the Member State in which the product is retailed. Member States may make these particulars compulsory within their territory either for materials or articles where specific Directives apply, or where similar national provisions apply. They may also make the additional requirement that retailers provide information in a language easily understood by the purchaser in the form of a notice placed in the vicinity of the goods.

<u>Verification</u>

Sampling and analysis of substances should be determined in accordance with the consultation procedure involving the Standing Committee for Foodstuffs.

Amendments to the lists of substances authorised by specific Directives may be adopted subject to consultation with the Scientific Committee for Food.

The Directive does not apply to materials and articles intended for export outside the Community.

Timetable

Member States were required to comply with the Directive by April 1978. Member States were required to authorise trade in materials and articles complying with the Directive by November 1980. Trade in and use of materials and articles not complying with the Directive was prohibited by November 1981. Member States could prohibit the manufacture of materials and articles not complying with the Directive by 9 December 1980.

The full text was published in OJL 340, 9.12.76.

Council Directive 78/142/EEC of 30 January 1978 on the approximation of the laws of the Member States relating to materials and articles which contain vinyl chloride monomer and are intended to come into contact with foodstuffs.

Analysis methods:
Commission Directive 80/766/EEC, see OJL 213, 16.8.80
Commission Directive 81/432/EEC, see OJL 167, 24.6.81

Summary

Directive 76/893/EEC established general rules, applicable horizontally to all products intended to come into contact with foodstuffs. Within the meaning of Directive 76/893/EEC, this Directive sets out specific criteria concerning materials and articles containing vinyl chloride monomer and possible migration from materials and articles prepared with vinyl chloride polymers or copolymers which are intended to come into contact with foodstuffs.

The Directive establishes a maximum level of one milligram per kilogram of vinyl chloride monomer which may be contained in the final product of materials and articles intended to come into contact with food.

<u>Verification</u>

Materials and articles must not pass onto foodstuffs any vinyl chloride monomer detectable by a method of analysis which complies with the criteria that:

- the level of vinyl chloride in materials and articles and the level of vinyl chloride released by materials and articles to foodstuffs are determined by means of gas-phase chromatography using the "headspace" method.

- the detection limit shall be 0.01 mg/kg;

- when the determination of vinyl chloride in certain foodstuffs is shown to be impossible for technical reasons, Member States may permit determination by stimulants for these particular foodstuffs.

The method of analysis used to check compliance with this criteria was laid down by Commission Directives 80/766/EEC and 81/432/EEC.

Timetable

Member States were required to comply with this Directive no later than 26 November 1979.

The full text was published in OJL 44, 15.2.78.

Commission Directive 80/590/EEC of 9 June 1980 determining the symbol that may accompany materials and articles intended to come into contact with foodstuffs.

Summary

Directive 80/590/EEC determining the symbol that may accompany materials and articles intended to come into contact with foodstuffs illustrates that symbol.

Timetable

Member States were required to take measures necessary to authorise use of that symbol by 1 January 1981.

The full text was published in OJL 151 of 19.6.80.

Council Directive 82/711/EEC of 18 October 1982 laying down the basic rules necessary for testing migration of the constituents of plastic materials and articles intended to come into contact with foodstuffs.

List of simulants to be used for migration tests laid down by:
Council Directive 85/572/EEC, see OJL 372, 31.12.85

Summary

Council Directive 76/893/EEC laid down that materials and articles must not transfer their constituents to foodstuffs in amounts which could endanger human health or bring about unacceptable changes to food. This Directive supplements Directive 76/893/EEC by establishing basic rules for verifying the migration of constituents of plastic containers and packaging which come into contact with foodstuffs.

The Directive applies specifically to those items consisting entirely of plastics, or consisting of two or more plastic materials bound together which are brought into contact with food. The Directive limits its definition of plastics to:

- organic macromelecular compounds obtained by polymerisation, polycondensation, polyaddition or similar processes from molecules with a lower molecular weight or by chemical alteration of natural macromolecules;

- silicones and other similar macromelecular compounds;

- macromelecular compounds to which other substances have been added.

The Directive does not apply to:

- varnished or unvarnished regenerated cellulose film;

- elastomers, natural and synthetic rubber;

- paper and paperboard;

- surface coatings obtained from paraffin waxes or mixtures of these waxes with each other or with plastics;

- materials composed of two or more articles, not all of which consist entirely of plastics.

Maximum migration levels for the constituents of plastic materials and articles are to be set out in lists of substances established by specific directives.

Verification

Where it is not possible to use the methods of analysis and verification specified in Directive 76/893/EEC, basic rules for testing migration in simulants are provided by this Directive. Directive 85/572/EEC lays down the list of simulants to be used for testing migration and the concentration of these simulants.

National derogations

If a Member State has grounds for establishing that the specified migration tests are unsuitable, it may temporarily introduce more appropriate tests provided that the Commission and other Member States are informed of its reasons for doing so. On the basis of this information and consultation with the Standing Committee for Foodstuffs, the Commission may introduce more appropriate provisions.

Timetable

Once specific directives have been adopted to establish maximum migration levels, Member States are required to comply with this Directive within the time limits set by those directives.

The full text was published in OJL 297, 23.10.82.

Council Directive 83/229/EEC of 25 April 1983 on the approximation of the laws of the Member States relating to materials and articles made of regenerated cellulose film intended to come into contact with foodstuffs.

As amended by:
Council Directive 86/388/EEC, see OJL 288, 14.8.86

Summary

Directive 76/893/EEC laid down rules preventing the transfer of the constituents of materials and articles on to or into foodstuffs in quantities which could endanger human health or bring about an unacceptable change in the composition of foodstuffs. In accordance with the provisions of Directive 76/893/EEC, the Directive on the approximation of the laws of the Member States relating to materials and articles made of regenerated cellulose film intended to come into contact with foodstuffs sets out specific instruments applicable to that substance.

The Directive applies to regenerated cellulose film which is either:

- a finished product;

- part of a finished product, containing other materials, which is likely to come into contact with food.

The Directive does not apply to:

- regenerated cellulose film which has a coating exceeding 50 mg/dm^2;

- synthetic castings of regenerated cellulose.

Regenerated cellulose film may be manufactured only from substances authorised in the Annex of the Directive. Additional substances may be used as colouring matter or adhesives provided that there is no trace of migration of these substances into foodstuffs.

Printed surfaces of regenerated cellulose film may not come into contact with food.

<u>National derogations</u>

Where a product is intended to come into contact with a foodstuff containing fat, Member States may refuse authorisation for the following substances in the manufacture of regenerated cellulose film:

- butylbenzylphthalate;

- butyl-methylcarboxybutyl-phthalate [= butylphthalyl butyl glycolate];

- di-n-butyl and di-isobutyl phthalate;

- dicyclohexyl phthalate;

- di(methyl-cyclohexyl) phthalate and its isomers [= sextolphalate];

- methyl-methylcarboxyethyl phthalate [= methyl-phthalyl ethyl glycolate].

The Council was required to decide on arrangements for these substances by 1 July 1986.

Timetable

Member States were required to authorise the marketing of products complying with this directive by 1 January 1985. The marketing of products not complying with this directive was prohibited after 1 January 1986.

The full text was published in OJL 123, 11.5.83.

Council Directive 84/500/EEC of 15 October 1984 on the approximation of the laws of the Member States relating to ceramic articles intended to come into contact with foodstuffs.

Summary

Directive 76/893/EEC established Community regulations applicable horizontally to all materials and articles intended to come into contact with foodstuffs. Directive 84/500/EEC is specific within the meaning of Directive 76/893/EEC by harmonizing the limit values and the test and analysis methods for ceramic articles intended to come into contact with foodstuffs.

The Directive relates to the possible migration of lead and cadmium from ceramic articles into foodstuffs. Fixed limits are set for permissible quantities of lead and cadmium extracted during test conditions. These limits are:

- Category 1: Pb 0.8 mg/dm^2; Cd 0.07 mg/dm^2.
  Applicable to articles which cannot be filled and articles which can be filled, the internal depth of which, measured from the lowest point to the horizontal plane passing through the upper rim, does not exceed 25mm;

- Category 2: Pb 4.0 mg/l; Cd 0.3 mg/l.
  Applicable to all other articles which can be filled;

- Category 3: Pb 1.5 mg/l; Cd 0.1 mg/l.

Where a ceramic article does not exceed these quantities by more than 50%, the article may be recognised as satisfying the requirements of the Directive if at least three other articles of the same shape, dimensions, decoration and glaze are found under test to have average quantities of lead or cadmium extracted which do not exceed the set limits by more than 50%.

Within three years the Council was required to:

- set limits to be imposed on those areas of ceramic articles which are intended to come into contact with the mouth;

- determine methods for checking that these limits are imposed;

- re-examine the limits set down by this Directive in the light of toxicological and technical data.

Timetable

Member States are required to permit trade in ceramic articles which comply with the Directive by 20 October 1987 and prohibit trade in articles which do not comply with the Directive by 20 October 1989.

The full text was published in OJL 277, 20.10.84.

PACKAGING - PROPOSED LEGISLATION

COM(87) 239 final. Amended proposal for a Council Directive on the approximation of the laws of the Member States relating to materials and articles intended to come into contact with foodstuffs.

Summary

Directive 76/893/EEC established general rules, applicable horizontally, to all materials and articles intended to come into contact with foodstuffs. COM(86) 90, the original Commission proposal to amend and codify Directive 76/893/EEC, had the objective of identifying sectors for which specific directives are to be drafted, and empowering the Commission to adopt specific directives and amend existing directives.

The proposed Directive relates to materials and articles intended to come into contact with foodstuffs. Covering or coating substances which form part of foodstuffs and may be consumed together with the food, such as cheese rinds, are exempt.

This subsequent amended proposal takes into account the opinion of the European Parliament.

Standing Committee on Foodstuffs

Directive 76/893/EEC required the adoption of specific directives to introduce special provisions for certain groups of materials and articles. The proposed framework Directive envisages empowering the Commission to adopt these specific Directives after consultation with the Standing Committee on Foodstuffs, and in doing so replacing the role of the Council in these cases.

Scientific Committee for Food

Where provisions may affect public health, adoption would be subject to prior consultation with the Scientific Committee for Food. In these cases it is proposed that general criteria must be met which require:

- approval for use only of those substances which are not transferred to foodstuffs in quantities likely to constitute a danger to human health under normal conditions;

- suitable toxicological testing and evaluation for all substances which appear on an authorised list;

- where there is no approved list, identification of those substances for which limits should be set down, based on the criterion set out above;

- account to be taken of the presence of a substance in other items which may contribute to a human being's daily intake.

Items subject to specific Directives

It is proposed that the following groups of materials and articles will be subject to specific Directives:

- plastics;

- regenerated cellulose film;

- elastomers and rubber;

- paper and board;

- ceramics;

- glass;

- metals and alloys;

- wood;

- paraffin wax or microcrystalline wax.

National derogations

Where Directive 76/893/EEC permits a Member State to provisionally authorise the use of a substance not included on an approved list, such exemptions will no longer be permitted by the proposed Directive. Member States will no longer be able to restrict trade in or usage of materials and articles which comply with the proposed Directive and specific Directives on grounds relating to composition, behaviour in the presence of a foodstuff or labelling.

In the case of materials and articles not yet subject to specific Directives, Member States will be able to require such items to be accompanied by a written declaration certifying that they comply with rules applying to them.

Where a Member State has detailed grounds for establishing that, despite complying with a specific Directive, a material endangers human health, use of that material may be temporarily restricted. The Commission will take appropriate measures after consultation with the Standing Committee for Foodstuffs.

Labelling

Retail trade in materials and articles will be prohibited unless labelling particulars required by Directive 76/893/EEC are in a language easily understood by purchasers.

Timetable

Member States will be required to permit trade in materials and articles complying with the Directive within 18 months of notification and prohibit trade in and use of materials not complying with the Directive within 36 months of notification.

Since this account was prepared, the Directive was adopted on 21.12.88 as 89/109/EEC, which repealed Directive 76/893/EEC.

The full text of the new Directive was published in OJL 40, 11.2.89.

COM(88) 750. Proposal for a Council Directive amending Directive 75/106/EEC on the approximation of the laws of the Member States relating to the making-up by volume of certain prepackaged liquids.

Summary

The proposal for a Directive on the approximation of the laws of the Member States relating to the making-up by volume of certain prepackaged liquids provides technical amendments to Directive 75/106/EEC in order to take account of developments in the vatting, bottling and labelling of wine.

At the time of writing the full text was not available in the OJC series.

ADDITIVES AND FLAVOURINGS - EXISTING LEGISLATION

Council Directive of 23 October 1962 on the approximation of the rules of the Member States concerning the colouring matters authorised for use in foodstuffs intended for human consumption.

As amended by:
Council Directive 65/469/EEC, see OJP 178, 26.10.65
Council Directive 67/653/EEC, see OJP 263, 30.10.67
Council Directive 70/358/EEC, see OJL 157, 18.7.70
Council Directive 76/399/EEC, see OJL 108, 26.4.76
Council Directive 78/144/EEC, see OJL 44, 15.2.78
Council Directive 81/712/EEC, see OJL 257, 10.9.81

Summary

The objective of the Directive on the approximation of the rules of the Member States concerning the colouring matters authorised for use in foodstuffs intended for human consumption is to ensure the protection of public health and consumer interests, while contributing to the free movement of foodstuffs in the Community.

Member States are required to prohibit the authorisation of any colouring in foodstuffs which is not listed in the Annex of the Directive. General and specific purity criteria are laid down for the authorised substances.

Member States may authorise the use of the following products for diluting or dissolving the colouring matters listed in the Annex:

- sodium carbonate and sodium hydrogen carbonate;

- sodium chloride;

- sodium sulphate;

- glucose;

- lactose;

- sucrose;

- dextrins;

- starches;

- ethanol;

- glycerol;

- sorbitol;

- edible oils and fats;

- beeswax;

- water;

- citric acid;

- tartaric acid;

- lactic acid;

- gelatine;

- pectins;

- ammonium, sodium and potassium alginates;

- L-ascorbic acid esters of the unbranched fatty acids C_{14}, C_{16} and C_{18} (authorised exclusively for colouring matters listed under E160 and E161).

<u>Labelling</u>

Authorised colouring matters may be placed on the market only if packaging or containers bear information relating to:

- the name and address of the manufacturer established within the Community;

- the official number of the colouring matter;

- the words "colouring matter for foodstuffs".

National derogations

The Directive does not affect national rules concerning natural substances which are used in the manufacture of certain foodstuffs because of their aromatic, sapid or nutritive properties but which also have a subsidiary colouring property.

The Directive does not affect national rules concerning colouring matters authorised for:

- the colouring of shells of hard boiled eggs, tobacco and manufactured tobacco;

- stamping meat, citrus fruit, cheese-rinds, the shells of eggs and other external parts not usually consumed with the foodstuffs.

Member States may authorise the use of pigmeat rubine and burnt amber, mixed with paraffin wax or other harmless substances, for the colouring of cheese-rinds.

The Directive applies to products imported into the Community.

Timetable

Member States were required to comply with the Directive by 11 November 1964.

The full text was published in OJL 115, 11.11.62.

Council Directive 64/54/EEC of 5 November 1963 on the approximation of the laws of the Member States concerning the preservatives authorised for use in foodstuffs intended for human consumption.

As amended by:
Directive 67/427/EEC, see OJP 148, 11.7.67
Directive 70/359/EEC, see OJL 157, 18.7.70
Directive 71/160/EEC, see OJL 87, 17.4.71
Directive 74/62/EEC, see OJL 38, 11.2.74
Directive 74/394/EEC, see OJL 208, 30.7.74
Directive 76/462/EEC, see OJL 126, 14.5.76
Directive 78/145/EEC, see OJL 44, 15.2.78
Directive 81/214/EEC, see OJL 101, 11.4.81
Directive 85/585/EEC, see OJL 372, 31.12.85

Specific criteria of purity:
Council Directive 65/66/EEC, see OJL 22, 9.2.65
As amended by:
Council Directive 67/428/EEC, see OJP 148, 11.7.67
Council Directive 76/463/EEC, see OJL 126, 14.5.76
Council Directive 85/585/EEC, see OJL 352, 13.12.86

Summary

The Directive on the approximation of the laws of the Member States concerning the preservatives authorised for use in foodstuffs intended for human consumption has as its objective the protection of public health and consumer interests, and the free movement of foodstuffs within the Community.

The Directive lays down in the Annex a list of preservatives which may be used in foodstuffs intended for human consumption. In specific cases, the Directive lays down additional conditions for the use of substances. Member States are required to ensure that conditions for use are complied with in these cases.

General purity criteria

Preservatives intended for use in foodstuffs must satisfy the following general purity criteria:

- they shall not contain a toxicologically dangerous amount of any element, in particular heavy metals;

- they shall not contain more than 3 mg/kg of arsenic or more than 10 mg/kg of lead;

- they shall not contain more than 50 mg/kg of copper and zinc taken together of which the zinc content must in no case exceed 25 mg/kg, subject to the specific criteria of purity.

Labelling

When placed on the market, preservatives intended for use in foodstuffs must contain the following information on packaging or containers:

- the name and address of the manufacturer or seller;

- the number and name of the preservative, as given in the Annex;

- the words "for foodstuffs (restricted use)";

- in the case of a mixture composed of a preservative and other products, the percentage of the preservative and the name of the mixture.

National derogations

A Member State may, for a maximum period of one year, suspend or restrict the use of a preservative on grounds that it may endanger human health. In this event, the Member State must inform the other Member States and the Commission of its reasons for doing so within one month. The Commission may decide to modify the list of authorised preservatives on the basis of consultations with the Standing Committee on Foodstuffs.

A Member State may authorise the smoking of certain foodstuffs only in smoke, or in liquid solutions of smoke, produced from wood or woody plants in the natural state and provided that this does not create additional risk to human health.

The Directive does not affect national laws concerning:

- foodstuffs to which preservatives may be added in so far as such provisions do not totally exclude the use of the preservative in foodstuffs;

- products used as foodstuffs, but which may have preservative properties;

- products used for coating foodstuffs;

- products used to protect plants and plant products against harmful organisms;

- anti-microbial products used for the treatment of drinking water;

- antioxidants.

The Directive is applicable to preservatives and foodstuffs imported into the Community.

The full text was published in OJL 12, 27.1.64.

Council Directive 70/357/EEC of 13 July 1970 on the approximation of the laws of the Member States concerning the antioxidants authorised for use in foodstuffs intended for human consumption.

As amended by:
Council Directive 87/55/EEC, see OJL 24, 27.1.87

Specific criteria of purity:
Council Directive 78/664/EEC, see OJL 223, 14.8.78
As amended by:
Council Directive 82/712/EEC, see OJL 297, 23.10.82

Summary

The Directive lays down a list of antioxidants which are authorised for use in foodstuffs intended for human consumption. These substances may be dissolved or diluted in:

- drinking water or demineralised water;
- distilled water;
- edible oils;
- edible fats;
- ethyl alcohol;
- glycerol;
- sorbitol;
- propylene glycol (1, 2-propanediol).

General purity criteria

Antioxidants intended for use in foodstuffs must not contain:

- more than 3 mg/kg of arsenic and not more than 10 mg/kg of lead;
- more than 50 mg/kg of copper and zinc taken together, of which the zinc content must be no higher than 25 mg/kg, subject to additional criteria specific to particular substances;

- any measurable trace of toxicologically dangerous elements, in particular other heavy metals, subject to specific criteria of purity.

Labelling

When placed on the market, substances listed in the Annex must contain the following information on packagings or containers:

- name and address of the manufacturer or seller;

- the number and name of the substance, as given in the Annex;

- the words "for foodstuffs (restricted use)";

- in the case of a mixture composed of substances listed in the Annex or including other substances, labelling must indicate the name or the number given in the Annex and percentages of the components, where one or more of the substances is diluted as an antioxidant, a substance capable of increasing the antioxidant effect of other substances, or a substance in which antioxidants may be dissolved or diluted.

National derogations

The Directive does not affect national laws which specify the foodstuffs to which antioxidants, or substances capable of increasing the antioxidant effect of other substances, may be added in so far as such provisions do not totally exclude the use of these substances in foodstuffs.

A Member State may, for a maximum period of one year, suspend the use of a substance authorised by this Directive on the grounds that it may endanger human health. In this event, the Member State must inform the Commission of its reasons for doing so within one month. After consultation within the Standing Committee for Foodstuffs, the Commission may decide to propose modifications to the list of authorised substances.

The Directive applies to substances or foodstuffs imported into the Community, but does not apply to substances or foodstuffs intended for export from the Community.

Timetable

Member States were required to amend national laws in accordance with the Directive by 18 July 1971. Amended national laws were required to come into force not later than 18 July 1972.

The full text was published in OJL 157, 18.7.70.

Council Directive 74/329/EEC of 18 June 1974 on the approximation of the laws of the Member States relating to emulsifiers, stabilisers, thickeners and gelling agents for use in foodstuffs.

As amended by:
Council Directive 78/612/EEC, see OJL 197, 22.7.78
Council Directive 80/597/EEC, see OJL 155, 23.6.80
Council Directive 86/102/EEC, see OJL 88, 3.4.86

Specific criteria of purity:
Council Directive 78/663/EEC, see OJL 223, 14.8.78
As amended by:
Council Directive 82/504/EEC, see OJL 230, 5.8.82

Summary

Directive 74/329/EEC on the approximation of the laws of the Member States relating to emulsifiers, stabilisers, thickeners and gelling agents for use in foodstuffs is based on the principle that Community legislation is necessary in order to ensure the protection of public health and consumer interests against falsification, while ensuring the free movement of goods between Member States.

Authorised substances

The Directive establishes a single list of agents which may be authorised for use in foodstuffs intended for human consumption and lays down a general criteria of purity. The list of authorised substances does not apply to:

- foodstuffs which have emulsifying, stabilising, thickening or gelling properties, for example eggs, flour, starches;

- emulsifiers used in release agents;

- acids, bases and salts which change or stabilise the pH when added to a foodstuff;

- blood plasma, modified starches, edible gelatine and hydrolysed food proteins and their salts.

General purity criteria

Substances authorised by the Directive must not contain:

- toxicologically dangerous amounts of an element, particularly heavy metals;

- more than 3 mg/kg of arsenic or more than 10 mg/kg of lead;

- more than 50 mg/kg of copper and zinc taken together, of which zinc must not exceed 25 mg/kg except where specified in the criteria of purity. The limit fixed for copper shall not apply to pectins, which shall be specified in the criteria of purity.

Substances listed under E 471, E 472(b), E473, E474, E475, and E477 must not contain more than 6% of sodium oleate, listed under E470.

Labelling

Substances listed by the Directive which are intended for use in foodstuffs must contain the following information on packaging:

- name and address of the manufacturer or the seller responsible. A person importing a product from a third country shall be regarded as the manufacturer;

- the name and number of the substance, as listed in the Directive;

- the statement "for foodstuffs (restricted use)";

- in the case of mixtures of listed substances, or where a listed substance has been mixed with other additives, or where other additives can be dissolved or diluted in a listed substance: the name of each component or where appropriate its listed number and the percentage of each component, where this is required.

National derogations

A Member State may suspend authorisation or reduce the maximum permitted levels of certain components of the substance for a period of one year on the grounds that a substance may endanger human health. The Commission may propose extending these measures for a further year, or may decide to withdraw the substance from the authorised list completely on the basis of consultations with the Standing Committee for Foodstuffs.

In the case of mixtures, Member States may make the additional requirement that, where national legislation limits the quantity of a substance permitted in foodstuffs, that substance should be expressed as a percentage, except when the same requirement applies to all components of a mixture. The Directive requires that the Council shall fix rules relating to the labelling of mixtures in the future.

Member States must not prohibit the introduction into their territory of substances which meet the requirements of this Directive concerning the labelling given on packaging or containers. However a Member State may require that this information is given in its own official language.

The Directive applies to substances intended for use in foodstuffs imported into the Community, but exempts substances or foodstuffs intended for export.

Timetable

Member States were required to comply with the Directive by 18 July 1975 and implement all necessary measures by 18 July 1976.

The full text was published in OJL 189, 18.6.74.

Council Directive 76/621/EEC of 20 July 1976 relating to the fixing of the maximum level of erucic acid in oils and fats intended as such for human consumption and in foodstuffs containing added oils and fats.

Analysis Methods:
Commission Directive 80/891/EEC, see OJL 254, 27.9.80

Summary

Directive 76/621/EEC relating to the fixing of the maximum level of erucic acid in oils and fats intended as such for human consumption and in foodstuffs containing added oils and fats stipulates that after 1 July 1977 the maximum level of erucic acid, calculated on the total level of fatty acids in a fat component, must not exceed 10%. After 1 July 1979 the level of erucic acid must not exceed 5%.

National derogations

Where a Member State has detailed grounds for requiring a lower level of erucic acid than that laid down by the Directive, a Member State may temporarily suspend or restrict application of the Directive. In these circumstances the Commission may authorise amendments to the Directive after consultation with the Standing Committee on Foodstuffs.

Timetable

Member States were required to apply provisions of the Directive to products put on the market after 1 July 1977 and 1 July 1979 respectively.

The full text was published in OJL 202, 28.7.76.

Commission Recommendation 78/358/EEC of 29 March 1978 to the Member States on the use of saccharin as a food ingredient and for sale as such in tablet form to the final consumer.

Summary

The Commission Recommendation on the use of saccharin as a food ingredient and for sale as such in tablet form to the final consumer endorses the opinion of the Scientific Committee for Food and recommends that:

- national rules on the use of saccharin in foodstuffs should be developed. Where necessary, this should be in accordance with the acceptable daily intake of 0 to 2.5 mg/kg body weight proposed by the Joint FAO/WHO Expert Committee on Food Additives. The intake of saccharin by children should be kept to a minimum;

- foodstuffs should be labelled in such a way that the presence of saccharin is specifically and clearly mentioned;

- labelling provisions for saccharin sold in tablet form should be implemented to inform the purchaser of the possible dangers of excessive consumption, particularly in the case of children and pregnant women.

Until specific Community provisions are introduced to implement these recommendations, the Commission's belief is that Member States should take all measures necessary to comply with the Committee's recommendations.

The full text was published in OJL 103, 15.4.78.

Commission Recommendation 80/1089/EEC of 11 November 1980 to the Member States concerning tests relating to the safety evaluation of food additives.

Summary

The Commission recommends to the Member States to comply with the Guidelines for the Assessment of Food Additives laid down by the Scientific Committee for Food for the conduct of tests and in the presentation of results for inclusion in a Community list.

The Commission further recommends to the Member States to incorporate the provisions of the guidelines into national rules governing food additives which are not yet the subject of Community legislation.

The full text was published in OJL 320, 27.11.80.

First Commission Directive 81/712/EEC of 28 July 1981 laying down Community methods of analysis for verifying that certain additives used in foodstuffs satisfy criteria of purity.

Summary

Commission Directive 81/712/EEC lays down the analysis methods necessary to verify that certain additives used in foodstuffs satisfy the general and specific criteria of purity. The scope of the Directive is laid down in Annex I. Analysis methods are laid down in Annex II.

Timetable

Member States were required to comply with the Directive by 20 February 1983.

The full text was published in OJL 257, 10.9.81.

Council Directive 88/344/EEC of 13 June 1988 on the approximation of the laws of the Member States on extraction solvents used in the production of foodstuffs and food ingredients.

Summary

The Directive on the approximation of the laws of the Member States on extraction solvents used in the production of foodstuffs and food ingredients lays down a list of those solvents which are authorised. Those extraction solvents authorised for use in compliance with good manufacturing practice are:

- propane;

- butane;

- butyl acetate;

- ethyl acetate;

- ethanol;

- carbon dioxide;

- acetone;

- nitrous oxide.

Extraction solvents authorised for use in foodstuffs and food ingredients, subject to conditions of use and maximum residue limits specified in the Annex of the Directive, are:

- hexane;

- methyl acetate;

- ethylmethylketone;

- dichloromethane.

Extraction solvents authorised for use in foodstuffs and food ingredients, subject to conditions of use specified in the Annex of the Directive, are:

- diethyl ether;

- isobutane;

- hexane;

- cyclohexane;

- methyl acetate;

- butan-1-ol;

- butan-2-ol;

- ethylmethylketone;

- dichloromethane;

- methyl-propan-1-ol.

The Council is required to decide within two years whether the residues in this third list should refer to flavourings rather than foodstuffs.

Purity criteria

Extraction solvents listed in the Directive must meet the following purity criteria:

- they must not contain a toxicologically dangerous amount of any element or substance;

- they must not contain more than 1 mg/kg of arsenic or more than 1 mg/kg of lead, except where provided for by specific purity criteria;

- they must satisfy the specific purity criteria, to be determined in accordance with the consultation procedure with the Standing Committee for Foodstuffs.

Labelling

Member States are required to ensure that, when marketed, substances authorised by the Directive contain the following information on packaging, containers or labels in a language easily understood by purchasers:

- the commercial name of the substance;

- a clear indication that the material is of a quality suitable for use for the extraction of food or food ingredients;

- a reference by which the batch or lot may be identified;

- the name and address of the manufacturer, packer or seller established within the Community;

- the net quantity given as units of volume;

- any special storage conditions or conditions of use.

Alternatively, information given in compliance with the latter four points may be provided in trade documents supplied with or prior to delivery.

Member States must not lay down labelling requirements more stringent than those laid down in this Directive.

<u>Standing Committee for Foodstuffs</u>

The consultation procedure within the Standing Committee for Foodstuffs will be used in order to determine:

- methods of analysis necessary to verify compliance with the general and specific purity criteria;

- methods of sampling and analysis of the extraction solvents;

- where necessary, the specific purity criteria of extraction solvents.

The Committee is required to re-examine the status of the following substances, which at present are excluded from the provisions of the Directive:

- methanol, propan-1-ol and propan-2-ol (within three years);

- trichloroethylene (within seven years).

Within two years the Committee is required to re-examine the status of the following substances:

- butan-1-ol;
- butan-2-ol;
- methyl-propan-1-ol;
- methyl-propan-2-ol;
- methyl acetate;
- cyclohexane;
- dichloromethane;
- hexane;
- ethylmethylketone;
- isobutane;
- diethyl ether.

National derogations

A Member State may temporarily suspend or restrict use of an extraction solvent on the grounds that it may endanger human health. In this event, a Member State must inform the other Member States and the Commission of its reasons for doing so. Accordingly the Commission may, on the basis of consultation with the Standing Committee for Foodstuffs, decide to propose modifications to the list of authorised extraction solvents.

The Directive is applicable to extraction solvents used in foodstuffs or ingredients imported into the Community, but is not applicable to extraction solvents or foodstuffs intended for export.

Timetable

Member States are required to comply with the Directive by 24 June 1991.

The full text was published in OJL 157, 24.6.88.

Council Directive 88/388/EEC of 22 June 1988 on the approximation of the laws of the Member States relating to flavourings for use in foodstuffs and to source materials for their production.

Summary

Directive 88/388/EEC on the approximation of the laws of the Member States relating to flavourings for use in foodstuffs and to source materials for their production requires Member States to ensure that:

- flavourings do not contain any element or substance in a toxicologically dangerous quantity;

- flavourings do not contain more than 3 mg/kg of arsenic, 10 mg/kg of lead, 1 mg/kg of cadmium and 1 mg/kg of mercury. This provision is subject to exceptions provided for in the specific criteria of purity;

- the use of flavourings does not result in the presence in foodstuffs of benzopyrene in amounts greater than those laid down in the Annex of the Directive;

- the use of flavourings and other food ingredients with flavouring properties does not result in the presence in foodstuffs of certain other undesirable substances in amounts greater than those laid down in the Annex of the Directive.

The Council, acting by qualified majority voting, will adopt at a later date:

- special provisions relating to use and production of categories of flavourings and source materials laid down by a Commission inventory;

- special provisions relating to the use and production of flavourings and source materials necessary for the protection of public health or trade;

- amendments concerning maximum limits of those substances laid down in the Annex of the Directive.

Council Decision 88/389/EEC requires the Commission to establish by June 1990 an inventory of the following categories of source materials and substances used in the preparation of flavourings:

- flavouring sources composed of foodstuffs and of herbs and spices not normally considered as foods;

- flavouring sources composed of vegetable or animal raw materials not normally considered as foods;

- flavouring substances obtained by appropriate physical processes or by enzymatic or microbiological processes from vegetable or animal raw materials;

- chemically synthesised or chemically isolated flavouring substances chemically identical to flavouring substances naturally present in foodstuffs or in herbs and spices normally considered as foods;

- chemically synthesised or chemically isolated flavouring substances chemically identical to flavouring substances naturally present in vegetable or animal raw materials not normally considered as foods;

- chemically synthesised or chemically isolated flavouring substances other than those referred to in the two previous categories;

- source materials used for the production of smoke flavourings or process flavourings, and the reaction conditions under which they are prepared.

The Commission, after consultation with the Standing Committee for Foodstuffs, is required to establish labelling rules for flavourings intended for sale to the ultimate consumer by 1 July 1990, and lay down the list of substances or materials authorised as:

- additives necessary for the storage and use of flavourings;

- products used for dissolving and diluting flavourings;

- additives necessary for the production of flavourings (processing aids) where such additives are not covered by other Community provisions.

Where necessary the Commission, after consultation with the Standing Committee for Foodstuffs, is required to establish:

- analysis methods necessary to verify compliance with the maximum limits laid down for certain substances;

- the procedure for taking samples and the methods of qualitative or quantitative analysis of flavourings in or on foodstuffs;

- the specific criteria of purity for certain flavourings;

- the microbiological criteria applicable to flavourings;

- the designation criteria given to the more specific names.

Packaging information

Flavourings not intended for sale to the ultimate consumer may not be marketed unless packaging bears the following information in a language easily understood by the purchaser and in indelible marking:

- the name or business name and address of the manufacturer or packer, or a seller established within the Community;

- the sales description: either the word "flavouring" or a more specific name or description of the flavouring. Member States may maintain for a period of three years more specific names to designate flavourings composed of mixtures of flavouring preparations and flavouring substances;

- the statement "for foodstuffs" or a more specific reference to the foodstuff for which the flavouring is to be used;

- a list in descending order of weight of the categories of flavouring substances present;

- an indication of the maximum quantity of each component or group of components in a foodstuff which are subject to the Directive;

- a means of identifying the consignment;

- the nominal quantity expressed in units of mass or volume.

Information required on packaging or containers prior to sale to the ultimate consumer may be given merely on the trade documents relating to the consignment, provided an indication of this fact appears in a conspicuous part of the packaging.

Member States are required to refrain from laying down more stringent national provisions relating to packaging information for sale prior to sale to the ultimate consumer.

National derogations

Where a Member State has detailed grounds for establishing that a substance covered by the Directive constitutes a danger to human health, the Member State may temporarily suspend or restrict use of the substance in its territory. The Commission may take appropriate measures on the basis of consultation with the Standing Committee for Foodstuffs.

The Directive applies to flavourings and foodstuffs imported into the Community, but does not apply to flavourings or foodstuffs for export outside the Community.

Timetable

Member States are required to take measures necessary to comply with the Directive by 22 December 1989. Member States are required to authorise the marketing and use of flavourings complying with the Directive by 22 June 1990 and prohibit the marketing and use of flavourings not complying with the Directive by 22 June 1991.

The full text was published in OJL 184, 15.7.88.

The text of the corrigendum was published in OJL 345, 14.12.85.

The full text of Council Decision 88/389/EEC was published in OJL 184, 15.7.88.

ADDITIVES AND FLAVOURINGS - PROPOSED LEGISLATION

COM(84) 726. Proposal for a Council Directive on the approximation of the laws of the Member States relating to modified starches intended for human consumption.

Summary

The proposed Directive on the approximation of the laws of the Member States relating to modified starches intended for human consumption lays down an approved list of chemically modified starches, the use of which has been authorised in foodstuffs.

Member States are required to authorise the marketing and use as foodstuffs ingredients of the modified starches listed in the Annex of the Directive, and prohibit the marketing and use of all other chemically modified starches. Special provisions relating to infant formulae and follow-up milk are laid down in the Annex of the Directive.

<u>General purity criteria</u>

Member States are required to ensure that modified starches do not:

- contain any substances in quantities that are liable to endanger public health;

- contain moulds, insects, remains of insects or other impurities of an animal nature or origin;

- have an abnormal flavour or odour.

Member States are required to ensure that the following maximum contents are not exceeded:

- arsenic: 1 mg/kg;

- lead: 1mg/kg;

- cadmium: 0.1 mg/kg

- mercury: 0.05 mg/kg;

- sulphur dioxide: 50 mg/kg.

Moisture

- modified starches made from cereals: 15% m/m;

- modified starches made from potatoes: 21% m/m;

- modified starches of other origins: 18% m/m.

Proteins

- starches in general: 0.5%;

- amylase-rich starches: 2.0%.

Labelling

Labelling of modified starches will be required to consist solely of the following wording:

- either the term "modified starch" followed by the reference letter of the product indicated in the Annex; or the name of the modified starch given in the Annex. The constituents of a mixture are to be designated individually;

- the words "for human consumption" or an indication of the specific intended use of the modified starch;

- the net quantity, except in the case of products put up in bulk;

- the date of manufacture, or identification of the production batch;

- the name or business name and address of the manufacturer or packer, or of a vendor established within the Community.

Information relating to the name of the modified starch and the date of manufacture will be required to appear on the package or label. Information relating to an indication of specific use or net quantity will be required to appear either on the package or label, or on the commercial documents relating to the modified starch in question.

Analysis methods

Sampling and methods of analysis for checking the composition and manufacturing characteristics of modified starches will be adopted in accordance with the consultation procedure involving the Standing Committee on Foodstuffs.

National derogations

Where a Member State has detailed grounds for establishing that a modified starch authorised by the Directive constitutes a hazard to public health, the Member State may suspend or restrict authorisation within its territory. The Commission will be required to adopt appropriate measures after consultation with the Standing Committee on Foodstuffs.

A Member State will be able to authorise the marketing and use within its territory of a modified starch not listed in the Annex of the Directive for a maximum period of three years. The Member State must ensure that foodstuffs containing additionally authorised modified starch are officially monitored. All such foodstuffs will be required to bear a specific indication of its status. Within three years the Member State may request that the Commission include the substance in the Annex of the Directive. The Commission will be required to adopt appropriate measures after consultation with the Standing Committee on Foodstuffs.

Timetable

Member States will be required to permit the marketing of products complying with the Directive by 1 August 1986 and prohibit the marketing of products not complying with the Directive by 1 February 1988.

The full text was published in OJC 31, 1.2.85.

COM(87) 243. Amended proposal for a Council Directive on the approximation of the laws of the Member States concerning food additives authorised for use in foodstuffs intended for human consumption.

Summary

Commission proposal COM(86) 87 for a Directive on the approximation of the laws of the Member States concerning food additives authorised for use in foodstuffs intended for human consumption set out to harmonise trade in food additives by requiring compliance with the provisions of a framework Directive and subsequent Directives on specific food additives. This subsequent amended proposal takes into account the opinion of the European Parliament by accepting technical amendments consistent with achieving a framework Directive on food additives.

The proposed Directive intends that those additives authorised for use as ingredients during the manufacture or preparation of a foodstuffs be categorised in accordance with the principal function of that additive. Authorised categories of food additives are listed in the Annex, and will appear in subsequent specific Directives. Additives may only be included in the list if the requirements of the general purity criteria are met.

The proposed Directive does not apply to:

- processing aids;

- substances used in the protection of plants and plant products which are covered by Community rules relating to plant health;

- flavourings for use in foodstuffs which are covered by Community rules relating to flavourings.

The framework Directive

Provisions relating to each listed additive will be laid down in a framework Directive, which may be drawn up in stages. The framework Directive will be adopted in accordance with the consultation procedure with the Standing Committee on Foodstuffs.

The framework Directive will include:

- a list of authorised substances;

- the purity criteria;

- where appropriate, a list of the foodstuffs to which substances may be added and conditions of use;

- methods of analysis needed to verify that the purity criteria are satisfied;

- the procedure for taking samples and methods of analysis of additives in and on foodstuffs;

- other rules necessary to ensure compliance;

- where necessary the purpose may be restricted.

<u>Labelling</u>

Prior to sale to the ultimate consumer, food additives may only be marketed if the following information is contained on packaging or containers:

- the name of the additive and its EEC number, or a description of the product that is sufficiently precise to enable it to be distinguished from similar products;

- the words "food for use", or a more specific reference to its intended food use;

- where necessary, special storage conditions or conditions of use;

- an identifying batch or lot number;

- the name and address of the manufacturer, packer or seller established within the Community;

- an indication of the percentage of any component subject to a quantitative limitation in a food;

- the nominal net quantity expressed in units of mass or volume.

Additives intended for sale to the ultimate consumer will be required to contain the following additional information on packaging or containers:

- the name under which the product is sold;

- the date of minimum durability;

- any other information provided for in the comprehensive Directive.

These requirements are without prejudice to more detailed or extensive laws regarding weights and measures, or to laws relating to dangerous substances.

National derogations

A Member State may suspend or restrict the use of a food additive on the grounds that it may endanger human health. In this event, the Member State must inform the other Member States and the Commission of its reasons for doing so. The Commission may, on the basis of consultation with the Standing Committee on Foodstuffs, propose amendments to the framework Directive, or the specific Directive.

Timetable

Member States will be required to permit trade in and the use of food additives complying with this Directive by 12 December 1988 and prohibit trade in and the use of food not complying with this Directive by 12 June 1990.

The full text was published in OJC 154, 12.6.87.

The full text of the original proposal, COM(86) 87, was published in OJC 116, 16.5.86.

COM(88) 221. Re-examined proposal for a Council Directive on the approximation of the laws of the Member States relating to flavourings for use in foodstuffs and to source materials for their production.

Summary

The original proposal for a Directive relating to flavourings for use in foodstuffs and to source materials for their production, COM(80) 286, was amended following the opinion given by the Parliament. The amended proposal, COM(82) 166 was submitted to the Council. The Council agreed its common position in October 1987 and transmitted the proposal to the Parliament. The Parliament put forward a number of amendments. This re-examined proposal incorporates those amendments which the Commission found acceptable.

The proposed Directive is applicable to flavouring agents used or intended for use in or on foodstuffs to impart odour or taste, and to natural flavouring materials and other source materials used for the production of flavourings.

The proposed Directive is not applicable to:

- substances and products intended to be consumed as such, with or without reconstitution;

- natural flavouring materials, except those specified in the Directive;

- substances and products which have exclusively a sweet, sour or salt taste;

- protein hydrolysates obtained by the autolysis or hydrolysis of protein rich foods, or food proteins, without the addition of other substances.

Member States are required to take all measures necessary to ensure that:

- flavourings comply with the general purity criteria laid down in the Annex;

- the use of natural flavouring materials and/or natural flavouring preparations may not result in the presence in food of any substance listed in the Annex in a quantity greater than the limit specified.

The Council is required to adopt appropriate provisions concerning:

- artificial flavouring substances;

- nature-identical flavouring substances;

- source materials for the production of natural flavouring preparations and natural flavouring substances;

- source materials for the production of artificial flavouring preparations.

The following measures will be adopted by the Commission in accordance with the consultation procedure involving the Standing Committee for Foodstuffs:

- a list of additives authorised for the production and storage of flavourings;

- a list of products authorised for dissolving and diluting flavourings;

- a list of processing aids (for example, extraction solvents) authorised for the production of flavourings;

- technical amendments to the Annexes considered necessary on the basis of scientific and technical knowledge;

- the microbiological criteria applicable to flavourings;

- the designation criteria given to the more specific names referred to in the Directive;

- the physical processes for the production of natural flavouring preparations and natural flavouring substances.

Provisions which may have effects on public health may be adopted only after consultation with the Standing Committee on Foodstuffs.

Labelling

Flavourings may only be sold if packaging bears the following information:

- the name or business name and address of the manufacturer or packager, or the seller established in the Community;

- either the word "flavouring" or a more specific name or description of the flavouring;

- either the statement "for foodstuffs" or a more specific reference to its intended food use;

- in the case of mixtures of flavourings, a list of the categories of flavourings present in accordance with the definitions laid down in the Directive, in order of proportion by weight which each category bears in total;

- in the case of flavourings containing additives necessary for the production and storage of flavourings, products used for dissolving and diluting flavourings, or processing aids necessary for the production of flavourings: the name of any such substances or material or its "E" number, and the percentage of such substances where this requirement is stipulated in provisions relating to other categories of additives;

- an indication of the maximum amount present of any natural flavouring materials or natural flavouring preparations listed in the Annex;

- in the case of pre-packaged flavourings, the net quantity.

The word "natural" or any word having the same meaning may only be used for flavourings where the flavouring component contains exclusively natural flavourings.

Where flavouring contains nature-identical flavouring substances, any reference to the type of flavour must be accompanied by the word "reproduced". Where artificial flavouring substances are used, this indication must be replaced by the word "artificial".

Where flavourings are not intended for retail sale, certain information may be given on trade documents only.

Member States are required to refrain from requiring labelling requirements more detailed than those laid down in the Directive.

National derogations

Where a Member State has detailed grounds for establishing that the use of an approved flavouring endangers human health, the Member State may temporarily suspend or restrict application of the provisions in question in its territory. It must immediately inform the Commission and other Member States of its reasons for doing so. The Commission will take appropriate measures on the basis of consultations with the Standing Committee for Foodstuffs.

Non-harmonised national provisions may be justified on grounds of:

- protection of public health;

- prevention of fraud;

- protection of industrial and commercial property.

The Directive is applicable to flavourings intended for use in foodstuffs and to foodstuffs imported into the Community. The Directive is not applicable to flavourings or foodstuffs intended for export outside the Community.

The proposal was adopted by the Council on 21.12.88 as Directive 89/107/EEC.

The full text was published in OJL 40, 11.2.88.

COM(88) 322. Proposal for a Council Directive amending for the fifth time Directive 74/329/EEC on the approximation of the laws of the Member States relating to emulsifiers, stabilisers, thickeners and gelling agents for use in foodstuffs.

Summary

The Commission proposes the removal of temporary authorisation for tragacanth gum and karaya gum, and the reintroduction of these substances to the authorised list.

The full text was published in OJC 214, 16.8.88.

FOOD FOR SPECIAL NUTRITIONAL USES - EXISTING LEGISLATION

Council Directive 77/94/EEC of 21 December 1976 on the approximation of the laws of the Member States relating to foodstuffs for particular nutritional uses.

Summary

Directive 77/94/EEC on the approximation of the laws of the Member States relating to foodstuffs for particular nutritional uses is applicable to products which are distinguishable from foodstuffs for normal consumption due to their special composition or manufacturing process and are marketed in such a way as to indicate their suitability for specific nutritional purposes.

A product with nutritional use may be characterised as "dietetic" or "dietary" if it meets the nutritional requirements of:

- persons whose digestive processes or metabolism are disturbed;

- persons who may benefit from a controlled consumption of a particular foodstuff due to the nature of their physiological condition;

- infants or young children in good health.

Member States may restrict the use of the terms "dietetic" or "dietary" to products which meet the nutritional requirements of either the first or the first two of these groups. However, foodstuffs intended for normal consumption which may be used for a particular nutritional use may indicate this fact. Products with a particular nutritional use must also comply with mandatory provisions applicable to foodstuffs for normal consumption, except where changes made to them are permitted by a specific Directive or national provisions.

Labelling

Labelling of foodstuffs with particular nutritional uses must provide:

- details of the particular nutritional characteristics accompanying the description or, in the case of the nutritional requirements of infants and young children, a reference to the purpose for which they are intended;

- the particular elements of the qualitative and quantitative composition, or the special manufacturing process which gives the product its national characteristics;

- the available energy value expressed in kJ and kcal, and the carbohydrate, protein and fat content per 100ml of the product as marketed and, where appropriate, per specified quantity of the products proposed for consumption. Where the energy value is less than 50kJ (12 kcal) per 100 g or 100 ml of the product, these particulars may be replaced by an indication of this fact;

- the net quantity;

- any other particulars required by specific Directives or, where appropriate, by national provisions.

The labelling, advertising or presentation of products must not attribute to the foodstuff any properties for the prevention, treatment or cure of human disease, except where necessary to inform persons qualified in medicine, nutrition or pharmacy.

Specific Directives or, where appropriate, national provisions may lay down conditions under which reference may be made to a diet or a category of persons in the labelling, presentation or advertising of a particular foodstuff.

Prepackaged foodstuffs

Products intended for particular nutritional uses may only be made available on the retail market in prepackaged form, with packaging completely covering the foodstuff. Member States may exempt products intended for the retail trade from this provision provided that the product is accompanied by the required information at the time of sale.

Purity criteria

On the basis of a Commission proposal and consultation with the Standing Committee for Foodstuffs, the Council was required to lay down purity criteria for additives authorised for use in foodstuffs for particular nutritional uses.

National derogations

Non-harmonised national provisions may be justified only on ground of:

- protection of public health;
- prevention of fraud;
- protection of industrial and commercial property.

The Directive does not affect the status of national laws which provide for:

- a list of ingredients;
- date-marking.

Timetable

Member States were required to comply with the Directive by 31 July 1978 and permit trade in all products complying with the Directive by 31 January 1979. Trade in products not complying with the Directive was prohibited after 31 January 1980.

The full text was published in OJL 26, 31.1.77.

FOOD FOR SPECIAL NUTRITIONAL USES - PROPOSED LEGISLATION

COM(87) 241. Amended proposal for a Council Directive on the approximation of the laws of the Member States relating to foodstuffs intended for particular nutritional uses.

Summary

The original proposal for a Directive on foodstuffs intended for particular nutritional uses, COM(86) 91, was considered necessary in order to amend and replace Directive 77/94/EEC. This amended proposal takes account of the opinion of the European Parliament.

The proposed Directive defines foodstuffs for particular nutritional uses as foodstuffs which, owing to their special composition or manufacturing process, are clearly distinguishable from foodstuffs for normal consumption, which are suitable for their claimed nutritional purposes and which are marketed in such a way as to indicate such suitability.

A particular nutritional use must fulfil the nutritional requirements of:

- certain categories of persons whose digestive processes or metabolism are disturbed (which may be characterised as "dietetic" or "dietary" food); or

- certain categories of persons who are in a special physiological condition and who could benefit from controlled consumption of certain substances ("dietetic" or "dietary" food); or

- infants or children in good health.

The nature or composition of the foodstuff must be such that the products are appropriate for the particular nutritional use intended.

Labelling

In the case of labelling, presentation and advertising of foodstuffs for normal consumption, the following will be prohibited:

- use of the adjectives "dietetic" or "dietary" either alone or in conjunction with other words, to designate these foodstuffs;

- all other markings or any presentation likely to give the impression that a foodstuff for particular nutritional use is involved.

Foodstuffs for normal consumption may indicate suitability for a particular nutritional use in accordance with the consultation procedure involving the Standing Committee for Foodstuffs.

The labelling, presentation and advertising of foodstuffs within the scope of the Directive must not attribute properties for the prevention, treatment or cure of human disease, except in cases defined in accordance with the consultation procedure involving the Standing Committee for Foodstuffs. However, this requirement will not prevent the dissemination of any useful information or recommendations exclusively intended for persons qualified in medicine, nutrition or pharmacy.

The designation under which a product is sold must be accompanied by an indication of its particular nutritional characteristics. In the case of foodstuffs which fulfil the nutritional requirements of infants or young children, this reference must be replaced by a reference to the purpose for which they are intended.

In the case of products for which no specific Directive has been adopted, labelling information must include:

- the particular elements of the qualitative and quantitative composition or the special manufacturing process which give the product its nutritional characteristics;

- the available energy value expressed in kJ and kcal and the carbohydrate, protein and fat content per 100 g or 100 ml of the product as marketed and, where appropriate, per specified quantity of the product as proposed for consumption;

Where the energy value is less than 50 kJ (12kcal) per 100 g or 1000 ml of the product as marketed, these particulars may be replaced either by the words "energy value less than 50 kJ (12kcal) per 100 g", or the words "energy value less than 100 ml".

Where products are covered by a specific Directive, particular labelling requirements will also be adopted.

Packaging

Foodstuffs for particular nutritional uses must only be allowed on the retail market in prepackaged form. The packaging must completely cover the product.

Specific Directives

Specific provisions will be laid down for the following groups of foods:

- infant formulae;

- follow-up milk and other follow-up foods;

- baby foods;

- low energy and energy reduced foods.

Specific Directives may include:

- essential requirements as to the nature or composition of the products;

- quality of raw materials;

- hygienic requirements;

- permitted changes to ensure conformity with the definitions of foodstuffs for particular nutritional uses;

- lists of substances with a specific nutritional purpose including purity criteria for those substances;

- lists of additives;

- labelling, presentation and advertising;

- conditions under which any reference may be made in labelling, presentation and advertising to a diet or to a category of persons for which the particular nutritional use is intended;

- sampling procedures and methods of analysis necessary for checking compliance with the requirements of specific Directives.

Conditions under which reference may be made to a category of persons for which a product is intended may be adopted in accordance with the procedure involving the Standing Committee for Foodstuffs.

National derogations

Member States must not restrict trade in products which comply with the Directive and specific Directives on grounds relating to their composition, manufacturing specifications, presentation or labelling.

Where a Member State has detailed grounds for establishing that a foodstuff intended for particular nutritional use endangers human health although it complies with the relevant specific Directive, the Member State may temporarily suspend or restrict application of the provisions in question within its territory. It must immediately inform the Commission and other Member States of its reasons for doing so. The Commission will take appropriate action on the basis of consultations with the Standing Committee for Food.

The proposal was adopted by the Council on 14.10.88.

The full text is published in OJC 161, 19.6.87.

The full text of the original proposal, COM(86) 91, was published in OJC 124, 1986.

COM(86) 564. Modified proposal for a Council Directive on the approximation of the laws of the Member States relating to infant formulae and follow-up milks.

Summary

The Commission's original proposal for a Council Directive on the approximation of the laws of the Member States relating to infant formulae and follow-up milks, COM(84) 703, aimed to establish regulations governing the essential composition of such products. In taking into account the opinion of the European Parliament, this amended proposal envisages strengthening Community commitment in the areas of marketing, information and responsibilities of health authorities.

The proposed Directive authorises the marketing of all infant formulae which satisfy the nutritional requirements of infants during the first four to six months of life.

Infant formulae and follow-up milk must comply with the compositional criteria laid down in the Annex of the proposed Directive, except in the case of infant formulae not exclusively manufactured from cows' milk proteins, which will be specified at a later date. The Annex of the proposed Directive lays down the additives which may be used and those substances which may be used for the enrichment of infant formulae and follow-up milks with :

- mineral substances;

- vitamins;

- amino acids and other nitrogen compounds;

- other substances having a particular nutritional purpose.

Infant formulae and follow-up milks must not contain levels of any substances capable of endangering the health of infants after a date to be established by the Council.

Labelling

In addition to the labelling requirements of Directive 79/112/EEC, the proposed Directive requires the labelling of infant formulae and follow-up milks to carry to following information:

- in the case of infant formulae, a statement to the effect that a product is suitable for particular nutritional use where breastfeeding is not possible, or where the mother chooses not to breastfeed;

- in the case of infant formulae which do not contain added iron, a statement to the effect that infants over the age of six months must have iron requirements met from other sources;

- in the case of follow-up milks, a statement that the product is only of particular use to infants over the age of four months and that it should not be used as a replacement for breast milk during the first four months of life;

- available energy value, expressed in kJ and kcal, and the content of proteins, liquids and carbohydrates per 100 ml of the product ready for use;

- average quantity of each mineral substance and of each vitamin listed in the Annex of the Directive, and of chlorine per 100 ml of the product ready for use;

- instructions for preparing the product and a warning against the health hazards for inappropriate preparation;

- batch identification information.

The proposed Directive requires the labelling, presentation and advertising of infant formula milk contain the following information:

- a statement concerning the superiority of breastfeeding;

- a statement recommending that the product be used only on the advice of persons having qualifications in medicine, nutrition or pharmacy;

- a warning concerning the negative effect on breastfeeding of introducing partial bottle-feeding;

- a warning concerning the difficulty of reversing a decision not to breastfeed.

The labelling, presentation and advertising of infant formulae and follow-up milks will require the provision of information concerning the appropriate use of the product and in order not to discourage breastfeeding. The use of the terms "humanised", "materialised", "adapted" or similar terms will be prohibited.

Pictures of infants or any pictures or text which would idealise the product will not be permitted in the labelling of infant formulae. The use of graphics for easy identification or for illustrating methods of preparation will be permitted.

An indication will be required of:

- social and financial implications of product use;

- health hazards of inappropriate foods or feeding methods;

- health hazards of unnecessary or improper use of infant formulae.

Articles for use in conjunction of with infant-formulae and follow-up milk, such as specially-designed feeding equipment, will also be required to comply with the provisions of the proposed Directive.

Advertising

Advertisements promoting the use of infant formulae and follow-up milk will be subject to the provisions of the Directive. The Directive will restrict the advertising of infant-formulae to publications which specialise in baby care. Information contained in advertisements must be of a purely scientific and factual nature and must not imply that bottle-feeding is equivalent to or better than breastfeeding.

The Directive will not permit point-of-sale advertising, the giving of samples or other promotional devices to induce sales of infant formulae to the consumer at the retail level, or the use of promotional devices via the health care system. Donations or low-priced sales of infant formulae to institutions or organisations may only be distributed for infants fed on infant formulae and only for as long as required by such infants.

Member States will be required to ensure that donations of informational or educational equipment or materials by manufacturers or distributors are made only at the request, and with the written approval of, the national authority or within the guidelines set by that authority. Equipment or materials may bear the company name or logo, but must not refer to a brand name. Distribution may be made only through the health care system.

National derogations

National derogations from provisions laid down in the Annex of the Directive will be permitted for a maximum period of three years. A Member State will be required to carry out an official check of products manufactured on the basis of the additional authorisation. Products covered by the authorisation must bear information explaining this fact.

Within two months the Member State making the authorisation will be required to submit to the Commission and other Member States a text of the authorisation. Within three years the Member States may submit to the Commission reasons for including the elements subject to authorisation in the Directive. A decision will be reached after consultation with the Scientific Committee for Food and the Standing Committee for Foodstuffs.

A Member State may restrict or suspend the use of a substance or the maximum permissible concentration of the substance authorised by the Directive where there are detailed grounds that it endangers human health. The Commission will re-examine the status of the substance on the basis of consultations with the Standing Committee for Foodstuffs.

The full text was published in OJC 285, 12.11.86.

The full text of the original proposal, COM(84) 703, was published in OJC 28, 30.1.86.

GENERAL FOOD LEGISLATION - EXISTING

Council Directive 79/581/EEC of 19 June 1979 on consumer protection in the indication of the prices of foodstuffs.

As amended by:
Council Directive 88/315/EEC, see OJL 142, 9.6.88

Summary

The Directive on consumer protection in the indication of the prices of foodstuffs lays down rules relating to the indication of the selling price and the price per unit of measurement of foodstuffs which are to be supplied to the final consumer, or which are advertised with their prices stated.

The Directive is applicable to foodstuffs sold in bulk or prepackaged, but is not applicable to:

- foodstuffs sold in hotels, restaurants, cafes, public houses, hospitals, canteens and similar establishments and consumed on the premises;

- foodstuffs bought for the purpose of a trade or commercial activity;

- foodstuffs supplied in the course of the provision of a service;

- foodstuffs sold on the farm or to private sales.

<u>Labelling</u>

Foodstuffs which fall within the scope of the Directive must bear an indication of the selling price in a form which is unambiguous, easily identifiable and clearly legible. A Member State may lay down specific national provisions for such an indication of price.

Foodstuffs pre-packaged in quantities listed in the Annex of the Directive and foodstuffs pre-packaged in variable quantities must also bear an indication of the unit price.

A written or printed advertisement or catalogue which mentions the selling price of foodstuffs must also indicate the unit price.

Unit price

The unit price must be expressed as a price per litre for foodstuffs sold by volume and as a price per kilogram for foodstuffs sold by weight.

In the case of foodstuffs marketed by volume, a Member State may authorise that the unit price will refer to a quantity of 100 millilitres, 10 centilitres, one decilitre or 0.1 litre. In the case of foodstuffs marketed by weight, the unit price may refer to quantity of 100 grams.

In the case of pre-packaged foodstuffs, the unit price must refer to the quantity declared in accordance with national and Community provisions.

In the case of two or more quantities declared on the packaging, a Member State may determine which one is to be used to calculate the unit price.

A Member State may waive the requirement to indicate the unit price for foodstuffs marketed in bulk or pre-packaged foodstuffs where such an indication would be meaningless. In particular, such an indication would be meaningless in the case of:

- foodstuffs exempt from the obligation to indicate weight or volume;

- different foodstuffs sold in a single package;

- foodstuffs sold from automatic dispensers;

- prepared dishes or dishes for preparation contained in a single package;

- fancy products;

- multiple packs, made up of individual items corresponding to one of the values in a Community quality range.

Where highly perishable foodstuffs are sold at a reduced price due to the danger of distortion, these items may be exempted from the requirement to indicate the new unit price.

In the case of foodstuffs weighing less than 50 grams or 50 millilitres and foodstuffs weighing more than 10 kilograms or 10 litres, a Member State may waive the requirement to indicate the unit price.

The obligation to indicate the unit price of foodstuffs pre-packaged in pre-established quantities is not applicable in certain instances to foodstuffs which fall within the scope of the following Directives:

- Council Directive 73/241/EEC;
- Council Directive 73/437/EEC;
- Council Directive 77/436/EEC;
- Council Directive 75/106/EEC;
- Council Directive 80/232/EEC.

A Member State may waive the obligation to indicate the unit price of foodstuffs pre-packaged in pre-established quantities in the case of certain foodstuffs which fall within the scope of the following Directives:

- Council Directive 75/106/EEC;
- Council Directive 80/232/EEC.

Transitional measures

National measures and practices which exist at the date of adoption of Directive 88/314/EEC may be maintained until June 1995. Until this date, the use of the imperial system of units in national authorities in Ireland and the UK will determine for each foodstuff the units of mass or volume in which the unit price is compulsory.

National derogations

Member States may waive the obligation to indicate unit price in the case of foodstuffs which are sold by certain small retail businesses and handed directly by the seller to the purchaser. This exemption will apply where the indication of unit price is:

- likely to constitute an excessive burden for such businesses;

- be impractical owing to the number of foodstuffs offered for sale, the sales area, its layout or conditions peculiar to certain forms of trading.

Timetable

Member States were required to comply with the original Directive by 26 June 1979 and are required to comply with the amendments of Directive 88/315/EEC by 26 June 1990.

The full text was published in OJL 158, 26.6.79.

Council Directive 85/591/EEC of 20 December 1985 concerning the introduction of Community methods of sampling and analysis for the monitoring of foodstuffs intended for human consumption.

Summary

The Directive concerning the introduction of Community methods of sampling and analysis for the monitoring of foodstuffs intended for human consumption provides that the Commission may adopt Community methods of sampling and analysis when considered necessary after consultation with the Standing Committee for Foodstuffs.

The Commission will adopt methods of sampling and analysis where:

- this is deemed necessary to ensure that Community law is uniformly applied;

- barriers exist to intra-Community trade.

National derogations

A Member State may use methods of sampling and analysis other than Community methods provided that this does not hinder the free movement of products which comply with Community methods.

Where a Member State has detailed grounds for establishing that Community methods are inappropriate for technical reasons or due to insufficient examination of an important health question, the Member State may temporarily suspend the Community measure in its territory.

The Commission may amend Community methods on the basis of consultation with the Standing Committee for Foodstuffs.

Timetable

Member States were required to take all measures necessary to comply with the Directive by 31 December 1987.

The full text was published in OJL 372, 31.12.85.

GENERAL FOOD LEGISLATION - PROPOSED

COM(85) 514. Amended proposal for a Council Directive of the laws of the Member States relating to quick-frozen foodstuffs for human consumption.

Summary

The original proposal for a Directive on quick-frozen foodstuffs, COM(84) 489, was amended following the opinion delivered by the Parliament. The amended proposal is applicable to all foodstuffs put up for sale which have undergone a quick-freezing process, whereby the temperature zone of maximum crystallisation is spanned as rapidly as necessary, with the result that the temperature at the centre of the product is -18 degrees centigrade or lower. The Directive is applicable to:

- the common organisation of agricultural and fisheries markets;

- veterinary hygiene.

The Directive is not applicable to ice-cream or other edible ices.

The proposed Directive requires Member States to ensure that:

- raw materials used in the manufacture of quick-frozen foodstuffs are of sound merchantable quality;

- the quick-freezing operation is carried out with the aid of appropriate equipment;

- the quick-freezing takes place immediately after preparation of the product.

Authorised cryogenic fluids

A list of cryogenic fluids authorised for use in direct contact with quick-frozen foodstuffs will be adopted by the Council. The list must specify:

- the purity criteria to be satisfied by the fluids;

- the maximum permissible content of the residues of these fluids in quick-frozen foodstuffs.

Amendments to the list of authorised fluids will be adopted after consultation with the Scientific Committee for Food.

Storage temperature

During the storage, transportation and display of quick-frozen foods, the temperature must be maintained at -18 degrees or lower at the centre of the product. Brief upward fluctuations in the temperature of the product in accordance with good storage and distribution practices will be permitted provided that they do not exceed:

- 3 degrees centigrade during storage and transport other than local distribution;

- 6 degrees centigrade during local distribution and in retail display cabinets.

Where the permitted upward fluctuations are accidentally or unforeseeably exceeded, the product in question must be examined to determine the use to which it may be put. Thawed products or those in which the thawing process has begun must carry a clear warning on labelling.

Labelling

The sale name of quick-frozen foodstuffs intended for retail sale must be supplemented by the words "quick-frozen" or "quick-frozen foodstuff".

An indication must be made of the period during which they may be stored in the home of the consumer, together with an indication of the storage temperature or the type of storage equipment required.

In the case of quick-frozen foodstuffs not intended for retail sale, labelling need only display the following information:

- the sale name in accordance with Directive 79/112/EEC and supplemented be an indication that the product has been quick-frozen;

- the net quantity, except for products sold in bulk;

- the date or manufacture or some means of identifying the batch;

- the name or business name and address of the manufacturer or packer, or of a vendor established within the Community.

The particulars listed above must appear on the package or on a label attached to the package. Particulars relating to the sale name, net quantity and date of manufacture may appear only on the shipping documents for the product in question.

Packaging

Quick-frozen foodstuffs intended for retail sale must be packed by the manufacturer or packer in suitable sealed packages which:

- protect the products from any harmful influence;

- must be delivered intact to the consumer.

Verification

Member States are required to conduct random official checks on:

- equipment used for freezing;

- temperatures of the foodstuffs during storage and transport and in retail display cabinets.

Methods of sampling and analysis for the monitoring of temperature will be laid down in accordance with the consultation procedure involving the Standing Committee for Foodstuffs.

Member States may not make additional requirements that compliance with the conditions of the Directive be met by means of an official certificate.

The proposal was adopted by the Council on 21.12.88 as Directive 89/108/EEC.

The full text was published in OJL 40, 11.2.89.

COM(88) 88. Amended proposal for a Council Directive on the official inspection of foodstuffs.

Summary

The original proposal for a Directive on the official inspection of foodstuffs, COM(86) 747, intended to establish Community regulations for official inspections in order to protect the health and economic interests of consumers, and facilitate the free movement of foodstuffs within the Community. This amended proposal takes account of the opinion of the European Parliament.

The proposed Directive lays down general principles for the official inspection of:

- foodstuffs;

- materials and articles intended to come into contact with foodstuffs.

The Directive would require Member States to:

- take all measures necessary to ensure that inspections conform with the Directive;

- ensure that products intended for another Member State are inspected in the same way as those intended for their own territory;

- inspect products intended for export outside the Community.

Inspections must be carried out regularly and where non-conformity is suspected. Inspection may be carried out without prior warning and may be carried out during:

- production;

- manufacture;

- import into the Community;

- storage;

- transport;

- distribution and trade.

The competent national authority must select the stage at which examination will be carried out.

Inspection must consist of one or more of the following:

- inspection;
- sampling or analysis;
- examination of the staff;
- examination of written and documentary material;
- examination of any verification systems set up by the undertaking.

Inspection may be carried out on:

- the site, premises, offices, plant, means of transport, machinery and equipment;
- raw materials, ingredients, additives and technological aids used for the manufacture of foodstuffs;
- semi-finished products;
- finished products;
- packaging materials;
- cleaning and maintenance products and procedures;
- processes used for the manufacture or processing of foodstuffs;
- labelling and presentation of foodstuffs.

Inspections may be supplemented by:

- interviews from the head of the undertaking and his staff;
- the reading of values regarded by measuring instruments installed by the undertaking;

- checking by the competent authority with its own instruments of measurements registered by instruments installed by the undertaking.

Sampling and analysis methods

Samples may be taken for the purposes of analysis. A second sample from each product must be taken and left at the undertaking. The undertaking may have an independent check carried out if it so wishes.

Analyses must be carried out at official laboratories.

Inspection of personnel

Persons who come into contact, either directly or indirectly, with materials or articles which are subject to inspection as a result of the Directive will be subject to inspection.

Procedure

Officials responsible for the inspection may take note of written and documentary material held by physical and legal persons at all stages of inspection. Written and documentary material dealing with manufacturing processes will not be subject to examination.

Officials responsible for the inspection may take extracts of written and documentary material submitted to them for examination. Officials must be bound by professional secrecy.

Competent authorities in the Member States must draw up an annual programme for sampling which will establish the minimum number of samples to be taken for each category of foodstuff.

Timetable

Member States will be required to bring into force laws, regulations and administrative provisions 12 months after notification and comply with the Directive 24 months after notification.

The full text was published in OJC 88, 5.4.88.

The full text of the original proposal, COM(86) 747, was published in OJC 20, 27.1.87.

COM(88) 654. Proposal for a Council Directive on the approximation of the laws of the Member States concerning foods and food ingredients treated with ionising radiation.

Summary

The proposal for a Directive concerning foods and food ingredients treated with ionising radiation requires the Member States to take all measures necessary to ensure that irradiated foodstuffs are marketed only if they comply with the provisions laid down in the Directive.

Member States may not prohibit the marketing of irradiated foodstuffs on grounds relating to ionising radiation, if the process use complies with the requirements of the Directive.

Foodstuffs authorised for irradiation treatment are listed in the Annex of the Directive. The list of authorised foodstuffs may be amended in accordance with the general criteria laid down in the Annex.

Authorised radiation sources, requirements for good irradiation practice and calculation of the overall absorbed dose will be calculated in accordance with the Annex of the Directive.

Foodstuffs must not be re-irradiated. However, the complete dose needed to fulfil a technological function may be given as several fractioned doses. Irradiation may be used in conjunction with other processes.

Exceptions to the above paragraph will be decided in accordance with the procedure involving the Standing Committee for Foodstuffs. The Standing Veterinary Committee or the Standing Committee on Plant Health will be consulted where appropriate.

Labelling

Member States are required to ensure that the packages of irradiated foodstuffs intended for sale to the ultimate consumer bear the information required by Directive 79/112/EEC.

The packages of foodstuffs not intended for sale to the ultimate consumer must bear the following information:

- a statement, in the format laid down in Directive 79/112/EEC, that the food has been irradiated;

- the identity and address of the unit which has carried out the irradiation or its reference number, as established by the Directive;

- a lot or batch number;

- the logo laid down in the Annex;

- in the case of non-irradiated foodstuffs which contain ingredients which have been irradiated, a statement in the format laid down in Directive 79/112/EEC for products sold to the ultimate consumer. Such a statement is not required if the irradiated ingredients are identified in the list of ingredients.

Packaging

Materials used for the packaging of foodstuffs for irradiation must be appropriate for that purpose.

Competent national authorities

Designated competent authorities in the Member States will be responsible for:

- prior approval of the units for irradiation;

- granting an official reference number;

- providing official control and inspection;

- the withdrawal or modification of an approval.

Approved establishments

Establishments must meet the requirements of the Joint FAO/WHO Codex Alimentarius Commission recommended international code of practice for the operation of irradiation facilities. Additional requirements may be made on the basis of the consultation procedure involving the Standing Committee for Foodstuffs.

Each establishment must keep a record for each lot of foodstuff treated, indicating:

- the nature and quantity of foodstuffs irradiated;

- the lot number;

- the consignee;

- the date of irradiation;

- the type of packaging used during treatment;

- the data for control of the irradiation process in accordance with the Annex of the Directive

- data on the checks carried out and the results obtained, with details of the upper and lower limits of the dose absorbed and the type of ionising radiation;

- the initial dose validation measurements;

- any supplementary information required by the Directive.

The above records must be preserved for five years.

Imports from third countries

Irradiated foodstuffs may not be imported from third countries unless:

- they comply with the provisions of the Directive; documents accompanying the consignment must indicate the name and address of the establishment which carried out the irradiation, in addition to the documentary requirements listed above;

- it has been officially confirmed that official supervision is exercised in the third country.

The Commission may enter into arrangements with third countries regarding the mutual notification of irradiation plants, and may arrange for Community inspection of establishments.

National derogations

Where a Member State has detailed grounds for establishing that the authorised irradiation of a foodstuff endangers human health, that Member State may temporarily suspend or restrict application of the provisions in question. The Member State will immediately inform the Commission and other Member States of its reasons for doing so. The Commission will take appropriate action on the basis of the consultation procedure involving the Standing Committee for Foodstuffs.

The full text is published in OJC 336, 31.12.88.

COMPOSITION OF FOODSTUFFS - EXISTING LEGISLATION

Council Directive 73/241/EEC of 24 July 1973 on the approximation of the laws of the Member States relating to cocoa and chocolate products intended for human consumption.

As amended by:
Council Directive 75/115/EEC, see OJL 64, 11.3.75
Council Directive 76/628/EEC, see OJL 223, 16.8.76
Council Directive 78/609/EEC, see OJL 197, 22.7.78
Council Directive 78/842/EEC, see OJL 291, 17.10.78
Council Directive 80/608/EEC, see OJL 170, 3.7.80

Summary

The Council Directive on the approximation of the laws of the Member States relating to cocoa and chocolate products intended for human consumption requires compliance with the rules and definitions laid in the Annex of the Directive, as amended by Directive 75/115/EEC and Directive 78/609/EEC.

The Annex of the Directive lays down descriptive names which must be used to designate a particular cocoa or chocolate product. The descriptive name must be applied only to products as defined in the Annex. Exceptions to this requirement exist in the case of:

- the names "pralina" or "cioccolatino", which may be used in Italy;

- the name "a chocolate", which may be used in Ireland and the UK to describe chocolate, plain chocolate, gianduja nut chocolate, milk chocolate with high milk content, gianduja nut milk chocolate or white chocolate in single-mouthful sizes;

- the name "milk chocolate", which may be used in Ireland and the UK to describe products defined in the Annex of the Directive as milk chocolate or milk chocolate with high milk content, provided that the term is accompanied by an indication of the amount of milk solids obtained by evaporation;

- the name "filled chocolate", which may be replaced in English by "chocolate with....filling" or "chocolate with....centre".

Purity criteria for cocoa-butter

The Directive required that the Council determine:

- the list of solvents which may be used for extracting cocoa-butter;

- the purity criteria for cocoa-butter, for solvents used in its extraction and for other products used as additives or for treatment.

Until the implementation of a purity criteria Member States were required to permit only the use of petroleum spirit 60/75 (Essence B) or its pure principal fraction. However, Member States may retain national provisions authorising the use of other solvents in respect of products marketed in their territory until the implementation of uniform measures.

Analysis methods

In accordance with the consultation procedure with the Standing Committee for Foodstuffs, the Commission was required to lay down measures for sampling and methods of analysis necessary to verify compliance with the Directive.

Marketable weights

In the case of chocolate, plain chocolate, gianduja nut chocolate, milk chocolate, milk chocolate with high milk content, gianduja nut milk chocolate, white chocolate and filled chocolate in the form of bars weighing not less than 85g and not more than 500g, only the following individual weights may be used: 85g, 100g, 125g, 150g, 200g, 250g, 300g, 400g, 500g.

In the case of cocoa and cocoa powder, sweetened fat-reduced cocoa, sweetened fat-reduced cocoa powder and fat-reduced drinking chocolate packaged in units with an individual weight less than 50g and not more than 1 kg, only the following individual net weights may be used: 50g, 75g, 125g, 250g, 500g, 750g, 1 kg.

Labelling

The following information is compulsory on the packages, containers or labels of products covered by the Directive:

- the name designated to a product in the Annex of the Directive;

- in the case of products designated as sweetened cocoa or sweetened cocoa powder, drinking chocolate, sweetened fat reduced cocoa or sweetened fat reduced cocoa powder, fat-reduced drinking chocolate, chocolate, plain chocolate, milk chocolate, or milk chocolate with high milk content, an indication of the total dry cocoa content;

- in the case of filled chocolate and chocolates obtained from chocolate products other than chocolate and couverture chocolate, an indication of the type of chocolate used;

- where appropriate, the declarations required by the Annex of the Directive;

- the net weight. In the case of products weighing less than 50g per unit and presented in packages containing two or more such products, the net weight must be clearly legible on the outer wrapper. In the case of hollow moulded products, the net weight may be replaced by the minimum net weight;

- the name or trade name and the address or registered office of the manufacturer or packer, or of a seller established within the Community.

Adjectives relating to quality may supplement the names "chocolate" and "milk chocolate" only if:

- chocolate has a total dry cocoa solids content of at least 43%, including a minimum of 26% cocoa butter;

- milk chocolate contains not more than 50% sucrose and a minimum of 30% total dry cocoa solids, at least 30% total dry cocoa solids and 18% milk solids obtained by evaporation (including at least 4.5% butter fat).

National derogations

Member States may retain national provisions relating to labelling which require an indication of:

- the factory in respect of home production;
- the country of origin, although this information may not be required for products manufactured within the Community.

Member States may prohibit trade in:

- products covered by the Directive if the following information is not shown on one side of wrapping in the national language: the product name, where appropriate the declarations of content required by the Annex of the Directive and, in the case of certain products, an indication of total dry cocoa content;
- milk chocolate with high milk content, if the description "milk chocolate" appears on the wrapping.

Non-harmonised national provisions may be retained on grounds of:

- protection of public health;
- prevention of fraud;
- protection of industrial or commercial property.

In addition, the Directive does not affect national laws relating to:

- the use of vegetable fats other than cocoa butter in chocolate products;
- the retail sale of various chocolate products without wrapping;
- the marketing of chocolate bars weighing between 75g and 85g;
- less stringent regulations relating to labelling in the retail sale of fancy products such as figurines;
- the sale of chocolate under the names "cream chocolate" or "skimmed chocolate".

The Directive is applicable to products imported into the Community, but is not applicable to products intended for export to third countries.

Timetable

Member States were required to take measures necessary to comply with the Directive by 1 July 1975. Trade in all products complying with the Directive was permitted after 1 January 1976, while trade in products not complying with the Directive was prohibited after 1 January 1977.

The full text was published in OJL 228, 16.8.73.

Council Directive 73/437/EEC of 11 December 1973 on the approximation of the laws of the Member States concerning certain sugars intended for human consumption.

Analysis Methods:
Council Directive 79/796/EEC, see OJL 239, 24.12.79

Summary

The Directive on the approximation of the laws of the Member States concerning certain sugars intended for human consumption requires Member States to take measures necessary to ensure that products defined in the Directive conform with specified composition rules.

The Directive is applicable to:

- semi-white sugar;

- sugar or white sugar;

- extra white sugar;

- sugar solution;

- invert sugar solution;

- glucose syrup;

- dried glucose syrup;

- dextrose monohydrate;

- dextrose anhydrous.

The Directive is not applicable to the categories listed above where products are in the form of:

- impalpable sugars;

- candy sugars;

- sugars in loaf form.

Descriptive names laid down by the Directive must only be applied to products which meet the requirements of the Directive.

The term "white sugar" must only be used for:

- sugar solution where the colour in solution does not exceed 25 ICUMSA units, determined in accordance with the analysis methods set down in the Annex of the Directive;

- invert sugar solution and invert sugar syrup where the ash content does not exceed 0.1 % and colour in solution does not exceed 25 ICUMSA units.

Products covered by the Directive must not be submitted to the blueing process, but may contain colourants which are intended for use in other foodstuffs, subject to specific rules relating to colouring matter.

Products defined by the Directive as glucose syrup or dried glucose syrup must not be offered for retail sale where sulphur dioxide content exceeds 20 mg/kg.

<u>Marketable weights</u>

In the case of semi-white sugar, sugar or white sugar and extra white sugar packed in a net individual weight of between 100g and 5 kg, these products may only be offered for sale in the following individual net weights: 125g, 250g, 500g, 750g, 1 kg, 1.5 kg, 2 kg, 2.5 kg, 3 kg, 4 kg and 5 kg.

Labelling

The following information must appear on the packages, containers or labels of products covered by the Directive:

- the description by which the products are designated in the Directive;

- the net weight, except where products weigh less than 50g. This exception does not apply to products weighing less than 50g which are contained in packages of two or more products and have a total weight of more than 50g;

- the name or trade name and the address or registered office of the manufacturer or packer, or of the seller established within the Community;

- an indication of the true content of dry matter and invert sugar in the case of sugar solution, invert sugar solution, and invert sugar syrup;

- the term "crystallised" for invert sugar syrup incorporating crystals in the solution;

- in the case of glucose syrup or dried glucose syrup of which the sulphur dioxide content exceeds 20 mg/kg, a reference to the foodstuff for the manufacture of which it is intended. The maximum sulphur dioxide content of the product must be indicated in accompanying documents.

In the case of products contained in packages of a net weight equal to or exceeding 10 kg and not offered for retail sale, an indication of net weight, the specific labelling requirements for sugar solution and invert sugar solution, and an indication of sulphur dioxide content may appear on accompanying documents only.

Member States may prohibit trade in products if labelling statutory labelling requirements are not met by displaying information on one side of the wrapping or container in the national language or, where appropriate, in accompanying documents.

National derogations

Member States are permitted to impose additional descriptive requirements, provided that such descriptions are not liable to mislead the consumer.

Member States may retain national provisions relating to labelling which require an indication of:

- the factory, in respect of home production;

- the country of origin, although this information may not be required for products manufactured within the Community.

Non-harmonised national provisions may be retained on grounds of:

- protection of public health;

- prevention of fraud;

- protection of industrial and commercial property.

The Directive does not apply to products intended for export to third countries.

Timetable

Member States were required to amend national laws in accordance with the Directive by 27 December 1974. Amended laws were applicable to all products offered for sale in the Community after 27 December 1975.

The full text was published in OJL 356, 27.12.73.

Council Directive 74/409/EEC of 22 July 1974 on the harmonisation of the laws of the Member States relating to honey.

Summary

The Directive on the harmonisation of the laws of the Member States relating to honey lays down rules and definitions which Member States must take all measures necessary to ensure compliance with.

The following terms may be applied only to products which meet the definitions given in the Directive:

- honey;
- blossom honey;
- honeydew honey;
- comb honey;
- chunk honey;
- drained honey;
- extracted honey;
- pressed honey.

No product other than honey may be added to honey offered for sale.

Compositional criteria

All honey marketed in the Community must comply with the compositional criteria laid down in the Annex of the Directive. The compositional criteria lays down permissible levels for:

- apparent reducing sugar content, calculated as invert sugar;
- moisture content;
- apparent sucrose content;
- water-insoluble solids content;
- mineral content (ash);
- acidity;
- diastase activity and HMF content determined after processing and blending.

In addition, honey must as far as possible be free from organic or inorganic matters foreign to its composition, such as mould or insects, when marketed or used in any product for human consumption. The honey must not:

- have any foreign tastes or odours;

- have begun to ferment or effervesce;

- have been heated to such an extent that its natural enzymes are destroyed or made inactive;

- have an artificially changed acidity;

- contain any substance in such a quantity as to endanger human health.

Honey may be marketed as "baker's honey" or "industrial honey" if it is suitable for human consumption but:

- it has foreign tastes or odours, has begun to ferment or effervesce, or has been heated to such an extent that its natural enzymes are destroyed or made inactive; or

- its diastase activity or HMF content does not comply with the limits laid down in the Annex of the Directive.

<u>Labelling</u>

The following information must appear on the packages, containers or labels of honey in a conspicuous, clearly legible and indelible form:

- the term "honey" or one of the names listed in the Directive:

- the net weight, expressed in grammes or kilograms;

- the name or trade name and address or registered office of the producer, packer or seller established in the Community.

The term "honey" or one of the names listed in the Directive may be supplemented by:

- a reference to the origin, whether blossom or plant, provided the product comes predominantly from the source indicated;

- a regional name, provided that the product originates entirely from that area.

In the case of honey packaged in amounts of 10 kilograms or more, information relating to the net weight and the name of producer or packer may appear only on accompanying trade documents.

National derogations

National provisions which require an indication of the country of origin may be retained, but this information may no longer be required for honey originating in the Community.
Member States may prohibit trade in honey if the term "honey" or one of the names listed in the Directive is not shown on one side of the package in the national language.

Non-harmonised national provisions may be retained on grounds of:

- protection of public health;

- prevention of fraud;

- protection of industrial or commercial property.

By way of derogation from the maximum levels of moisture content laid down by the compositional criteria, Member States may authorise the marketing of heather honey, "baker's honey" or "industrial honey" with a maximum moisture content of 25%, if this is the result of natural conditions of production.

The Directive is not applicable to products intended for export to third countries.

Timetable

Member States were required to amend laws in accordance with the Directive by 12 August 1975. Amended laws were applicable to all products sold in the Community after 12 August 1976.

The full text was published in OJL 221, 12.8.74.

Council Directive 75/726/EEC of 17 November 1975 on the approximation of the laws of the Member States concerning fruit juices and certain similar products.

As amended by;
Council Directive 79/168/EEC, see OJL 37, 13.2.79
Council Directive 81/487/EEC, see OJL 189, 11.7.81

Summary

The Directive on the approximation of the laws of the Member States concerning fruit juices and certain similar products requires that such products may be marketed only if they comply with the compositional requirements of the Directive. The Directive is applicable to:

- fruit juice intended for direct consumption;

- concentrated fruit juice intended for direct consumption;

- fruit nectar intended for direct consumption;

- dried fruit juice intended for direct consumption;

- concentrated fruit juice used for the production of fruit juice or nectar intended for direct consumption;

- fruit juice used for the production of fruit nectar intended for direct consumption.

The following processes are authorised for the production of fruit juices:

- the mixing of fruit juices;

- treatment with:

    - L-ascorbic acid (E 300) in the amount necessary to produce an anti-oxidant effect. The addition of L-ascorbic acid does not authorise any reference to Vitamin C,

    - nitrogen,

    - carbon dioxide (E 290),

    - pectolytic enzymes,

- proteolytic enzymes,

- amylolytic enzymes,

- edible gelatine,

- tannins,

- bentonite,

- silica aerogel,

- kaolin,

- charcoal,

- inert filtration adjuvants;

- the usual physical processes and treatments such as heat treatments such as heat treatments, centrifuging and filtering.

The use of quantities of substances which may be dangerous to human health is prohibited.

Sugars

Sugars may be added to fruit juices other than pear and grape juice:

- in a quantity, expressed as dry matter, not greater than 15g per litre of juice, in order to correct them;

- in a quantity, expressed as dry matter, not greater than 40g per litre of apple juice; 200g per litre of lemon, lime, bergamot, and red, white and blackcurrant juices; and 100g per litre of other juices for the purpose of sweetening.

Treatment of grape juice

The treatment of grape juice is permitted with:

- sulphur dioxide (E 220);

- sodium sulphite (E 221);

- acid sodium sulphite (E 222);

- sodium disulphite (E223);

- potassium disulphite (E224);

- calcium sulphite (E226);

- acid calcium sulphite (E227);

- desulphiting by physical processes;

- clarification by means of casein, white of egg and other animal albumins;

- partial deacidification by means of neutral potassium tartrate, or calcium carbonate to which may be added small quantities of double calcium salt of D-tartaric and L-malic acids.

Treatment of pineapple juice

The addition of citric acid (E330) to pineapple juice is permitted in a maximum quantity of 3g per litre.

Acid

The addition of both sugars and acid to the same fruit juice is prohibited.

Where more than one acid is added to the same fruit juice or nectar, the sum quantity of each acid must not exceed 100% of the maximum authorised quantity.

Sulphur dioxide

Unless otherwise laid down in the Directive, the sulphur dioxide content of a fruit juice must not exceed 10 mg per litre of juice.

Fruit nectars

In addition to the processes authorised for the production of fruit juices, the following are authorised for the production of fruit nectars:

- the addition of sugars in a quantity not greater than 20% by weight of the total weight of the finished product;

- the addition of water in a quantity such that the fruit juice and/or fruit puree content and the total acidity of the product are not less than the levels specified by the Annex of the Directive, as amended.

Concentrated fruit juices

In addition to the general processes authorised for the production of fruit juices, the following processes are permitted for the manufacture of concentrated fruit juices:

- partial dehydration of the fruit juice by a physical treatment or process other than by direct flame;

- restoration of its aroma by means of the volatiles collected during the concentration process.

Dried fruit juice

The Directive authorises the almost total dehydration of fruit juice by processes other than direct flame.

Restoration of the essential volatiles from fruits of the same kind is compulsory.

Labelling

Where a product is marketed prior to delivery to the ultimate consumer, Member States may remain free to determine labelling rules without prejudice to Community labelling rules.

Products may only be marketed under the descriptive name reserved for them except where:

- a Member State designates use of the name "fruit nectar";

- a product is defined as dried fruit juice. This name may be replaced by "powdered" fruit juice and may be accompanied by particulars of the specific process used.

The name under which a product may be sold will be supplemented:

- in the case of products manufactured from two or more kinds of fruit, except as regards the use of lemon juice, by a list of the fruits used;

- in the case of products with added sugar, by the description "sweetened" followed by an indication of the maximum quantity of sugars added.

The obligation to apply the list of ingredients is subject to certain derogations. Substances used for the following purposes need not be listed as ingredients:

- the restoration of fruit juice from concentrated fruit juice or concentrated fruit puree, and the restoration of the flavour to concentrated fruit juice or dried fruit juice;

- substances authorised for use in grape juice. These substances will also not be listed as ingredients of fruit juice, concentrated fruit juice, fruit nectar or dried fruit juice provided that sulphur dioxide content does not exceed 10 mg per litre.

An indication of the following particulars will be required in specific cases:

- in the case of fruit juice and nectar obtained wholly or partially from a concentrated product, the declaration "contains....made from concentrate", together with the name of the concentrated product used;

- in the case of fruit juice, concentrated fruit juice and fruit nectar where the carbon dioxide content is greater than 2 g per litre, the description "carbonated";

- in the case of fruit juice and dried fruit juice, an indication of the quantity of water to be added to restore the product;

- in the case of fruit nectars, the actual minimum content of fruit juice, fruit puree or a mixture of these ingredients, the declaration "fruit content....% minimum".

National derogations

Non-harmonised national provisions may be retained on grounds of:

- protection of public health;
- prevention of fraud;
- protection of industrial and commercial property.

National provisions may be retained in order to determine:

- the vitaminisation of products;
- the process of diffusion authorised for the manufacture of juices other than grape, citrus fruit, pineapple, pear, peach and apricot intended for the manufacture of concentrated fruit juices;
- sulphur dioxide may be added to pineapple, apple, orange and grapefruit juices in quantities not exceeding 50 mg per litre;
- sulphur dioxide may be added to lemon and lime juices in quantities not exceeding 350 mg per litre;
- dimethylpolysiloxane may be added to pineapple juice in quantities not exceeding 10 mg per litre;
- lactic acid may be added to fruit nectars obtained from apples or pears in quantities not exceeding 5g per litre;
- citric acid may be added to grape juice, where such addition is authorised at the time of notification of the Directive, or to apple juice in quantities not exceeding 3g per litre.

The Directive is not applicable to products intended for export from the Community.

Timetable

Member States were required to permit trade in products which comply with the Directive by 1 December 1977 and prohibit trade in products not complying with the Directive by 1 December 1978.

The full text was published in OJL 311, 1.12.75.

Council Directive 76/118/EEC of 18 December 1975 on the approximation of the laws of the Member States relating to certain partly or wholly dehydrated preserved milk for human consumption.

As amended by:
Council Directive 78/630/EEC, see OJL 206, 29.7.78
Council Directive 83/635/EEC, see OJL 357, 21.12.83

Methods of Analysis:
Commission Directive 79/1067/EEC, see OJL 327, 24.12.79

Methods of Sampling:
Council Directive 87/524/EEC, see OJL 306, 28.10.87

Summary

The Directive on the approximation of the laws of the Member States relating to certain partly or wholly dehydrated preserved milk for human consumption requires Member States to ensure that products defined in the Annex of the Directive conform to the definitions and rules stipulated. The Directive is applicable to the following products:

- unsweetened condensed milk;

- unsweetened condensed skimmed milk;

- unsweetened condensed partly skimmed milk;

- unsweetened condensed high-fat milk;

- sweetened condensed milk;

- sweetened condensed skimmed milk;

- sweetened condensed partly skimmed milk;

- dried whole milk or whole milk powder;

- dried skimmed milk or skimmed milk powder;

- dried partly skimmed milk or partly skimmed milk powder;

- dried high-fat milk or high-fat milk powder.

The Directive is not applicable to:

- dietetic products specifically prepared for babies and young children;

- products intended for export outside the Community.

The preservation of unsweetened condensed milk, unsweetened condensed skimmed milk, unsweetened condensed partly skimmed milk and unsweetened condensed high-fat milk must be achieved by sterilisation through heat treatment.

The preservation of sweetened condensed milk, sweetened condensed skimmed milk and sweetened condensed partly skimmed milk must be achieved by the addition of sucrose.

The preservation of wholly dehydrated milk must be achieved by dehydration.

In the manufacture of unsweetened condensed milk, unsweetened condensed skimmed milk, unsweetened condensed partly skimmed milk and unsweetened condensed high-fat milk only the following substances may be used:

- sodium and potassium carbonates listed in the Directive;

- diphosphates;

- in the case of UHT unsweetened partly dehydrated milk, triphosphates;

- in the case of UHT unsweetened partly dehydrated milk, linear polyphosphates containing not more than 8% cyclic compounds.

The total quantity of added substances in the finished product must not be greater than:

- 0.2% for products with a total dry matter content not exceeding 28%;

- 0.3% for products with a total dry matter content exceeding 28%.

In the case of UHT unsweetened partly dehydrated milk, the total triphosphate and linear polyphosphate content by weight must not exceed 0.1%.

In the case of products whose total dry matter content is less than 28%, total added phosphate content must not exceed 0.1%. In the case of products whose total dry matter content is more than 28%, total added phosphate content must not exceed 0.15%.

In the manufacture of sweetened condensed milk, sweetened condensed skimmed milk and sweetened condensed partly skimmed milk, only the following substances may be used:

- the substances approved for use in the manufacture of unsweetened condensed milk, provided that their total quantity by weight in the finished product does not exceed 0.2% and that total added phosphate content does not exceed 0.1%;

- lactose, provided that this is in a quantity less than 0.02 % by weight in the finished product. Tricalcium phosphate content must not exceed 10% of the lactose added;

In the manufacture of wholly dehydrated milk listed in the Annex of the Directive, only the following substances may be used:

- the substances authorised for use in the manufacture of unsweetened condensed milk, provided that the total quantity of these substances by weight is not greater than 0.5%, of which sodium and potassium bicarbonate content does not exceed 0.2%. Maximum sodium and potassium bicarbonate content may be raised to 0.3% in the case of "Hatmaker" or "Roller" wholly dehydrated milk not intended for sale, provided that none of the other substances authorised for use in unsweetened condensed milk are used. By way of derogation, the UK may authorise sale of these products within its territory;

- the substances authorised for use in the manufacture of unsweetened condensed milk, provided that the total added phosphate content does not exceed 0.25%.

Lactate content

Products defined in the Directive must not contain lactate in quantities which exceed 300 mg per 100g of milk solids not fat.

Labelling

The net quantity of products defined in the Annex must be expressed in units of mass. In the case of unsweetened condensed milk, unsweetened condensed skimmed milk, unsweetened condensed partly skimmed milk or unsweetened condensed high-fat milk which is packed in anything other than tubes or metal tins, net quantity may be expressed in units of mass and volume.

The following information must appear on packaging, containers or labels of all products covered by the Directive:

- the descriptive name of the product;

- the net quantity, expressed in kilograms or grams;

- the name or business name and address of the manufacturer, packer or seller within the Community;

- the name of the country of origin in the case of products imported from third countries;

- the date of manufacture or an indication of batch.

In addition, the following information may be required:

- the percentage of milk fat, expressed by weight in relation to the finished product (except in the case of unsweetened condensed skimmed milk, sweetened condensed skimmed milk or dried skimmed milk or skimmed milk powder), and the percentage of fat-free dried extract in the case of partly dehydrated milk;

- in the case of partly dehydrated milk, recommendations on the method of dilution or reconstitution;

- in the case of wholly dehydrated milk, recommendations on the method of dilution or reconstitution, including details of the fat content of the product in its reconstituted form (except in the case of dried skimmed milk or skimmed milk powder);

- in the case of unsweetened condensed milk, unsweetened condensed skimmed milk, unsweetened condensed partly skimmed milk or unsweetened condensed high-fat milk, the expression "UHT" or "ultra heated milk" where such treatment has been used.

Where products weighing less than 20g per unit are packed within outer packaging, labelling particulars need appear only on the outer package, except for the designation under which the product is to be sold. In the case of vitamins added to the product, Member States may require details of the nature and quality of the added vitamins on labelling. Member States may require the inclusion of a special warning concerning the use of wholly skimmed products as baby food.

Packaging

Partly or wholly dehydrated preserved milk must be packaged in sealed containers and must be delivered intact to the consumer.

National derogations

In the case of wholly dehydrated milk used in vending machines, Member States may authorise the use of additional additives. The addition of vitamins to all products covered by the Directive may be authorised by a Member State within its territory.

Non-harmonised national provisions may be justified only on grounds of:

- protection of public health;

- prevention of fraud;

- protection of industrial and commercial property.

Where a Member State has detailed grounds for establishing that the use of products covered by the Directive endangers human health, the Member State may temporarily suspend or restrict use of that product within its territory. The Commission is required to examine the grounds given by the Member State and take appropriate action on the basis of consultation with the Standing Committee on Foodstuffs.

The Directive does not affect national laws concerning an indication of quality.

Timetable

Member States were required to amend national laws necessary to comply with the Directive by 30 January 1977. Amended laws were applicable to all products put on the market after 30 January 1978.

The full text was published OJL 24, 30.1.76.

Council Directive 77/436/EEC of 27 June 1977 on the approximation of the laws of the Member States relating to coffee extracts and chicory extracts.

As amended by:
Council Directive 85/573/EEC, see OJL 372, 13.12.85

Analysis methods:
Commission Directive 79/1066/EEC, see OJL 327, 24.12.79

<u>Summary</u>

The Directive on the approximation of the laws of the Member States relating to coffee extracts and chicory extracts requires Member States to take measures necessary to ensure that products covered by the Directive comply with the definitions and rules stipulated. The Directive is applicable to:

- soluble coffee, instant coffee, dried coffee extract or dried extract of coffee;

- coffee extract paste;

- liquid coffee extract;

- dried chicory extract, soluble chicory or instant chicory;

- chicory extract paste;

- liquid chicory extract.

Blends of coffee extracts and chicory extracts, and extracts of blends of roasted coffee and roasted chicory may only be sold if:

- products comply "mutandis mutandis" with the definitions laid down in the Annex of the Directive;

- where sold in solid or paste form, they comply with the provisions of the Directive relating to packaging.

<u>Labelling</u>

In the case of products intended to be supplied to the ultimate consumer without further processing, labelling must indicate the name under which a product is sold. This may be supplemented by the term "concentrated" in the case of liquid coffee extract where coffee-based dry matter content is more than 25% by weight, or liquid chicory extract where chicory-based dry matter content is more than 45% by weight.

Provision of the following information will also required in appropriate cases:

- the term "decaffeinated" in the case of coffee extracts where the anhydrous coffee content does not exceed 0.3% by weight of coffee-based dry matter;

- in the case of liquid coffee extract or liquid chicory extract, the term "roasted with sugar", "with sugar", "preserved with sugar" or "with added sugar";

- in the case of coffee extract paste or liquid coffee extract, the minimum coffee-based dry matter content, expressed as a percentage by weight of the finished product;

- in the case of chicory extract paste or liquid chicory extract, the minimum chicory-based dry matter content, expressed as a percentage by weight of the finished product.

Products not intended for supply to the ultimate consumer need indicate only the following compulsory information:

- product name;

- nominal net quantity (except in the case of products in bulk);

- a means of identifying the batch;

- name or business name and address of the manufacturer, packager or seller established in the Community.

Packaging

Where coffee extracts or chicory extracts are sold in solid or in paste form and are packaged in individual containers exceeding 10 kg, they must be sold only in the following weights: 50g, 100g, 200g, 250g, 500g, 750g, 1 kg, 1.5 kg, 2 kg, 3 kg and multiples of a kilogram.

A Member State may prohibit individual packages of 250g provided that packages of 300g are permitted.

National derogations

Member States may authorise the use of anti-caking agents in its territory in the case of:

- soluble coffee, instant coffee, dried coffee extract or dried extract of coffee, where these products are used in vending machines;

- dried chicory extract, soluble chicory or instant chicory.

Non-harmonised national provisions may be justified only on grounds of:

- protection of public health;

- prevention of fraud;

- protection of industrial and commercial property.

Timetable

Member States were required to amend national laws in accordance with the Directive by 12 July 1978, permit trade in products complying with the Directive by 12 July 1979 and prohibit trade in products not complying with the Directive by 12 July 1980.

The full text was published in OJL 172, 12.7.77.

Council Directive 79/693/EEC of 24 July 1979 on the approximation of the laws of the Member States relating to fruit jams, jellies and marmalades and sweetened chestnut puree.

As amended by:
Council Directive 88/593/EEC, see OJL 318, 25.11.88

Summary

The Directive on the approximation of the laws of the Member States relating to fruit jams, jellies and marmalades and chestnut puree requires Member States to ensure that products conform to the definitions and rules stipulated. The Directive is applicable to:

- extra jam;

- jam;

- extra jelly;

- jelly;

- marmalade;

- sweetened chestnut puree.

The Directive is not applicable to products intended for the manufacture of fine bakers' wares, pastries and biscuits.

The descriptive names laid down in the Directive may only be applied to the products which meet the definitions laid down in the Annex, where the soluble dry matter content is not less than 60%. Member States may permit the use of products with a soluble dry matter content less than 60% within its own territory. The Council will decide on rules concerning the Community names applicable to the latter products before 1 January 1991.

Raw materials used in the manufacture of products covered by the Directive must meet the definitions laid down in the Annex. In addition, substances added to products covered by the Directive must meet the requirements laid down in the Annex.

The Directive lays down the maximum sulphur dioxide content which may be permitted in products.

Labelling

The following information must be given on the labelling of products defined within the Directive:

- the descriptive name of the product;

- an indication of the types of fruit used, in descending order of weight of the raw materials used;

- an indication of certain other specific ingredients listed in the Annex;

- the words "prepared with....g of fruit per 100g". In the case of extra jam, jam, extra jelly, jelly or sweetened chestnut puree an indication must be given of quantities of pulp, puree, juice and aqueous extracts. In the case of marmalade, an indication must be given of quantities of citrus fruit;

- the words "total sugar content....g per 100g";

- in the case of products with a soluble dry matter content of less than 63% the words "keep in a cool place once opened".

The following additional information may be required where appropriate:

- in the case of marmalade containing peel, an indication of the style of cut of that peel or in the case of marmalade not containing peel, an indication of this fact;

- in the case of jam, an indication of the content of dried apricots;

- in the case of jam or jelly, an indication of the content of red beetroot juice used to reinforce the colour;

- in the case of products containing more than one type of fruit, Member States may require only the word "fruit" to indicate the types of fruit used;

- in the case of a sulphur dioxide content exceeding 30 mg/kg, the words "residual sulphur dioxide" must appear on the list of ingredients, according to the percentage by weight of the residue in the finished product.

The addition of L-ascorbic acid to a product will not authorise reference to be made to vitamin C.

National derogations

Where products are not intended for sale to the final consumer, Member States may lay down national provisions regarding labelling.

Member States may introduce separate rules relating to dietetic products, subject to Community provisions in this field.

Non-harmonised national provisions may be justified on grounds of:

- protection of public health;

- prevention of fraud;

- protection of industrial and commercial property.

Timetable

Member States were required amend national laws in order to comply with the Directive, to permit trade in products complying with the Directive by 13 August 1981 and prohibit trade in products not complying with the Directive by 13 August 1982.

The full text was published in OJL 205, 13.8.79.

Council Directive 80/777/EEC of 15 July 1980 on the approximation of the laws of the Member States relating to the exploitation and marketing of natural mineral waters.

Summary

The Directive on the approximation of the laws of the Member States relating to the exploitation and marketing of natural mineral waters requires Member States to take measures necessary to ensure that all products marketed comply with the provisions of the Directive.

The Directive lays down definitions and criteria for substances extracted from the ground of a Member State or a third country, and recognised as natural mineral waters by the responsible authority of a Member State. In the case of natural mineral waters from a Member State, certification will be subject to regular checks to ensure compliance with the criteria laid down in the Annex of the Directive. In the case of natural mineral waters from third countries, certification will be subject to checks every two years.

The Directive is not applicable to:

- waters which are medicinal products within the meaning of Directive 65/65/EEC;

- natural mineral waters used at source for curative purposes in thermal or hydromineral establishments.

Treatment of natural mineral water

Except where used in the manufacture of soft drinks, natural mineral waters may only be subject to the following treatments:

- separation of unstable elements by filtration or decanting in so far as this treatment does not alter the composition of the water as regards the essential constituents which gave it its properties;

- total or partial elimination of free carbon dioxide by exclusively physical methods;

- introduction or reintroduction of carbon dioxide under the conditions laid down in the Annex of the Directive.

The Directive prohibits any disinfection treatment likely to change the viable colony count of the water.

Colony count

Revivable total colony count of a natural mineral water at source must conform to its normal viable colony count and provide evidence of the protection of the source against contamination.

After bottling, total colony count at source must not exceed 100 per millilitre at 20 to 22 degrees centigrade in 72 hours on agar-agar or an agar-gelatine mixture and 20 per millilitre at 37 degrees centigrade in 24 hours on agar-agar. Total colony count will be measured within 12 hours of bottling, the water being maintained at 4 degrees centigrade plus or minus 1 degree centigrade.

At source, total colony count at source should not exceed 20 per millilitre at 20 to 22 degrees centigrade in 72 hours and 5 per millilitre at 37 degrees centigrade in 24 hours. These figures at source are to be considered as a guide only.

Natural mineral water must be free from:

- parasites and pathogenic micro-organisms;

- Esherichia coli and other coliforms and faecal streptococci in any 250 ml sample examined;

- sporulated sulphite-reducing anaerobes in any 50 ml sample examined;

- Pseudomonas aeruginosa in any 250 ml sample examined.

At the marketing stage, revivable total colony count must only be that resulting from the normal increase in bacteria content which it had at source, while organoleptic defects must not be presented.

Sales description

The sales description "natural mineral water" must be used for products defined in the Directive. Where appropriate the following terms may be used:

- "naturally carbonated mineral water";

- "natural mineral water fortified with gas from the spring";

- "carbonated natural mineral water";

- "fully de-carbonated";

- "partially de-carbonated".

Labelling

The following information must be indicated:

- either the words "composition in accordance with the results of officially recognised analysis of....(date of analysis)", or a statement of analytical composition;

- the name of the spring and the place where the spring is exploited.

A Member State may also:

- retain provisions which require the country of origin to be indicated. In the case of natural mineral waters from the territory of a Member State, this information cannot be demanded;

- require information on the separation of unstable elements.

The name of a locality may occur in the wording of a trade description, provided that this is not misleading as to the place of exploitation of the spring.

Where labelling includes a trade description different from the name of the spring or the place of its exploitation, this place or the name of the spring must be indicated in letters at least one and a half times the height and width of the largest of the letters used for trade description.

The Directive prohibits any indication which:

- suggests a characteristic which the water does not possess. Information must not be misleading as regards the origin of the product, the date of authorisation to exploit it, results of the analyses or any references to guarantees of authority;

- descriptions liable to cause confusion with mineral waters in the case of packaged drinking water which does not meet the requirements laid down in the Directive.

The Directive prohibits indications which attribute to natural mineral water properties relating to the prevention, treatment or cure of a human illness.

Packaging

Containers used for packaging natural mineral waters must be fitted with closures designed to avoid adulteration or contamination.

National derogations

Member States may adopt special rules regarding the provision of information relating to the suitability of a natural mineral water for the feeding of infants. National provisions may also concern the properties of the water which determine the use of such information.

Non-harmonised national provisions may be retained on grounds of:

- protection of public health;

- prevention of fraud;

- protection of industrial and commercial property.

The Directive is not applicable to natural mineral waters intended for export to third countries.

Timetable

Member States were required to permit trade in products complying with the Directive by 30 August 1982 and prohibit trade in products not complying with the Directive by 30 August 1984.

The full text was published in OJL 229, 30.8.80.

Council Directive 83/417/EEC of 25 July 1983 on the approximation of the laws of the Member States relating to certain lactoproteins (caseins and caseinates) intended for human consumption.

Analysis Methods:
Commission Directive OJL 308, 20.11.85

Sampling Methods:
Commission Directive OJL 243, 28.8.86

Summary

The Directive on the approximation of the laws of the Member States relating to certain lactoproteins (caseins and caseinates) intended for human consumption requires Member States to ensure that products defined in the Annex of the Directive are marketed only if they conform to the definitions and rules stipulated. Products which do not satisfy these criteria must be named and labelled in such a way that the buyer is not misled as to their nature, quality or use.

The basic materials referred to in the Annexes of the Directive must be subject to heat treatment which will render the photophatase negative.

Labelling

The following information must be given on the packages, containers or labels of products in a form which is clearly visible, easily legible and indelible:

- the descriptive name of the product;

- in the case of mixtures, the words "mixture of ...." followed by names of the products which make up the mixture, an indication of the cations in the case of caseinates, and the protein content in the case of mixtures containing caseinates;

- the net quantity expressed as grams or kilograms;

- the name or business name and the address of the manufacturer, packager or seller established in the Community;

- in the case of products imported from third countries, the name of the country of origin;

- the date of manufacture or some marking by which the batch can be identified.

National derogations

Non-harmonised national provisions may be retained on grounds of:

- protection of public health;

- prevention of fraud;

- protection of industrial and commercial property.

Where a Member State has detailed grounds for establishing that one of the substances used in the products authorised by the Directive constitutes a danger to human health, the Member State may temporarily suspend or restrict use of that substance. The Commission will then take appropriate measures on the basis of consultation with the Standing Committee for Foodstuffs.

The Directive is not applicable to products intended for export to third countries.

Timetable

Member States were required to amend national provisions in order to permit trade in products complying with the Directive by 26 August 1985 and prohibit trade in products not complying with the Directive by 26 August 1986.

The full text was published in OJL 237, 26.8.83.

COMPOSITION OF FOODSTUFFS - PROPOSED LEGISLATION

COM(86) 159. Amended proposal for a Council Regulation laying down general rules on the definition, description and presentation of spirituous beverages.

Summary

The original Commission proposal for a Regulation laying down general rules on the definition, description and presentation of spirituous beverages, COM(82) 328, set out common rules for the labelling of alcoholic drinks. This amended proposal takes account of the Opinions of the European Parliament and the Economic and Social Committee.

The proposed Regulation lays down definitions and requirements with which each category of spirituous beverage would have to comply. The addition of any substance other than those authorised by the Regulation would disqualify the beverage from using the restricted name listed.

Minimum alcoholic strength

The following minimum levels of alcoholic strength would be required by the Regulation:

- for whisky/whiskey: 40% by volume;

- for rum, spirits, gin and distilled gin, vodka, grappa, aquavit, ouzo, Roggenbrand, Kornbrand and Weizenbrand: 37.5% by volume;

- for Korn and Kornbranntwein: 32% by volume;

- for juniper-flavoured spirituous beverages other than gin and distilled gin, for cumin-flavoured spirituous beverages other than aquavit, and for aniseed-flavoured spirituous beverages other than ouzo: 30% by volume;

- for amers and bitters: 15% by volume.

A minimum alcoholic strength by volume in excess to that laid down for each category may be fixed for each of the spirituous beverages listed in the Annex. Acting on a proposal from the Commission, the Council will determine these minimum alcoholic strengths by volume.

Water

The addition of water will be authorised in the preparation of spirituous beverages. Water must be of a quality which meets the requirements of Directives 80/777/EEC and 80/778/EEC, and must not alter the nature of the spirituous beverage.

Ethyl alcohol

Ethyl alcohol used in the preparation of spirituous beverages must be solely of agricultural origin and must comply with the specifications laid down in the Annex.

Only natural aromatic substances, substances identical with natural aromatic substances and natural aromatic preparations may be used as flavourings in the preparation of spirituous beverages.

Geographical ascriptions

Geographical ascriptions laid down in the Annex may be used in addition or instead of the designated names of spirituous beverages. Such ascriptions may be used only by the territories to which they refer, provided that the production stage during which the product acquired its character and definitive qualities took place in the geographical area concerned. Specific national rules on production will continue to be applied where such rules are compatible with Community law.

Additions to the list of designated names of spirituous beverages may be made by the Council in order to protect producers against unfair competition and to prevent consumers from being mislead or deceived.

Special Provisions

Special provisions for spirituous beverages may be adopted on:

- the use of certain words, initial or signs;

- the use of certain composite names including the word "brandy";

- the names of mixed beverages and mixtures of spirituous beverages.

Labelling

The name under which the product is sold must be the designated name of the spirituous beverage. Alcoholic strength must be expressed as a percentage of the volume and rounded off to the nearest half percent.

The list of ingredients need not mention:

- distillates of natural fermented liquids;

- ethyl alcohol produced by distillation;

- water.

In the case of labelling which refers to the raw material used to produce the ethyl alcohol of agricultural origin, each type of alcohol must be mentioned in decreasing order of quantity used.

Where the product has been subjected to the addition of alcohol, the product name must be supplemented by an indication of this fact and may be supplemented by the term "blend" where the product has undergone blending.

A maturation period may be specified only where it refers to the youngest alcoholic component and provided that the product was aged under revenue supervision or supervision affording equivalent guarantees.

Where a spirituous beverage has been defined, expressions such as "like", "type" or "style" must not be used to describe other spirituous beverages.

Added alcohol

A spirituous beverage must not contain added alcohol where the product is offered for sale for human consumption under one of the following names:

- rum
- whisky/whiskey
- grain spirit
- brandy
- Weinbrand
- grape marc spirit
- grappa
- fruit spirit
- cider spirit
- perry spirit.

Implementation Committee for Spirituous Beverages

In accordance with the procedure involving the Implementation Procedure for Spirituous Beverages, the following will be determined:

- conditions under which the labelling may specify a maturation period and those relating to the raw materials used;
- conditions governing the use of trade descriptions which imply that the product has been aged;
- special provisions to govern the use of terms referring to a certain property of the product such as the method by which it was prepared;

- rules governing the labelling of products in containers not intended for the final consumer, including derogations.

Exports

The Regulation is not applicable to spirituous beverages intended for export from the Community, except those listed in the Annex.

In the case of spirituous beverages listed in the Annex, the Commission is required to adopt a system of certificates or export in order to prevent imitations.

Additional rules or derogations may be adopted in respect of spirituous beverages intended for export if this is required by the legislation of third countries.

Timetable

The full text was published in OJC 269, 25.10.86.

The text of the original proposal COM(82) 328 is published in OJC 189, 23.7.82.

COM(87) 581. Proposal for a Council Directive amending for the ninth time Directive 73/241/EEC on the approximation of the laws of the Member States relating to cocoa and chocolate products intended for human consumption.

Summary

The proposal for a Directive amending Directive 73/241/EEC on cocoa and chocolate products intended for human consumption lays down that the 1973 Directive will not affect national provisions which authorise the marketing under the name "chocolate familiar a la taza" and "chocolate a la taza" of chocolate not defined in the Annex of the 1973 Directive as containing starchy substances and intended for consumption with milk after cooking.

The proposal was adopted by the Council in December 1988.

The full text was published in OJC 16, 21.1.88.

FOOD LEGISLATION NOT YET PROPOSED

Revision of labelling rules for food drawn up in view of a uniform EEC label. Proposal expected 1989. Delay vis-a-vis timetable in White Paper.

Groups of foods for particular nutritional uses for which specific provisions shall be laid down by specific directives in accordance with the Directive replacing Directive 77/94/EEC:

Baby foods (proposal not yet announced).

Low energy foods (proposal not yet announced).

8. REMOVAL OF FISCAL BARRIERS

BACKGROUND

VAT

The individual Member States charge value added tax (VAT) and excise duties on the import of goods, with tax relief for exports, and there is a large variation in the rates charged by different States on different goods. The Third VAT Directive laid the foundations for harmonisation in 1969, by requiring Member States to introduce value added tax as a replacement for their existing turnover taxes. Since then, a large number of measures have been introduced toward harmonisation. The most significant single directive is the Sixth VAT Directive of 1977, which provides for a uniform basis of assessment.

The Commission is concerned that there must be an end to the distortion of trade which is maintained by the continued variation in indirect taxation. As moves are made toward the abolition of physical border controls, any real differences in VAT rates would give rise to unacceptable distortion of competition, fraud and tax evasion by purchase of goods in countries with low VAT, without the requirement to pay further VAT on import into the home State. There are a number of proposals still outstanding on the question of VAT, since there is fundamental disagreement between Member States on the necessity for harmonisation.

The major proposals concern the removal of fiscal frontiers - the abolition of the present system of charging VAT on imports from another EC Member State and exempting VAT on imports; and harmonisation of VAT rates into two bands.

Abolition of fiscal frontiers

The Member States each charge VAT on goods and services supplied within their own borders, and also on the import of goods; while exports are exempt from VAT. This is felt by the Commission to be not compatible with the concept of the single market without frontier controls. The Commission has proposed that Member States should adopt measures to establish a clearing-house for VAT on sales within the Community.

VAT revenue will therefore continue to be assigned to the State where the goods or services are consumed.

Approximation of VAT rates

The abolition of differences between the VAT rates of Member States is seen by the Commission as crucial to the completion of the internal market. During the latter part of his term as Commission Vice President, Lord Cockfield attached the greatest importance to this aim of the 1985 White Paper. The proposal is that the present variety of VAT rates throughout the Community should be replaced by two bands: of 4-9% for essential goods and services, and 14-20% for the remainder.

The UK Government is opposed to approximation of VAT rates, as it considers the variation in VAT rates is small in relation to the other factors affecting price levels. In September 1988 the UK Chancellor Nigel Lawson proposed an alternative scheme with minimised tax controls at frontiers, intending that countries with high VAT should reduce the level to one more comparable with that of their neighbours. The scheme did not meet with the support of the other Member States, but the Commission did agree to revise the proposal to take account of criticism.

The UK Government was particularly concerned about the absence of zero rating, which it had applied to a number of sectors including most foods. The Commission maintained that zero rating was a temporary measure which would be removed with the completion of the internal market. Following protracted argument throughout 1988, the Commission is now understood to be considering the recommendation of the European Parliament, that the lower rate should be from 0-7%.

Excise duties

The Commission's intention to harmonise the structures of excise duties goes back to its proposals of 1972. It was indicated then that the duties on manufactured tobacco, spirits, wine, beer and mineral oils should be harmonised at Community level, and that the other excise duties should be phased out as far as they involved tax adjustments at internal frontiers. Proposals to harmonise the structures of excise duties on these commodities were made in 1972 for the first four, and for mineral oils in 1973. A further two proposals made in 1985 completed the group on excise structures. The proposed harmonisation of structures for French traditional rum from its overseas departments was adopted in April 1988, but very little progress has been made on the other structure proposals.

Together with the proposals for the harmonisation of VAT, the objective of these measures was to abolish fiscal frontiers. The Commission has taken the view that flexibility in the harmonised rates should be in the province of VAT rather than excise duties. This is because VAT applies to far more types of goods, and is therefore more important for the national budgets of Member States. Having thus proposed a range for harmonised VAT, the Commission has proposed specific rates of excise duties for the four types of goods above; calculated according to the circumstances of each in order to cause the minimum of disruption to each sector. To have allowed a range of excise duty rates would have permitted price differentials of well over 5% as a result of indirect taxation.

For spirits, the proposed rate for excise duty is the Community arithmetic average. This method was, however, found to be highly disruptive if used for wine and beer, when consumption was taken into account. These types of drinks are therefore proposed to be taxed equally per litre.

The 1985 White Paper proposed that the rates of excise duties of Member States for tobacco, alcoholic drinks and mineral oils should be brought closer together, that they should be abolished for other types of goods, and that a system should be developed to link the bonded warehouses of the Member States.

Under the existing system, imported goods which are subject to excise duties are retained in bonded warehouses until the duties are paid; when they are released to the distributor or customer. Conversely, exported goods are allowed cancellation of excise duties, after proof of export has been produced. The advantage of the system is that duty is charged in the country where the goods are consumed. Abolition of the existing border controls would make the continuation of the bonded warehouse system impossible, since it would then be wide open to abuse. It would be easy for goods to be exported through a bonded warehouse in a country with relatively low excise duty, taken out of bond and transported for consumption in a high rate country. It is for this reason that it is proposed to link the national bonded warehouses of Member States.

Standstill and convergence

In 1987 the Commission proposed a "Convergence" directive in relation to both VAT and excise duties. The effect of this is to ensure that any changes made by the Member States to their indirect taxation of these types tends towards the rates which will apply after 1992, rather than diverging from them. The presentation of the convergence proposal and the group of proposals on harmonisation of VAT, the Community VAT clearing mechanism and the excise duty rates, has enabled the existing proposals for a VAT standstill and intermediate harmonisation measures (the 14th VAT directive) to be withdrawn.

Effect of harmonised VAT and excise duties on national revenue

The Commission demonstrated in its 1985 White Paper that the revenue generated by VAT and excise duties on tobacco products, beer, wine, spirits and mineral oils was remarkably consistent for nine Member States, at an average of 10.68% of GDP. (Data for Greece was not available.) However, there was much greater variation between the relative contribution of VAT and of excises when considered separately.

The Commission has requested that Member States should supply information on the nature and extent of any compensatory policies that they might adopt in order to moderate the effects of tax harmonisation. Studies of the likely effects are under way, and subject to their outcome, the Commission has indicated the following likely changes to national income from VAT and excise duties:

Substantial increase: Luxembourg, Spain, Portugal
Small/moderate increase: UK, West Germany, Greece
Same as present level: Belgium, Italy, Netherlands
Small decrease: France
Substantial decrease: Denmark, Ireland.

There is likely to be considerable political difficulty in reaching agreement between the Member States on a single rate for excise duties. The UK has serious reservations for several reasons. Firstly the proposal would be very limiting to the control exercised by the Chancellor over Budget revenue. Secondly, the proposed duty rates are between 40 and 85% lower than the present UK rates for alcoholic drinks. The loss in revenue from this and from the differences in duties on tobacco and oils would be considerable. There is an added aspect; that the fall in excise duty would generate an increase in consumption of alcoholic drinks and tobacco, which is at variance with the Government's health programme.

VAT LEGISLATION

Due to the very large number of VAT measures, only the directives of general importance and those of particular relevance to the food industry are outlined in the section which follows. The references to the full published text are given for these and also for those of peripheral interest, to enable further study.

EXISTING VAT LEGISLATION

First Council Directive 67/227/EEC of 11 April 1967 on the harmonisation of legislation of Member States concerning turnover taxes.

As amended by:
Council Directive 69/463/EEC, see OJL 320 of 20.12.69
Council Directive 77/388/EEC, see OJL 145 of 13.6.77.

This Directive was the first move toward harmonisation of indirect taxation in the Member States. The text is published in OJL 71 of 14.4.67.

Council Directive 68/221/EEC of 30 April 1968 on a common method for calculating the average rates provided for in Article 97 of the Treaty.

The full text is published in OJL 115 of 18.5.88.

Third Council Directive 69/463/EEC of 9 December 1969 on the harmonisation of legislation of Member States concerning turnover taxes - introduction of value added tax in Member States.

The Third VAT Directive required Member States to introduce a system of VAT to replace their existing turnover taxes. It is published in OJL 320 of 20.12.69.

Sixth Council Directive 77/388/EEC of 17 May 1977 on the harmonisation of the laws of Member States relating to turnover taxes - common system of value added tax: uniform basis of assessment.

As amended by:
Council Directive 80/368/EEC, see OJL 90 of 3.4.80
Council Directive 84/517/EEC, see OJL 285 of 30.10.84
Council Directive 84/386/EEC, see OJL 208 of 3.8.84

Council Directive 87/400/EEC, see OJL 213 of 4.8.87

The Sixth VAT Directive gave the basis for harmonisation of VAT by providing the uniform basis of assessment. It is published in OJL 145 of 13.6.77.

Ninth Council Directive 78/583/EEC of 26 June 1978 on the harmonisation of the laws of Member States relating to turnover taxes.

This is published in OJL 194 of 19.7.78.

PROPOSED VAT LEGISLATION

COM(87) 321. Proposal for a Council Directive supplementing the common system of value added tax and amending Directive 77/388/EEC - approximation of VAT rates.

Summary

The proposal is that Member States should operate two ranges of VAT rate, a standard rate and a reduced rate. The reduced rate is to be in the range 4-9%, and will apply to:

- food (not including alcoholic drinks)
- energy for heating and lighting
- water
- pharmaceuticals
- books
- newspapers and periodicals
- passenger transport.

The standard rate is to be between 14-20%, and will apply to all other goods and services.

The European Parliament has been critical of the proposal, alleging that the Commission has failed to assess the changes in consumption patterns, or the social, economic and public health impact which would be caused by the proposed changes. The Parliament proposed that after such effects have been taken into account, it might be possible to consider setting two bands for VAT at 0-7% and 14-22%.

Timetable

The new Commissioner with responsibility for indirect taxation, Mme Scrivener, has requested time for further study of the proposal before it is debated in the European Parliament; and this is now likely to arise in the plenary session of April 1989.

COM(87) 322. Proposal for a Council Directive completing and amending Directive 77/388/EEC - Removal of fiscal frontiers.

Summary

The purpose of the proposal is to enable tax charged in one Member State to be deductible in another Member State, and to end the current system where the exports from one Member State to others are not subject to VAT, while imports from other Member States are.

The terms of the proposal are that only imports from non-EC countries will be subject to VAT, and the only exports exempted from VAT will be those to non-EC countries. As a result of these changes, amendments are made to the right of Member States to deduct input tax. The Council is also required, on a proposal from the Commission, to take steps to establish a clearing-house mechanism for VAT on sales within the Community.

Timetable

Member States are required to comply with the Directive, and cease the operation of transitional measures, by 31 December 1992, at the latest.

The full text is published in OJC 252 of 22.9.87.

COM(87) 324. Proposal for a Council Directive instituting a process of convergence of rates of value added tax and excise duties.

Summary

This proposal aims to prevent further differences being created between the rates of VAT and excise duties of the various Member States. It requires Member States not to alter the number and level of rates except according to the terms of this Directive. The Member States may alter the number of rates of VAT to two, and may amend the levels of VAT within these rates, provided that the changes bring the levels closer to the proposed ranges of 4-9% and 14-20%.

The requirements on excise duties are that Member States shall not introduce new excise duties or comparable indirect taxes; nor increase the rates nor enlarge the scope of existing duties. The excise duties on manufactured tobacco, alcoholic drinks and mineral oils are, however, exempt from these requirements, and here Member States may amend the rates of excise duties, provided that the changes bring the rates closer to the levels given in this Directive.

The proposal replaces the earlier proposal for a standstill on VAT and excise duties, which provided the option to apply two or three ranges of VAT (COM(87) 17, published in OJC 30 of 7.2.87).

The UK Government is not content with this proposal, since it could not reasonably be adopted in the absence of agreement on the general principles of a harmonised taxation system. The proposal would make limitations on the Government's ability to make changes to the tax system until the time of full approximation of taxes. The proposed levels for excise duties are also significantly lower than those currently existing in the UK, and would therefore cause a loss of revenue.

Timetable

Member States are required to refrain from making changes to their rates and levels of VAT and excise duties from the date of adoption of the Directive.

The full text is given in OJC 250 of 18.9.87.

COM(86) 444. Proposal for a Council Directive amending Directive 77/388/EEC on the harmonisation of the laws of Member States relating to turnover taxes in respect of the common value added tax scheme applicable to small and medium-sized businesses.

As amended by:
COM(87) 524, see OJC 310 of 20.22.87.

Summary

The objective of this proposal is to bring the VAT systems of Member States closer together in regard to the small and medium-sized enterprises. Companies with an annual turnover of less than ECU 10,000 are to be exempt from VAT, and those with an annual turnover of less than ECU 35,000 may be exempted at the option of individual Member States. A simplified VAT scheme is to be introduced for businesses with an annual turnover of less than ECU 200,000. (This was ECU 150,000 in the original proposal COM(86) 444).

The simplified scheme is to work on the basis of annual returns and quarterly or monthly advance payments. The levels for exemption are to be revised annually by the Commission, which will also fix annually their equivalents in national currencies.

Timetable

Member States were required by the original proposal to comply with the Directive by no later than 1 April 1987.

LEGISLATION NOT YET PROPOSED

Proposals under the internal market programme are yet to be made for VAT clearing house system. This will enable VAT to be charged by a vendor at the rate in his home country, on goods for export to another Member State; and the VAT would be deducted by the purchaser in the Member State of importation. The clearing system will then compensate the output tax with the input tax collected at the point of consumption.

EXCISE DUTIES LEGISLATION

Proposals for the harmonisation of the structure of excise duties go back to 1972, but only that relating to the structure of duties on French rum has been adopted. There is likely to be substantial revision to the remaining proposals before they can be adopted.

Proposals on the rates of the duties were made in 1987, after the 1985 White Paper had set a deadline of 1992 for their harmonisation.

As for the legislation on VAT, only the proposals of general importance or particular relevance to the food and drink industry are detailed below. Measures relating to tobacco are also included, although strictly outside the scope of this study.

EXISTING EXCISE DUTIES LEGISLATION

Council Directive 72/464/EEC of 19 December 1972 on taxes other than turnover taxes which affect the consumption of manufactured tobacco.

As amended by:
Council Directive 318/74/EEC, see OJL 180 of 3.7.74
Council Directive 786/75/EEC, see OJL 330 of 24.12.75
Council Directive 911/76/EEC, see OJL 354 of 24.12.76
Council Directive 805/77/EEC, see OJL 338 of 28.12.77
Council Directive 1275/80/EEC, see OJL 375 of 31.12.80
Council Directive 246/86/EEC, see OJL 164 of 20.6.86

The text is published in OJL 303 of 31.12.72.

Second Council Directive 79/32/EEC of 18 December 1978 on taxes other than turnover taxes which affect the consumption of manufactured tobacco.

The text is published in OJL 10 of 16.1.79.

Council Directive 80/369/EEC of 26 March 1980 authorising the French Republic not to apply in the French overseas departments Directives 72/464/EEC and 79/32/EEC on taxes other than turnover taxes which affect the consumption of manufactured tobacco.

The text is published in OJL 90 of 3.4.80.

Council Decision 88/245/EEC of 19 April 1988 authorising the French Republic to apply in its overseas departments and in Metropolitan France, by way of derogation from Article 95 of the Treaty, a reduced rate of the revenue duty imposed on the consumption of 'traditional' rum produced in those departments.

The text is published in OJL 106 of 27.4.88.

PROPOSED LEGISLATION - STRUCTURES OF EXCISE DUTIES

Proposal for a Council Directive on the harmonisation of excise duties on alcohol.

Summary

The proposal specifies that a single rate of duty will be charged for ethyl alcohol other than beer, wine, cider and similar fermented drinks. There will be a reduced rate of duty for grape must, liqueur wines, vermouths and similar products with an alcoholic strength up to 22 degrees C.

No excise duty shall be applied to ethyl alcohol used for the production of vinegar, medicines, cosmetics and products for non-human uses, on alcohol for medicinal use, or on denatured alcohol.

The European Parliament has approved the proposal, with the recommendation that an exemption is granted for ethyl alcohol for use in foodstuffs and for confectionery with an alcohol content of less than 6%.

Timetable

The adoption of the proposal awaits the corresponding proposal on the rate of duty for alcohol.

The full text is given in OJC 43 of 29.4.72.

COM(72) 225/3. Proposal for a Council Directive concerning a harmonised excise duty on wine

Summary

The proposal requires Member States to apply a harmonised excise duty to wine, and defines wine, sparkling wine and other wines.

The full text is published in OJC 43 of 29.4.72.

Proposal for a Council Directive concerning a harmonised excise duty on beer

The full text is published in OJC 43 of 29.4.72.

Proposal for a Council Directive on the harmonisation of the structure of excise duty on cigarettes.

This proposal, published in OJC 264 of 1980, has since been withdrawn in favour of a combined measure on VAT and excise duties. It proposed excise duties of between 10% and 35% of the total tax burden levied on cigarettes.

COM(85) 150. Proposal for a Council Directive laying down certain rules on indirect taxes which affect the consumption of alcoholic drinks.

Summary

Member States applying excise duty to still wine shall use a single rate, based on volume. Still wine is defined as table wines, quality wines, and non-sparkling beverages with an alcoholic content of between 8.5% and 15% by volume. The rate of duty on a given quantity of still wine must not exceed that on the same volume of beer of the category most sold, pro rata to their respective alcoholic strengths.

The text is published in OJC 114 of 8.5.85.

COM(85) 151. Proposal for a Council Directive concerning the harmonisation of excise duties on fortified wine and similar products.

Summary

The proposal requires Member States to apply a single rate of excise duty to fortified wines and similar products known as intermediate products. The duty is to be determined by actual volume and alcoholic strength by volume, and the total duty is to be between 20% and 65% of the duty on the same volume of pure alcohol. There is to be a lower rate applicable to certain French quality wines; the vins doux naturels.

The text is published in OJC 114 of 8.5.85.

PROPOSED LEGISLATION - RATES OF EXCISE DUTIES

COM(87) 328. Proposal for a Council Directive on approximation of the rates of excise duty on alcoholic drinks and on the alcohol content contained in other products.

Summary

The proposal requires that all Member States apply a common rate of excise duty to alcohol, at the following levels:

    spirits and alcohol in foodstuffs   - ECU 1271 per hl pure alcohol

    undenatured ethyl alcohol in
    perfumes, toiletries and cosmetics - ECU 424 per hl pure alcohol

intermediate products such as fortified wines	- ECU 85 per hl
still wine	- ECU 17 per hl
sparkling wine	- ECU 30 per hl
beer	- ECU 1.36 per hl per degree Plato at 15 degrees C

The rates will be adjusted by the Commission from time to time.

Timetable

Member States are required to comply with the directive by 31 December 1992.

The proposal is published in OJC 250 of 18.9.87.

COM(87) 325. Proposal for a Council Directive on the approximation of taxes on cigarettes.

Summary

This proposal is a combined measure to harmonise both VAT and excise duties for cigarettes.

The intention is to apply to cigarettes:

- specific excise duty of ECU 19.5 per 1000 cigarettes
- proportional excise duty fixed so that this duty plus the VAT comes between 52% and 54% of the retail selling price including all taxes.
- VAT proportional to the retail selling price.

Timetable

Member States are required to comply with the Directive by 31 December 1992.

The text is published in OJC 251 of 19.9.87.

COM(87) 326. Proposal for a Council Directive on the approximation of taxes on manufactured tobacco other than cigarettes.

Summary

Rates are given for excise duties to be applied to the following types of manufactured tobacco, such that the total tax burden of VAT plus excise duty will be:

    cigars and cigarillos   - 34% - 36%

    smoking tobacco   - 54% - 56%

    chewing tobacco and snuff   - 41% - 43%

Timetable

Member States will be required to comply with the Directive by 31 December 1992.

The full text is published in OJC 251 of 19.9.87.

Proposal for a Council Decision setting up a Committee on Excise Duties.

Summary

This Committee is to be set up under the chairmanship of the Commission and with representatives of the Member States, to consider and express opinions on the drafts of implementing directives for the harmonisation of excise duties.

The text is published in OJC 43 of 29.4.72.

LEGISLATION ON EXCISE DUTIES NOT YET PROPOSED

Two proposals on excise duties remain to be proposed in the internal market programme:

- the gradual abolition or reduction of excises not covered by the common system and giving rise to border formalities

- the introduction of a linkage between national bonded warehouses for excise goods.

9. IMPLICATIONS OF A SINGLE EUROPEAN MARKET FOR THE FOOD AND DRINK INDUSTRY

BACKGROUND

Since ratification of the Single European Act in July 1987, considerable progress has been made towards the Commission's objective of reaching agreement on the 279 proposals for Community legislation by 31 December 1992. In the foodstuffs sector, significant achievements have been made with the adoption of measures designed to remove technical barriers to free trade in foodstuffs. While divergent national food laws on the production and marketing of foodstuffs have in the past been problematic, mutual recognition of national standards has proved a successful strategy.

The Commission has expressed disappointment that progress to remove physical barriers to trade has been less successful. However, the Commission is optimistic that the harmonisation of health and hygiene conditions for agricultural products will be completed by the 1992 deadline.

Achievement of the Commission's proposals to remove fiscal barriers to trade by harmonising VAT and excise duty rates seems less likely. Despite strong pressures from the Commission and other Member States, retention of unanimous voting in the Council on fiscal matters makes UK opposition to fiscal harmonisation a continuing problem.

IMPLICATIONS OF THE INTERNAL MARKET PROGRAMME

Labelling

The amendments to the 1979 Directive on the labelling, presentation and advertising of foodstuffs were adopted at the end of 1988. The objective is to complete the harmonisation of foodstuffs labelling regulations and remove all remaining national derogations which prevent the uniform provision of consumer information.

In general, the principle upon which Community labelling regulations are now based is that consumers must be adequately informed and, in addition, producers must be protected against unfair competition in order to remove remaining barriers to the free movement of foodstuffs.

Amendments extend the scope of the 1979 Directive to include foodstuffs intended for use in restaurants, hospitals and canteens, with exceptions provided for charity organisations and the armed forces. In the case of highly perishable foodstuffs, the Directive recommends that the "sell by" date should be replaced by the "best before" date. However, the Directive also lists products which, by their very nature, do not require an indication of the "sell by" date.

The intended impact of changes to the labelling Directive is that remaining barriers to trade will be removed, while the highest possible standards of labelling and "fair trading" will be ensured throughout the Community.

Materials and articles in contact with food

Amendments to the 1976 Directive on materials and articles in contact with food aim to create harmonised Community legislation on all such materials and articles. The Commission has proposed that a "framework" directive be adopted by the Council, with powers to adopt subsequent vertical directives on approved lists of materials acceptable for packaging foodstuffs delegated to the Commission. The Commission would base its decisions on consultations with the Standing Committee on Foodstuffs and the Scientific Committee for Food.

The major concern of the food industry is that new procedures to delegate powers to the Commission will provide fewer opportunities for consultations on the vertical directives. There are also fears that the Commission's desire to provide adequate consumer information where possible will lead to unreasonable requirements for a "for food use" declaration to be placed on all materials and articles likely to come into contact with food. However, the major impact of proposed amendments is of a technical nature only.

Packaging

In an attempt to achieve standardisation in distribution packaging throughout the Community, cooperation has already begun in Denmark, West Germany and the Netherlands. In December 1988, the European Confederation for the Retail Trade (CECD) initiated a working committee to discuss cooperation on uniform distribution packaging at a Community level. The achievement of this objective would benefit intra-Community trade by simplifying storage and transportation procedures.

Additives

Differing national regulations which determine the use of additives in foodstuffs constitute an effective barrier to Community trade in foodstuffs. Complete harmonisation has yet to be achieved since each Member State may legitimately introduce controls which restrict the use of specific additives on grounds of Article 36 of the Treaty - the protection of health and life of humans.

While existing directives set out lists of additives authorised for use in foodstuffs, legislation to determine the uses of these additives is still awaited. The Commission's intention is that mutual recognition of national regulations will remove such barriers to Community trade.

The Commission proposal is for the adoption of a "framework" Directive for harmonising national provisions on all additives by making provision for adoption by the Commission of "specific" directives laying down lists of acceptable additives and conditions of use. At present, lists of acceptable additives exist only in the case of colouring matter, antioxidants, emulsifiers and stabilisers, preservatives and extraction solvents.

Specific directives will lay down a system of evaluating use and will require an indication of the presence of an additive on labelling. The Commission's criteria for establishing status of a particular additive will not be based primarily on technological "need". Instead, the primary consideration will be to establish that the use of an additive complies with Community health and safety requirements.

Foodstuffs for particular nutritional uses

The Council has adopted a Directive which amends and replaces the 1977 Directive on foodstuffs for particular nutritional uses. The new Directive sets out provisions relating to labelling, presentation and advertising which will have implications for the marketing of such foodstuffs. The Directive determines the groups of foodstuffs for which "specific" directives will be adopted by the Commission in accordance with the powers delegated to it by the Council.

The Directive lays down a new definition for foodstuffs of "particular nutritional needs". However, this definition has been criticised by manufacturers for failing to make clear the distinction between foodstuffs with a medical use and those intended for ordinary use.

Composition of foodstuffs

Since 1983 no Community legislation has been adopted which lays down the composition of specific types of food. Proposals for directives determining the composition of foodstuffs were abandoned since it was considered both a complex and unnecessary method of ensuring consumer protection and harmonising national regulations.

Food manufacturers in those countries which operated more stringent legislation on the content of foodstuffs feared that this move would result in a reduction in quality standards. Within the principle of mutual recognition, foodstuffs manufactured in a Member State may be freely sold throughout the Community. However, foodstuffs manufactured and sold in a domestic market must still comply with national regulations. Adequate labelling is now considered sufficient to inform the consumer about the compositional standards of foodstuffs.

Spirit drinks

In December 1988 the Council, after six years of negotiations, reached agreement on legislation which will protect the quality of spirit drinks by defining standards for production and specifying minimum strength. The new regulations will prevent the use of names such as "whisky" for imitations which do not meet recognised standards.

The Scottish whisky industry would benefit considerably from the implementation of Commission proposals to harmonise excise duties. At present the whisky industry, which sells 45% of its exports in the Community, faces barriers to trade caused by divergent excise duty rates, which vary dramatically between high rates in Denmark to very low rates in Greece. Progress on the harmonisation of excise duties remains far from certain, since fiscal matters still require unanimous agreement by the Member States.

Official inspection of foodstuffs

The purpose of a Community-wide system of inspection is to prevent risks to health, ensure consumer protection and facilitate the free movement of goods.

The current emphasis on retail inspection is considered by the Commission to be an insufficient means of verification where modes of mass production are in operation. It is anticipated that future Community-wide systems of inspection will place greater emphasis on inspection at the manufacturing level.

The UK food industry has voiced its preference for a partial shift of inspection procedures to the manufacturing level. However, the extent to which the Commission will be successful in its proposals for a comprehensive factory enforcement system is not yet clear.

Information procedure: standards and technical regulations

The EEC information procedure in the field of standards and technical regulations, previously applicable in the industrial sector, is now applicable to foodstuffs and agricultural products.

The procedure requires a Member State to inform the Commission and other Member States of national technical regulations which it intends to introduce. Accordingly, the Commission and the other Member States must assess whether Community regulations in this field are necessary. If this is the case, a Member State must suspend plans to introduce national regulations and comply with Community standards when they are adopted.

The new information procedure limits the ability of a Member State to introduce technical regulations at a national level. Yet in terms of free trade in foodstuffs and agricultural produce, the procedure is clearly consistent with completion of the internal market since it will prevent the imposition of divergent national technical standards.

Metrication

The 1979 Directive on the harmonisation of units of measurement provided ten-year derogations for the UK and Ireland in order to allow the continued use of imperial measurements. The new proposed Directive to amend these provisions has not yet been formally published, but discussion is already under way between the twelve Member States. An increase in the use of metric units can be expected, since the Commission is committed to harmonise units of measurement for economic, health and safety and administrative purposes.

Petrol, do-it-yourself supplies, pre-packed food (including fruit, vegetables and meat made up in packages) and drinks appear likely to be sold in metric units by 1994. The harmonisation of measurements for these goods is consistent with the Commission's overall aim of removing non-tariff barriers to intra-Community trade.

The opinion of the Department of Trade and Industry is that goods which are not traded across borders, such as the pint bottle of milk or the pint of beer should be exempt from the metrication requirements since they are intended for the domestic market. The Commission is also considering allowing foodstuffs sold loose, such as fruit and vegetables, to be given until 1999 before metrication is imposed in order to protect the small trader.

The most likely immediate implications for the food and drink industry will be in the packaging sector, where new packaging sizes will be required. Further problems will arise if the Commission insists that the 1.2 billion imperially measured returnable bottles in UK circulation must be scrapped in the next ten years.

Agricultural products

The Commission's aim is to remove all barriers to the free movement of meat and meat products, fruit and vegetables by raising health and hygiene standards to the highest possible level.

In terms of meat and meat products, the Commission's policy is at an early stage of development. The intention is that meat plants throughout the Community will operate to uniform hygiene standards. Compliance with standards agreed at the Community level will be verified by independent Commission inspectors.

The Commission has acknowledged that some plants will be unable to comply with the high standards for meat establishments due to economic constraints. Consequently, it is anticipated that derogations will be allowed for small processing plants which produce for a "local market".

The objective of harmonised health checks for meat and meat products is that inspections, in the form of samples, should be carried out at the place of destination in order to remove unnecessary delays to the transportation of meat at national frontiers.

The European Court clarified its interpretation of Community law on health checks of imported fresh meat in September 1988. In Case 190/87: <u>Oberkreisdirektor v. Handelsonderneming Moormann BV</u>, the Court ruled that systematic checks on poultrymeat carried out on the entry into a Member State constitute measures having an equivalent effect to quantitative restrictions. The case reinforces the principle that meat inspections must be in the form of samples, in accordance with the procedures laid down in the directives.

Community legislation relating to pesticide residues on fruit and vegetables is well established. Future legislation is anticipated in order to align national standards, suppress plant health certificates and reinforce Community controls of harmful organisms. This legislation will be consistent with the Commission's overall objective of removing all remaining barriers to trade in agricultural products.

The free movement of agricultural products remains constrained by the administrative delays and price structures imposed by Monetary Compensatory Amounts (MCAs). In recognising that MCAs caused an additional barrier to free trade, the Commission announced in 1985 its intention to gradually phase them out completely.

The maintenance of health checks at border posts remains one of the most tangible examples of barriers to trade in the Community. In order to remove the need for border checks for non-processed food products, the Commission anticipates that health checks will be limited to the place of departure, and a Community health mark issued for products which comply with EC standards. Checks at the place of destination will be limited to an inspection of health certificates. Consequently, the necessity for checks at border posts will be removed.

Transport

The removal of administrative delays at border posts has been a consistent cause of delays and additional handling charges for intra-Community trade in goods. The introduction of the Single Administrative Document (SAD) on 1 January 1988, which standardised the documentation required at border posts, went a long way to alleviate administrative delays.

Even so, significant restrictions remain, particularly with regard to the number of journeys that hauliers can undertake within another Member State. The Commission intends to curtail the use of all such quota systems. Technical restrictions have similarly proved to be an impediment to the transportation of foodstuffs on a pan-European scale. Once again the Commission anticipates that, with the adoption of common transportation safety rules, there will be no justification for maintaining additional national regulations which restrict access to national markets.

TRENDS IN THE EUROPEAN FOOD INDUSTRY

Despite being one of the largest industries in the Community, covering all activities from the processing of agricultural products to the marketing of retail goods, employing 2.5 million people and with a turnover exceeding ECU 360 billion, the European food industry has traditionally been considered highly fragmented.

The structural diversity of the industry is due only partly to barriers to free movement of goods. Limited trade in food products between the Member States is more easily attributable to variations in market demand and cultural factors which determine food consumption trends. Moves towards convergent consumption trends have been slow. This has led multinational food manufacturers to concentrate on the production of foodstuffs locally for local consumption patterns. Such determining factors of production prevent relocation of manufacturing plants.

Overall, it appears that the cultural and demographic barriers to intra-Community trade will prove more difficult to remove than technical and physical barriers. While the Community food market remains no more than a collection of national food markets, the potential for exporting national brands on a Community wide basis will remain limited.

Despite the determining effect of structural and demographic factors in the food industry generally, there is an increasing interpenetration of rival European markets by large national producers. Common trends in food consumption are apparent which indicate growth in processed products, convenience foods and health foods. However, these trends are manifesting themselves only slowly. The steady decline in expenditure throughout the decade indicates that, in general terms, the market has become stagnant.

However, the trend towards increased concentration in most sectors of the industry has continued, with a tendency for larger companies dominating sectors of the market. In terms of capital, production experience and management skills, multi-national companies have retained their market advantage.

The stagnation of traditional markets for foodstuffs has led companies to diversify into sectors which are developing more rapidly. In the case of

Unilever this has involved expansion of its non-foodstuff concerns. Elsewhere, large firms have tended to diversify into areas of specialised foodstuff production traditionally occupied by small companies. The range of production has also increased as firms have extended their activities at national, Community and international levels.

While the threat to small food manufacturers from large concerns remains a possibility, smaller companies still retain an advantage in their ability to react with a more flexible approach and more innovation to rapidly changing market demands. The development of private label products has created valuable niche markets for small and medium sized companies. Even so, small firms remain totally dependent on large-scale distribution networks and may fare badly during the market restructuring which the industry is experiencing.

Market restructuring

The prospect of a Single European Market by 1992 has provided the impetus for the food and drink industry to begin the modernisation of manufacturing equipment, the introduction of technological processes and a general trend towards mergers and acquisitions in the market.

With the exception of Unilever, Nestle and BSN, the European food industry is not in a position to compete with the financial strength of the major US food companies. While companies such as BSN, which has been operating a pan-European strategy in recent years and has expanded considerably in Spain and Italy, are well placed to take advantage of a Single Market, food companies in Europe have in general remained relatively small operations. Comparatively speaking, the major US companies such as Kraft, Heinz, Kellogg, CPC and Quaker Oats are already well established in pan-European food markets and have the financial and technological resources to expand further when opportunities created by the internal market programme present themselves.

The shortage of finance to facilitate technological developments in the European food industry is particularly problematic for small and medium sized manufacturers. This indicates one reason for an increasing trend towards market concentration and the dominance of large concerns.

In comparison with its competitors in continental Europe, the UK food industry retains a strong market position, with Cadbury Schweppes, Associated British Foods, United Biscuits, Unigate, Dalgety, Tate and Lyle and RHM among the leading European food companies. However, despite strong positions in the domestic market, only Cadbury Schweppes has major operations in continental Europe. Traditionally, the overseas interests of UK food companies have focused instead upon US and Canadian niche markets. In addition, UK companies still indicate a greater interest in consolidating their domestic markets than expanding into continental Europe. Most recently, developments in the UK industry have involved RHM's acquisition of Nabisco's UK breakfast cereals business and Associated British Foods' growing interest in United Biscuits. The absence of a strong presence in continental Europe may prevent the industry from utilising an established base on which to build post-1992.

The absence of pan-European brand strength is particularly noticeable in virtually all product sectors. The Commission's Cecchini Report on the benefits of the internal market has predicted the emergence of new major companies which will enjoy high brand strength over wide geographic areas of the Community. The Report acknowledges, however, that such movements into new markets may trigger major consolidation and restructuring of the market of a similar type to the events which been apparent in the US.

The trend towards restructuring goes much further than the food manufacturing sector. In early 1989, the Commission stated its intention not to intervene in the proposed Anglo-French merger between Metalbox Packaging, the packaging interest of MB Group, and French packaging company Carnaud. The intention to create CBM, a packaging organisation on a European scale, indicates a desire to exploit opportunities for greater access to the EC market as technical and commercial barriers to European business cooperation become increasingly less significant.

In the distribution sector, the British company Polly Peck International has increased its activities in Continental Europe by acquiring three companies in different Member States: Van Den Brink (Netherlands), Frio Mediteraneo (Spain) and Fruco (West Germany).

Implications for retail distribution

The Community's legislative programme to remove barriers to intra-Community trade will not directly affect the retail sector. Even so, the implications of technical regulations (labelling, materials in contact with food, additives) and the simplification of transportation procedures will clearly have implications. The removal of border controls will enable the use of wider sources of supply. Harmonisation of VAT rates will, if achieved, involve a short-term fall in demand in those countries where taxation on food is at present low or zero rated.

It can be anticipated that free access to the European market will enable retailers to obtain products from a wider variety of sources. In addition, an increasing tendency towards more centralised purturing and distribution networks may increase the bargaining position of the retail sector in its relations with food manufacturers.

In the long-term, the removal of barriers to trade will increase opportunities for establishing branches in other Member States, particularly on a selective basis. Marks and Spencer, the retail group, has already announced plans to investigate the possibility of acquiring stores in major European cities, which could then be turned into M and S concerns.

Overall, trends in retail distribution echo those apparent in the food manufacturing sector. Despite the continuing rise in consumer spending, market saturation for UK food retailers is an impending prospect for the early 1990s. In a generally static market, retail groups will continue to undertake mergers, acquisitions and joint ventures in order to increase market share.

TRENDS IN THE EUROPEAN DRINKS INDUSTRY

Wines and spirits

The Community currently produces one-third of the world supply of spirit drinks; twice as much as the United States. In terms of wine, the Community accounts for half of world production. EC wine and spirits industries are continuing with stable patterns of growth due to the opening up of new markets and an increased sophistication in tastes. This pattern is particularly apparent in the case of products with strong brand names. The introduction of new technology and the desire to improve competitiveness have led to increasing centralisation of production.

Merger and acquisition activity has increased in the favourable climate created by the internal market programme, most recently with the Guinness-Agache joint acquisition of Louis Vuitton-Moet Hennessy. However, future activity may be influenced by the European Commission's intervention in the consortium bid for Irish Distillers in July 1988. The Commission blocked the bid by GC & C Brands, the consortium backed by Grand Metropolitan, Allied-Lyons and Guinness, on grounds that the link-up was designed to eliminate competition from rival bidders. The decision left Grand Met to bid against Pernod Ricard for Irish Distillers in the open market and may deter future consortium offers in the highly concentrated drinks sector.

The market continues to be dominated by four companies: Grand Metropolitan, Allied-Lyons, Guinness and Seagram. Their considerable brand strength and distribution facilities indicate that they will also be the best placed to benefit from the Single European Market.

While the harmonisation of technical standards may have implications for labelling, packaging and transportation of wines and spirits, the impact of 1992 on the sector will be limited unless agreement can be reached on the harmonisation of VAT and excise duties.

Beer

The recent performance of Community brewers has been less successful. Annual EC beer production in the 1980s has fallen behind growth patterns in the world market. Community beer production is now only slightly ahead of the US.

The West German market for beer is the largest in the EC. However, since the 1987 European Court ruling that the German "Rheinheitsgebot" beer purity law constituted an unfair barrier to intra-Community trade, the large German beer industry has faced open competition in its home market for the first time. Even so, consumer preference for local beers has meant that the German market remains highly fragmented and dominated by local brewers. Consumer trends and poor distribution networks may prove prohibitive for large EC brewers considering expansion into the German market.

In the highly profitable UK market, traditional draught beers still account for the majority of sales. The market is dominated by six brewers, but all leading European brands now have a presence in the UK through licensing agreements with the major brewers. The success of such joint ventures indicates that the trend will continue to provide an access point for overseas producers. Alternatively, some activity in mergers and acquisitions may be expected of the type seen in the Elders/Courage deal, where Courage had already established the market for Elders' major brand before being acquired.

Fast growth in the Spanish market has led major EC brewers Heineken, BSN and Carlsberg to purchase the leading local brands. These companies are well placed to exploit potential for market development.

Three EC markets are dominated by large brewers with Carlsberg (Denmark), Heineken (Greece) and Guinness (Ireland) in strong positions. In other Community markets, the trend for two or three large brewers dominating the market continues with: BSN and Heineken (France); Birra Peroni, BSN and Heineken (Italy); Heineken, Grolsch and Artois Piedboeuf and Allied Breweries (Benelux).

Completion of the internal market is not likely to have significant implications for European brewers. The only major impact of the 1992 programme would come from the harmonisation of VAT and excise duties. This would have short-term implications for profitability, but it appears increasingly unlikely that harmonisation will be achieved within the 1992 deadline.

General trends will continue, with an increase in imported major brands in national markets, an emphasis on improving efficiency and the acquisition of local production and distribution networks for brand-name beers. A continued growth in the activities of non-European brewers Elders, Bond, Anheuser-Busch and Miller (Philip Morris) may also be anticipated.

IMPLICATIONS FOR THIRD COUNTRIES

Since progress towards completion of the internal market gained momentum, major food companies based in non-EC countries have increased their activities in the Community. By setting up operations within the EC, food companies from outside the Community will have free access to the Single European Market. Any product lawfully produced and marketed in a Member State will be able to be marketed throughout the Community provided that EC rules are observed.

The general trend amongst non-EC companies which require access to EC markets is to undertake acquisitions of established companies in the Member States. In this context, it can be anticipated that Nestle's acquisition of Rowntree will be the first of many such moves for established EC food companies. A marked increase in merger and acquisition activity is certainly apparent. However, it would be premature to suggest that such activity is motivated by the a desire to be on the "inside" in 1992, since mergers and acquisitions have always played a major role in the development of the food industry.

An alternative strategy for access to European markets was demonstrated by Mrs Fields, the US cookie manufacturer, in December 1988. The US company announced the formation of a joint venture with Midial, the French food company. Midial took a 99 per cent share of a new company, Mrs Fields Europe, and in return agreed to pay the US company a fee of $5 million for a product licence agreement to sell the products throughout Europe. Association agreements of this type may become an increasingly common characteristic of the industry as the 1992 deadline approaches.

The strength of US food companies will clearly pose a major threat to EC companies. While the largest EC companies - with financial, production and management resources at their disposal - will benefit from the internal market, small and intermediate-sized companies face serious threats from competitors outside the Community.

Indications are that Japanese manufacturers such as Suntory, Snow, and Kao are also ready to enter the European market on a large scale.

Import restrictions - impact on third countries

With the creation of a Single European Market, implications for non-EC countries which traditionally import goods into the Community may be serious. Moves to unify the Community market have upset the status quo of import arrangements which have traditionally allowed the access of non-European foodstuffs and agricultural products into the EC.

The implications of the Community's internal market programme for trade with non-EC countries has been underlined by the dispute with the United States which began in December 1988. The Council had previously adopted a Directive banning imports of hormone-treated meat from 1 January 1989 on grounds that it presented a danger to human health. The United States claimed that the measure was unjustified in the case of five hormones which are not harmful. However, the EC refused to reconsider the decision since GATT rules on free trade were not infringed: the measures taken did not discriminate between EC and non-EC products.

The US responded to the Community's decision by declaring its intention to impose custom duties on EC products, in particular certain low alcohol drinks and tomato preserves, amounting to $100 million. The US customs duties would be imposed on 1 January 1989. The Community responded by announcing its intention to introduce customs duties corresponding exactly to the US restrictions. The Community duties would be on nuts and dried fruits. The significance of the products chosen for custom duties was that Italy and West Germany, the countries most affected by the proposed US restrictions, were also the main importers of nuts and dried fruits.

Efforts to avert a trade war resulted in an announcement by the US on 16 January 1989 that entry into force of EC restrictions on hormone treated-meat would be postponed until 1 February. In addition, an exchange of letters between Washington and Brussels agreed in principle that a "travelling time" be allowed for products sent both ways before 1 January 1989. The intention was that US hormone-treated meat could enter the Community until 31 January if it was already being transported. Similarly, it was proposed that EC produce subject to US custom duties could enter the United States at normal rates until 31 January. At the time of writing, the United States has yet to comply with EC restrictions on hormone treated meat.

Progress towards a Single European Market has also had an impact on relations with other non-EC countries. The renewal of special terms which allow the importation of New Zealand butter into the UK encountered problems in Council at the end of 1988. A compromise was agreed which will allow a temporary authorisation for the butter until March 1989; however the issues which the New Zealand case raised indicates problems which may lie ahead for non-EC trading partners. The ACP countries in particular have voiced concern about the degree of access which non-EC agricultural produce will receive in the future.

10. STRATEGIC PLANNING FOR 1992

The final chapter of this book is devoted to the views of companies and institutions in the food industry on how they see the opportunities, problems and challenges of the single European market.

Eurofi would like to thank the authors of the following articles for their individual assessment of the implications.

SINGLE EC MARKET MUST NOT BE "TROJAN HORSE"

Rt. Hon. John Macgregor OBE MP
Minister of Agriculture, Fisheries & Food[1]

In her Bruges speech, the Prime Minister expressed, in very positive terms, her commitment to the commercial aspects of 1992. I share her belief that we must concentrate on the key measures that will develop the Community's potential as one of the world's largest internal free trading areas. It should be about removing obstacles and wherever possible deregulating, not creating new bureaucratic burdens or unnecessary central powers. We are in the business of promoting enterprise and creating jobs, not fostering State intervention.

The food and agriculture industry provides an excellent illustration of what is needed. The industry, a major contributor, in terms of jobs and value added, to the EEC economy, is still hampered by trade barriers. Indeed, intra-EC food trade only amounts to about 15% of EC food consumption.

The UK Government's support for the removal of barriers to intra-Community trade is not in question. Our attitude is a logical extension of our policy of deregulation. The removal of unnecessary constraints on business will provide a further stimulus to economic activity in the Community.

The greater freedom for market forces to operate and the more competitive commercial environment will help to ensure a more effective allocation of resources. They will encourage greater efficiency and allow businesses to benefit from greater economies of scale and reduced costs. 1992 is therefore a big commercial opportunity for UK business. For the consumer, it should mean greater choice than ever before.

In third countries there is concern that the development of the single market might become a "Trojan Horse" for increased protectionism. This must be resisted; we are concerned with strengthening the EEC's position in world trade. We must not permit our enthusiasm for completing the single market to conflict with Europe's responsibilities as a major trading block. It is in the UK interest that worldwide trading conditions should be liberalised rather than further constrained.

---

[1] Abridged version of an address given to the Institute of Directors on 10th October 1988.

For agriculture, 1992 involves two key issues.

Firstly, in 1987 the Commission set the objective of removing MCAs by 1992, and we strongly supported them. In this year's price fixing the Council of Agriculture Ministers and the Commission committed themselves to eliminating the remaining agrimonetary gaps by 1992. And at my insistence it was accepted that the arrangements must cover all Member States, whether they are in the EMS exchange rate mechanism or not. The first step for us will take place with the devaluations due on 1 January 1989.

Anyone who has ever been involved in the tortuous negotiations over MCAs will recognise that it will not be easy to complete this process. But for me it is an essential element in achieving a single market, and the UK Government strongly supports this commitment.

Secondly 1992 will have a major impact on our system of animal and plant health controls. Our health status is higher than in many other parts of the Community. On this basis, we have developed a thriving export trade in livestock and livestock products. Our aim is to facilitate this trade, while at the same time ensuring that the necessary health safeguards are retained. A start has been made on the harmonisation of health controls in the Community, but there is a great deal of work to be done.

In some areas, for example in the control of foot-and-mouth disease or classical swine fever, the Community already has harmonised rules which have enabled considerable progress towards eradication. The Community's efforts in this direction will need to be redoubled as, of course, with serious diseases such as these total eradication is by far the best basis for a simplification of the necessary controls. For other diseases, such as Aujeszky's disease, Member States are at different stages and the UK has so far relied on bilateral arrangements with other Member States in the absence of harmonised rules. In this case we shall be working to ensure that the arrangements, without being more onerous than they need to be, continue to safeguard what we have achieved.

On plant health, we have so far only received preliminary proposals from the Commission. It is too soon to forecast how their thinking will develop. However, we shall be making every effort to ensure that the measures which will be introduced will provide at least as much protection for the United Kingdom's health status as the existing Community regime.

For food and drink manufacturers, in the highly competitive environment which is likely to characterise the 1990s, it is obvious that the industry will need to retain and where possible improve its competitive edge. One of the Government's main objectives is to create the right business environment. It is up to manufacturers to identify the most appropriate structure for their company, identify new trends in their market, respond to the need for better quality and variety as well as greater convenience, and make the necessary acquisitions or restructuring. Certainly the opportunities will be there. For example, changes in German tax law that come into effect in 1990, will result in a number of small and medium sized companies being sold or floated on the stock exchange in the next two years.

Many British food companies have been quick to recognise the challenges of 1992 and beyond. Essential restructuring is already well under way, but companies in other Community countries as well as from elsewhere, and particularly the large multilaterals, are fully alert to the implications of the single market. Many of them will take 1992 as an opportunity to rationalise manufacturing capacity, or to increase their presence in the Community.

The message must be to keep one's eyes open and focus on the opportunities as well as the threats. The single market will test the marketing and innovative skills of companies. The extent of strategic planning, related to 1992, which is currently going on in food and drink companies gives me great confidence in the ability of the industry to confront the challenges ahead.

For my Ministry one of the main workload implications of 1992 is the accelerating focus on food law harmonisation. The general aim is not to lay down detailed and inhibiting compositional standards for foods. Instead it is, first, to seek to ensure that food is safe and wholesome; and second, to ensure that the consumer is provided with the information necessary to permit her to choose her foods for herself.

So far as the safety of food is concerned, we have now reached a common position on the framework Directives dealing with food additives and with materials in contact with food. Once consultation with the European Parliament is complete we can expect work to commence on the detailed consideration of individual additives and contact materials. We shall need to stay in very close touch with the industry in developing our negotiating positions on these aspects. In the case of food additives, we have to agree on the foodstuffs in which specific additives can be used and the levels to which they can be permitted. I understand that there has been some reluctance in parts of the UK industry to give information to my officials on patterns of usage for food additives. I do urge the industry to provide the information we need. It will be handled in confidence. These negotiations are going to be difficult. Other Member States take a much more restrictive attitude in this area than we do. Unless we have all the relevant information, we shall be handicapped from the outset, and that would not be in the interests of the industry.

So far as consumer information is concerned, we are moving rapidly towards decisions on the changes to food labelling. A major aspect of this is the change proposed in date marking. The UK "sell by" date will have in most cases to be replaced in due course by the existing "best before" system, which will apply throughout the Community. Foods which have a very short shelf life and are microbiologically sensitive will require a "use before" date. Other provisions under discussion relate to information on product labels. Here a compromise will have to be found between what is practical for the industry and what consumer groups regard as desirable.

There are a number of proposals yet to come from the Commission.

The most important of these are on the nutrition labelling of foods and on food irradiation. In both cases when the proposals are made to the Council, we will need help to establish our negotiating position. The Greek Presidency are giving a good deal of priority to pushing forward with food harmonisation and we can expect to see progress when the proposals are submitted.

The Commission White Paper stated that there would be no more food compositional law developed at Community level. Unfortunately, it gave no indication of what should happen to existing compositional law. The Commission has to address this issue. Some Member States, notably France and Germany, are still pressing for the development of common food quality standards. We do not think that these are necessary or desirable. It certainly does not follow that the abolition of an existing standard automatically leads to a fall in quality. It can often open the way to the development of new products to meet developing consumer needs.

Accurate labelling is a more effective means of permitting the consumer to maximise satisfaction. But there may be a case for assisting the consumer to judge foods which look alike but which are different in composition. The Commission is examining a scheme for the quantitative declaration of ingredients. This and other proposals should be examined with care. We must try to meet consumer needs without placing unnecessary burdens on manufacturers.

I don't want to dwell on the issue of VAT, but lest there should be any doubt, let me repeat that the Government does not consider tax approximation to be a necessary part of the completion of the internal market. We have committed ourselves on many occasions not to extend VAT to food and have made it clear that the UK could not accept proposals which restrict our right to apply zero rates. It is relevant that while most other areas where harmonisation might be involved are decided by qualified majority, changes to tax measures require the unanimous agreement of the Member States.

Developments in transport policy will also have significant implications for the food industry. At present within the Community, the free movement of goods is substantially inhibited. UK road hauliers are unable to pick up and deliver loads between other Member States. Access to some countries (France, West Germany, Italy and Spain) is heavily restricted by quotas. These restrictions increase costs by preventing the most economical use of transport. Without them, there should be major opportunities for companies involved in food distribution to extend their operations throughout the continent.

Community Transport Ministers have accepted that international road haulage will be liberalised by the end of 1992. All road haulage permits and quotas for trade between Member States will then be abolished. In the meantime, permit quotas will be progressively increased. Proposals to allow hauliers registered in one Member State to operate wholly within another are still under consideration, but the UK will be pushing strongly for further liberalisation.

An effective competition policy is an essential ingredient of a Single European Market. Widespread Community powers already exist in Articles 85 and 86 of the Treaty of Rome to prevent the distortion of competition. A proposal for a regulation on mergers is currently under consideration in Brussels, although it is too soon to say whether it will be adopted, still less in what form. We have well developed competition legislation in the United Kingdom. The Secretary of State for Trade and Industry has recently proposed some changes to speed up and improve the arrangements for handling acquisitions and mergers, and he has also issued proposals for more effective controls on restrictive trade practices, which would bring our approach to these practices close to that in the Treaty of Rome.

Some of the criticisms I have heard on our approach seem to arise from a belief that our mergers policy looks exclusively at national market shares. This is not the case.

UK competition legislation is framed in terms of the national jurisdiction; and the UK competition authorities must have regard to the effects of an acquisition on national customers and consumers. However, increasing account will have to be taken of the wider Community scene.

In many markets, particularly for goods which can be traded easily across national frontiers, a merger may create a situation in which there are only one or two major UK suppliers which have a very high share of the UK market and yet which do not pose a serious threat to competition because of the potential competition from imports. This is fully recognised.

Arguments about the prospective gains to efficiency, and to international competitiveness, from a merger certainly are considered in appropriate cases. The competition authorities have regard to the market that is relevant. It may be a very local market. It may be regional. It may be the UK as a whole. But equally it may be - and is likely increasingly to be - Europe as a whole or even a wider international market. If there is effective competition with products from the rest of Europe, then it does not matter if there is only one UK supplier because that supplier does face effective competition. This is a situation that could become increasingly common as barriers to trade within Europe are progressively dismantled and as our own competitive and enterprising companies seek the best ways of exploiting the wider opportunities.

Much of the effectiveness of a single market depends on the maintenance of effective competition, and this is particularly important at a time when companies are reconsidering and adapting their structures. It is important that in considering proposed mergers and acquisitions we attach considerable weight to the need for effective competition as a spur to efficiency and enterprise. We need to facilitate change provided competition does not suffer.

It is increasingly clear that industry must plan on the basis that progress towards the single market will result in free trade in foodstuffs by 1993. Some people may still have their doubts. We all can see the amount of work which remains to be done and people understandably question whether the political will exists. That will does exist, and it is going to happen. Much progress has been made since 1985. And since I have become Minister, I have noticed the accelerating impact which the commitment to 1992 is having on the number of harmonisation issues coming up to the Council of Ministers.

Many of the developments will affect each company which should keep in close touch with Government and Trade Associations. MAFF will play its part in trying to keep the industry informed. By co-operating with other European companies in the industry or through the trade associations, other governments are also kept aware of industry views.

It also is important that my officials are aware of your concerns. There will be opportunities to influence the shape of the measure still to come. Beyond this, I suspect that there is no single formula. Individual companies must identify what their needs are and decide how to exploit the opportunities. It will be necessary to look at issues as diverse as the company structure, the language abilities of staff, how raw material suppliers will be affected and the requirements of existing and potential customers.

1989 is Food and Farming Year and this is an ideal opportunity for our food industry to launch its offensive for 1992. It will provide an excellent platform for the industry, and may be a suitable occasion to invite existing or prospective overseas clients to visit the UK. It is also an opportunity to show British consumers what your company has to offer. The food industry has demonstrated its commitment to Food and Farming Year.

I also hope it will demonstrate its commitment to Food From Britain, which can help in the detailed planning for 1992 and in many other ways. It was because of the importance we attached to FFB's role that we agreed to restructure its finances. During the next two years, the Government will be paying all FFB's establishment costs, and on the strength of this, FFB has begun a major reorganisation.

Although they will be maintaining a significant level of activity at home, the majority of their resources will be directed towards the export market. This will be particularly so in those markets served by their country offices in France, Germany and Holland, where the FFB staff can provide advice and direct contacts with customers. Nevertheless, the finance for individual projects and marketing programmes must come from industry itself, and I hope that full support will be forthcoming.

To sum up, 1992 represents a major opportunity for the UK food industry. In 1992 many of the objectives will still be the same, but some of the rules may have changed and success will be even harder to achieve. Challenge and opportunity are the two words which best characterise the single market. Challenge, because the rate of change is going to get much faster. Opportunity, because substantial rewards exist for those who make the most of them.

COMMENTS ON THE COMMUNITY'S FOOD LAW
HARMONISATION PROGRAMME

Ministry of Agriculture, Fisheries and Food

The Community's food harmonisation programme is based on "framework" directives which cover such areas as food labelling, food additives, foods for particular nutritional uses, materials and articles in contact with food and the official inspection of foodstuffs. These "framework" directives set down broad principles and, where appropriate, provide for the introduction of further legislation on more detailed matters which could pose barriers to trade if left to national discretion.

Previous Community food law defined detailed requirements on the composition ("recipes") of specific foodstuffs. These compositional directives were complicated and proved difficult to agree. They stifled product innovation and restricted the range of products available to the consumer. The new approach concentrates on establishing a more informative system of food labelling, together with essential food safety and fair trading measures. We support the main thrust of the Community's food harmonisation programme. The new de-regulatory approach is speeding up progress towards the completion of the single market. This could not have been achieved under the restrictive and time-consuming old approach. However, concern has been expressed that the Community's move away from food compositional standards or "recipe law" towards more informative labelling may result in a lowering of standards and poorer quality food. But we do not believe that the abolition of standards automatically leads to a fall in quality. This has certainly not been the case for products not covered by such standards. Product availability is largely determined by demand and there is considerable demand for top quality premium foods as well as for cheaper alternatives. We think the shift away from recipe law and the removal of trade barriers will encourage product innovation and increased market flexibility. This should give consumers greater choice and variety - at both ends of the price scale.

We are sometimes asked (more often than not with scepticism) whether all the barriers on food law will be removed by 1993. Obviously this will depend on the Commission's detailed legislative programme being agreed in time. Agreement has now been reached on the main "framework" directives, but the necessary "secondary legislation" and other measures need to be in place to achieve a single market in foodstuffs by 1993. There remains a great deal of work to be done, but the Community is making good progress towards this. Industry must plan on the basis that progress towards the single market will result in free trade in foodstuffs in the Community by 1993.

We should not, however, expect 1993 to come upon us with a "big bang". There will be a steady stream of legislation up to 1993. Once achieved, the single market will have transformed the markets of the 12 Member States into a single market with 320 million "consumers"! This market will be a competitive one and it will be for individual businesses to rise to the challenge. Market research will obviously have a large part to play and in this respect the changing focus of food law brought about by the Community's harmonisation programme should leave manufacturers largely free to develop new product ranges and alter existing products to satisfy the wide ranging consumer demands within the enlarged market.

Food labelling

The framework directive on food labelling seeks to harmonise labelling rules in the Community, mainly by replacing national derogations by Community rules. Current datemarking exemptions, which the UK has used, covering ice cream, long life and frozen foods will go. The directive provides for "best before" to be the usual form of date marking, with "use by" for highly perishable foods. It will be for manufacturers to decide which is the appropriate form for their products. The "sell by" form of date marking currently permitted in the UK will be allowed for a limited period only.

The official inspection of foodstuffs

This framework directive sets down the general principles for the official inspection of foodstuffs. It provides for enforcement authorities to inspect not only products destined for home consumption but also those intended for other Member States. The aim is to work towards mutual confidence in food inspection systems, in order to break down related non-tariff barriers. To ensure effective control, the directive also enables export consignments to be inspected. It provides for inspections to be carried out at all stages of the manufacturing and distributive cycle. In the UK this is likely to mean more in-factory (as opposed to retail level) inspections which will, possibly, lead to a change of emphasis towards preventative control. The directive requires Member States to draw up forward inspection programmes and submit annual inspection statistics to the Commission. It also provides for the Commission to recommend a co-ordinated inspection programme at Community level.

Foods for particular nutritional uses

This Framework Directive seeks to harmonise the rules governing foods for particular nutritional uses by removing the scope for national departures from current Community rules and identifies categories of food for which more detailed Directives would be introduced. Those foods for which specific Directives are to be made would not be freely traded until the Directives were in force (in other words national legislation would continue to apply) but for other foods, which would be able to be traded once the framework Directive takes effect, a 'safeguard' clause, in addition to public health safeguards, has been included. The 'safeguard' provides that a manufacturer or importer must keep papers, including scientific data, justifying that the food is for the particular nutritional use which is claimed and that it complies with the Directive. These papers may be examined by the responsible authority of a Member State and if the authority considers that the product infringes the Directive it may be provisionally restricted or banned in that Member State. Such a decision has to be communicated to the Commission who would consider other Member States before confirming or lifting the restrictions.

Specific Directives will apply to main categories of food for particular nutritional use, namely infant and baby foods, low or reduced energy foods for weight control, dietary foods for special medical purposes, low sodium and gluten free foods, high energy foods intended especially for sportsmen, and diabetic foods.

1992 - STRATEGIC ISSUES FOR THE FOOD AND DRINK INDUSTRY

Food from Britian

In October 1988, Food from Britain, the Government and industry sponsored marketing organisation for the UK food and drink industry, mounted a major conference in London to explore the implications of 1992.

Over 200 senior executives representing both the major food groups and some smaller companies gathered to hear the thoughts of a distinguished line up of speakers.

This article draws on the key points of some of the papers given at that conference. Full proceedings of the conference are available from Food from Britain at Market Towers, New Covent Garden, London SW8 5NQ.

A boom in the use of microwave ovens in Europe could decide the success, or not, of the abolition of trade barriers and tariff walls in 1992, as far as the food and drink industry is concerned.

It is something as simple as this, the way in which eating habits may or may not change in Europe, coupled with how long housewives are prepared to stay in the kitchen cooking elaborate meals, which could determine the future expansion of the food industry after 1992.

These were the views of more than one speaker at the Food from Britain conference last October.

Mr Raymond Monbiot, former chairman and managing director of Campbell's UK, said that one way of expanding into the European market inside a group which was still 12 distinctly different nations, was to look for common factors. These were changes in the European scene and changing European lifestyles.

The common factor that was driving the engine for expansion was the percentage of working women. By the year 2000 in Britain 65% of women would be working, with 59% in France, 55% in West Germany and 50% in Italy. This, in turn, led to a growth in labour-saving and time saving gadgets, such as microwave ovens. "The reality is that people with money want manufacturers to save them time. People without money want manufacturers to save them money."

There was also a very strong correlation between the availability of microwaves and the amount of time spent in the kitchen. American women, for example, with 75% penetration of microwaves, spent only 20 minutes a day in the kitchen. In Britain 35% of households had microwaves and women spent an average of 75 minutes in the kitchen. But in France "there is still the great feeling of eyes boring into the housewife's back as she reaches for a convenience product, guiltily withdrawing her hand, and going to spend another three hours making soup for a husband who will go and have dinner with his mother if his wife does not produce a proper meal".

In France there are only 12% of households with microwaves and they spend 180 minutes a day in the kitchen.

To compete on equal terms against this background, he said, the Japanese, the Koreans, the Americans, and the European food manufacturers had got to achieve critical mass in Europe. This meant having production mass and market mass.

Production mass meant investing in state-of-the-art equipment capable of producing large quantities at a consistent quality almost continuously so that borrowings could be repaid by volume at low cost.

This was best illustrated by the Japanese car industry where Nissan produces three cars every 55 seconds, with every car ordered before it is produced. And as the Japanese move into the food industry - "and that is one of their main international thrusts" - they were unlikely to abandon a system which had made them the most successful manufacturing-led economy in the world.

Mr Monbiot said that there was no doubt that the Japanese were planning to do to the food industry in Europe what they had already done to cameras, electronics and wrist-watches. They had the advantage of a 120 million home market on which to base their expertise and from which "they have pushed out with their lessons learned to roll up one market after another".

They saw big opportunities in Europe because of the fragmented nature of the indigenous food industry. "How, for example, do the Belgians replicate Japanese performance when their population is one-third the size of Tokyo? Britain is better placed with 57 million people, but we are still a small base for today's commercial environment. So we need a larger base, and the EC provides one of 320 million potential customers to combat the threat from the outside and to realise the potential both inside and out."

There were challenges of both taste and tradition before the food industry could expand into the rest of Europe, he said. But the path was also strewn with obstacles. There were 218 non-tariff barriers in 10 food markets alone. They ranged from the type of wheat used in pasta to the ingredients of chocolate and beer. Some of these ideas were now being outdated and not upheld in the European courts, but there was still a big problem to overcome by investing in low-cost, high volume food manufacturing plants, "or we will be swamped by overseas competitors".

Returning to the Japanese threat, Mr Monbiot said that they understood product engineering probably better than anyone else on earth. "They are probably taking apart even now, some targeted food products from Europe, grain by grain. They will survey the customers, establish the perceived strengths and weaknesses and then design out the negatives. They will then launch it at a lower price if we let them. This is standard procedure in every market they attack, and if we let them do it to us then we only have ourselves to blame."

Mr Robert Tyrrell, Managing Director of the Henley Centre, said that spending power was increasing across Europe. There was rising affluence and a mass middle-class consumer market was being created. A three percent increase compounded over a decade was a growth of one-third in increased spending power. This was likely to continue in the 1990s and the rich, as in other parts of the world, were becoming richer in Europe as a whole.

Technology dictated life-styles. Although people obviously had free-will, as soon as technology came into the shops and prices came down, so people began to acquire things. Following a recent visit to France, and looking at the way in which the French shopped and thought - "reading into their minds through their supermarkets," - they were developing on a very similar pattern to the UK.

"One sees that as the institutional physical environment becomes more similar, so in many ways do life-styles. As the French ownership of microwaves rises, as it almost inevitably must do, will they use them differently? It will be one of those agents of change causing a convergence more than anything else."

Perhaps more importantly in the context of 1992, were suppliers acting without differentiating by country, Mr Tyrrell asked? An awful lot was in the hands of the food industry. If it decided that France and Germany and the UK were different and needed to be treated differently, to some extent they would reinforce their own expectations. If it decided that there was more similarity, again to some degree it would be reinforcing its own expectations.

Earlier, the conference chairman, Mr Walter Goldsmith, Chairman of Food from Britain, said that the British food and drink industry was, he thought, very well prepared for 1992. Fourteen of the top 23 European food and drink companies in the EC were British. "Our retailers are the most efficient in the world, and we are among the leaders in the field of processing technology."

The goal for 1992, he said, was to widen choice for the consumer, remove trade constraints, and deregulate.

The Minister of Agriculture, Mr John MacGregor, said that he shared the Prime Minister's belief that Britain must concentrate on the key measures that would develop the Community's potential as one of the world's largest internal free-trading areas. "It should be about removing obstacles and wherever possible deregulating, not creating, new bureaucratic burdens or unnecessary central powers."

Essential restructuring of food companies would also be important, he said, and as far as the Government was concerned there would be a focus on food law harmonisation. This was to ensure that food was safe and wholesome and to ensure that the consumer was provided with the information necessary to permit him or her to choose their food themselves.

Food additives and food labelling were all areas where there would have to be harmonisation. The UK "sell-by" date, for example, would be replaced by the existing "best-before" system, which would apply throughout the Community.

Mr MacGregor said that some Member States, notably France and Germany, were still pressing for the development of common food quality standards. "We do not think these are necessary or desirable. It certainly does not follow that the abolition of an existing standard automatically leads to a fall in quality. It can often be the other way, so that the development of new products meets developing consumer needs."

Turning to taxation, Mr MacGregor said that he stood by the Government's commitment not to extend VAT to food, and he had made it clear that the UK would not accept proposals that restricted our rights to apply zero rates. "It is relevant that while most product areas where harmonisation might be important are decided by a qualified majority, changes to tax measures require unanimous agreement of the Member States."

On company mergers in Europe, he said that if there was effective competition with products from the rest of Europe, then it did not matter if there was only one UK supplier. This was a situation which could become increasingly common as barriers to trade in Europe were progressively dismantled, and as companies sought the best way of exploiting the wider opportunities.

Effective competition needed to be maintained and "it is increasingly clear that industry must plan on the basis that progress towards a single market will result in a free trade in foodstuffs by 1993".

Mr Paul Judge, Chairman of Premier Brands Ltd, told the conference that any company that wanted to be a serious competitor in the EC had to be a serious player in the five major countries. These were West Germany, Italy, the UK, France and Spain. Even though the UK had made substantial economic progress in the last few years it was still fifth from the bottom in Europe in terms of GDP per capita. So there were countries which were obviously richer and which provided substantial opportunity. But it was not only a matter of money.

Money was spent on differing products in each European country so direct comparisons were, in fact, difficult. Total GDP in the Community was £2.4 thousand billion. Germany was top of the league with £607 billion, and the UK came fourth with £374 billion. Expansion was possible everywhere and total household food expenditure in the

Community totalled £260 billion, just over 10% of GDP. This averaged out at £15.50 per person a week, substantially more than food spending in the UK.

Britain, he said, was already exporting £5 billion worth of food and drink and with the sophisticated financial markets in Britain in the City of London, there was easier access for raising capital. But imports of foodstuffs were nearly £10 billion. Therefore the opportunities were threefold: to increase UK exports; to establish a greater overseas presence; to rationalise European production and take advantage of economies of scale.

Mr Judge added that even if all the trade barriers and tariffs were removed there still remained the barriers of culture, taste and language.

Also, food manufacturers in this country had to expand overseas. They had a 20% share of the UK market, but this translated in Community terms to only 3%. If one looked at the US market then no-one would take themselves seriously if they only had a 3% share of that market. "We have to begin to remember that we will not be taken seriously if we have only a 3% share in the new unified market."

Mr K W Clarke, Food and Drink Trading Director of ASDA, said that there were undoubtedly opportunities for expansion in Europe, by European firms. But "we must recognise that we are fooling ourselves if we think that saying something was made in Britain will actually make people buy it. We have to face the prospect of competing on quality of products rather than on short-sighted attitudes. Quite simply the majority of our customers do not care where a product comes from as long as it is the right quality and the right price".

"My own view, which has been expressed on many occasions, is that organisations such as Food From Britain must be strengthened to ensure that they are able to compete on the best terms in marketing British products on the basis of their quality and not on the basis they are British. This must also be the best export strategy as the suppliers strive to increase their share of the massive European market."

Mr Christopher Chamberlain, Commercial Director and Director of Special Operations, Express Foods Group, said he believed the initial response of the UK dairy industry to 1992, and especially to the great change in distribution, was going to be a largely defensive one. "We are all going to have to defend the home market before we really strike out elsewhere."

Earlier he had said that probably most people would recognise that the spirit of 1992 had been present for some time due to the much maligned Common Agricultural Policy. It was something that the Community had been subject to for a long time "and we in the UK have been subject to it since we first fully joined the Community in 1978".

COMPLETION OF THE INTERNAL MARKET AND THE FOOD INDUSTRY

Pierre Mathijsen
Delegue General
CIAA
(Confederation of the Food and Drink Industries of the EEC)

If the by-now-famous "White Paper"[1] issued by the Commission in June 1985 concerns the elimination of internal frontiers for all goods, persons, services and capital, the Commission also recognised that the specificity of foodstuffs required, in order to make this elimination possible, a particular approach for the food-processing industry. It therefore issued, in November 1985, the so-called "White Paper bis"[2], on "Completion of the internal market: Community legislation on foodstuffs". The completion of the internal market has therefore a particular meaning for the food industry which, on the other hand, has seen its products play a vanguard role in the opening up of many a national market. And indeed, free movement of goods is - as is well known - based upon Articles 30 to 36 of the EEC Treaty, whose interpretation by the European Court of Justice became known through the "Cassis de Dijon" case. It was preceded and followed by many judgements concerning processed foods and drinks - remember the "beer" case - to such an extent that it can safely be said that by "forcing" its way onto the markets of the Member States, the European food processing industry has contributed more to the completion of the internal market than any other single economic group.

It follows that with regard to foodstuffs this "completion" in fact started long before "1992" became a slogan and it also shows that this industrial sector has, for many years, actively sought to exploit the advantages of a common market. This basic "European" behaviour cannot be explained solely by the multinational character of the large food processing companies - although that certainly played a role - but first and foremost by the fact that the food and drink industry has always been, is and always will be export oriented: in fact, the world is its market. The latter explains why CIAA is keenly interested in the reform of the Common Agricultural Policy (CAP) and in the GATT Uruguay Round multilateral negotiations, which should eliminate the obstacles which hamper world trade.

---

[1] COM (85) 310 final

[2] COM (85) 603 final

The purpose of this short article is to illustrate two of the aspects just mentioned: the regulatory basis for the internal food market and the results already obtained through the many court cases concerning the implementation of free-trade principles in the processed food sector.

It follows from the previous remarks that the so-often-referred-to date of 1992 is not a point in time after which nothing will be the same, but rather the end of a "transition" period during which all obstacles to free trade will be gradually abolished, with the result that the area within which goods, services and capital can freely circulate will, by then, really exist.

With regard to foodstuffs, free entry into a given Member State is still very often hampered, if not refused point-blank, with the pretext that public health or the consumer or fair trade must be protected and that the product in question constitutes a danger to these imperative requirements. Whether the worries of the public authorities are genuine or simply inspired by the will to protect national production, is not always possible to ascertain; what is important, however, is to make sure that in the future such national interference with trade between the Member States can only occur when provided for by Community legislation.

This is the reason why the food and drink industry of the EEC is cooperating very closely with the Community institutions -Commission, Parliament, and Council - in preparing and passing the necessary legislation. With about two years to go before the end of 1992, the Member States will need another two years to incorporate the Community rules into their national legislative system - most of this legislation has already either been passed or presented in draft form. It concerns a number of subjects of enormous importance for the industry, since it will determine many of the conditions under which it will be able to produce and commercialise within the Community in the years to come.

The list of items[1] being regulated speaks for itself:

1) protection of public health, more particularly the establishment of a positive list of additives and Community conditions for their use, materials and articles in contact with foodstuffs, foodstuffs intended for particular nutritional uses ("dietetic foods") and various processed for the manufacture and treatment

---

[1] This passage is taken in part from the White paper bis.

of foods such as deepfreezing, irradiation and certain biotechnological processes.

2) Consumer information and protection in matters other than health, in particular labelling of foods including presentation and advertising, so that the consumer may be protected against misleading practices; in this field nutritional information deserves special attention and the Commission has just proposed what is considered by industry to be excessive legislation;

3) Fair trade: producers must be protected against unfair competition and a matter of particular importance in this field is the composition and denomination of products. It is well known that over and over again Member States have used this question as a pretext for preventing imports of foodstuffs. However, in its many judgements handed down on the free movement of goods, the Court of Justice has never accepted that a Member State's authority can prohibit the sale of a product which does not conform to its own compositional rules, but which has been lawfully manufactured and marketed in another Member State, i.e. in accordance with that State's own rules.

4) Official inspection of foodstuffs: the Commission has prepared a directive on the general principles that should govern public inspection in the area of health protection, since it is admitted that free movement of goods does not prevent national authorities from exercising appropriate and efficient control over trade in foodstuffs.

It is obvious that new and additional Community legislation in all these fields will greatly affect the food manufacturing industry. It will impose new or different obligations and restrictions on the methods of processing and the presentation of processed foods, but it will also eliminate innumerable obstacles which, until recently, prevented free access to markets in other Member States. The food and drink industry welcomes the elimination of all obstacles to trade, while realising that this operation cuts both ways: it creates opportunities but also new challenges. Practically speaking, this means re-thinking production methods, investigating cross-border sales and/or investments and examining the possibilities of cross-border cooperation with other producers. That the progressive completion of the internal market has already had important consequences for the structure of the food industry is no secret, and it seems obvious that this process will continue. In this area of rapid change it is not necessarily the strongest but the most competitive and imaginative who will survive.

As was already briefly mentioned, the Court of Justice of the European Communities has, over the past ten years, played a leading role in clarifying, explaining, interpreting and developing EEC rules with respect to free trade in cases concerning the interpretation and implementation of Articles 30 to 36 had to do with food or drink products: from Dassonville and Cassis de Dijon to yogurt and Edam via beer and pasta. This development occurred not only at the instigation of the Commission, but very often thanks to action brought by private companies in their national courts, which then referred the cases to the European institutions in Brussels. The lack of freedom of trade within the Community is due just as much to unwillingness on the part of national authorities as to ignorance of the economic operators. In other words, if producers and exporters were better informed about their rights and were ready to defend them, the internal market would, for all practical purposes, be a reality.

In conclusion, it might be too much to say that for the food processing industry, the completion of the internal market has already been achieved, but the opportunities and challenges are certainly there and the industry is going through a period of adaptation to the new conditions by restructuring measures which could have far-reaching consequences for its competitivity, not only within the Community but also world-wide. Plans have been on the drawing-board for many years to adapt production conditions and structures to a more open market economy in the food sector, and although there is no room here for complacency, it is only fair to say that the food processing industry is well aware of the necessity to adopt a new approach in light of the developments initiated by the completion of the internal market.

A last remark should be made here concerning some general economic conditions at the present time, both within and outside of the EEC. Obviously 1992 is not the only point on the Community's agenda, and measures taken or programmes in other fields will necessarily affect the food industry in the years to come. They concern, for instance, fiscal and monetary harmonisation, stricter rules concerning the protection of the environment, competition and, last but not least, the reform of the Common Agricultural Policy. The latter is obviously of enormous importance for an industry which processes nearly 70% of the Community's agricultural production. As for conditions prevailing outside the Community, the multilateral trade negotiations within GATT, the Uruguay Round, are of utmost importance to an industry for which, world-wide, exports are second nature. The completion of the internal market must therefore be viewed and accepted in a larger economic and political context than is usually the case.

Strategic Planning for 1992

THE TECHNICAL CHALLENGE OF 1992

David Jukes
Lecturer, Food Technology
Department of Food Science and Technology
University of Reading

Introduction

The publication catalogues the changes which are taking place in the approach to the creation of the Internal Market by the 31st December 1992. There are changes in technical standards, administrative systems and, above all, changes in attitudes. As a food technologist, I am going to concentrate on a consideration of the changes in technical standards and the effect these will have on the work of a food company. However, it must be stressed at the outset that the changes in attitudes are likely to have the greatest impact. These changes are already having a fundamental impact on the thinking of all involved in the food industry. There is a realisation that the creation of the internal market is going to offer benefits to industry and consumers and, in particular, that products manufactured in the United Kingdom should be able to be sold anywhere within the Community. The opportunity will be there - it is up to the UK food industry to ensure that it manufactures products which meet consumer demands throughout Europe.

Legislative Change

The food industry has over many years adapted to changes in the technical content of legislation. The last 30 years has seen a major growth in the controls applied to food production and marketing. The temporary legal controls of the Second World War were, during the fifties, incorporated into more permanent controls. This process included the passing of the 1955 Food and Drugs Act (and the equivalent legislation for Scotland and Northern Ireland). The regulations passed at the time introduced a number of compositional standards. These were greatly extended during the sixties and further regulations included the adoption of many of the modern controls on additives.

The seventies saw the United Kingdom joining the original six Member States of the Community. A result was that many of the United Kingdom's regulations had to be modified to incorporate the requirements of the Directives already agreed by the Community. Further compositional regulations were introduced following the passage of further Community directives. The slow pace of these developments though has meant that the eighties have seen a slowing down of the changes in legislation. However, this last decade saw the adoption of the controls required under the Food Labelling Directive. The requirement that all additives should now be declared led directly to the consumer reaction to additives. Major changes were thus made to recipes, not because of legislation, but because marketing departments felt the need to remove those additives most affected by the concern. As the decade closes, the clamour for natural additives seems to be passed its peak and consumer attention is shifting to other topics.

With the approach of the internal market, the pace of change is quickening again. The adoption of the main framework directives of the internal market programme will take place during 1989. Whilst these will have to be incorporated into UK legislation and hence cause some changes to current controls, it is the specific directives which will follow their adoption which will create the most work.

The European Direction

Each of the framework directives contain provisions, explicit to a greater or lesser extent, for future directives. Thus the food additive proposal specifies six areas of work for which the Council and the Commission will develop new requirements. Whether these will appear in a single large directive or many smaller ones is still to be seen. These areas include permitted additives, permitted levels of addition into specified foods, methods of analysis and purity criteria. When it is appreciated that these six areas will be considered for 24 different categories of additives (colour, preservative, sweetener, etc) then the task ahead seems massive. Other major directives in progress include that for foods for particular nutritional uses and that for food contact materials.

Whilst the amount of work does seem vast, it must be accepted that the Commission is not starting from scratch. The need for the development of these directives is simply due to the presence of such legislation in most Member States already. Thus the task is not creation of legislation but harmonisation of existing requirements. With a willingness to compromise and an acceptance that the safety of the consumer can be achieved by standards different to those currently specified in national legislation, the job can and will be achieved.

Each Member State has legislation to protect the health of its population. Since this is a permitted reason for the continuance of legislation under the Treaty of Rome (see Article 36) it is obviously essential for the Commission to concentrate on harmonising legislation in this area. It is interesting to speculate what would result if the internal market programme was not met. If Member States were to insist on maintaining their national legislation, a whole series of cases would inevitably be taken to European Court. It seems likely that the Court would become less willing to accept the maintenance of national provisions once 1992 has arrived. Thus Member States would be forced by the Court to harmonise. In the interim period, total confusion would prevail with both industry and enforcement officers being unwilling to take action. At this stage therefore, it is in everybody's interest to see that the momentum is maintained and agreement reached in time for all interests to be able to understand the marketing conditions which will operate beyond 1992.

Safety Hazards

As the programme develops, it is essential that all aspects related to the completion of the internal market are considered in detail so as to ensure that the benefits which are so obvious are not lost. It is possible that with the rush to meet the target date, governments and industry may ignore some of the problems. The food industry has spent the last five or six years trying to regain the initiative which it lost when the additive controversy arose. Consider the possible effect on consumers were major problems to arise after 1992. The signs are already there.

In the United Kingdom, in December 1988, media attention (already concentrated on food hazards in relation to eggs) made headline news out of reports of sub-standard meat arriving in Cornwall. The fact that this meat had arrived from overseas immediately caused an outcry about poor standards in other countries. However, this meat was from another Member State (Ireland as it happens) and the Community many years ago adopted Directives harmonising procedures on intra-Community trade in meat. Health inspection standards have been agreed and procedures for following up complaints have been standardised. Despite this, as a result of the media attention, it would not be surprising if many consumers are left believing that the Community legislation in this area is unsatisfactory.

The Community has not been free of problems over the years. During 1985 and 1986 it became apparent that wine from a number of regions and countries was contaminated with diethylene glycol. Further problems arose when it was realised that certain other wine was being contaminated with methanol. Again, the Community has had extensive legislation on wines since its formation. This legislation failed to prevent the abuses.

It is likely therefore that with the reduction (if not removal) of frontier checks, the spread of hazardous foods is likely to be greater. When a hazard is uncovered, whether accidental or deliberate, a far greater population is potentially at risk and the media coverage will be that much greater. The media attention given to beef imports at the end of last year is likely to seem very mild by comparison. Consumer confidence in the system of mutual recognition of controls will be undermined. Industry and government would again be forced onto the defensive at a time when attention should be given to consolidating the internal market.

Quality Protection

The potential threats to the consumer acceptance of the internal market must be considered carefully during the next few years if the internal market is to succeed. It is important to appreciate what causes the consumer to purchase a particular product. Great emphasis is currently being put upon the need for quality products. Certainly, in an enlarged market where the potential for an increase in consumer choice exists, consumers will be able to select products which meet their perception of quality. Of course the definition of quality will vary between consumers.

Many aspects of quality are designed into products at the time of their development. Such aspects as colour, flavour and texture will be defined by the marketing departments to meet a perceived market demand. However, the trend over the last decade has been towards stressing other aspects which are not positive features of the product but indicate potential negative aspects of competitors' products. Examples of these include freedom from artificial additives ("contains no artificial anything" is an example) and freedom from pesticides and herbicides (organic foods).

The growth in these negative claims has caused much concern in technical quarters. For many years the scientists and technologists have been trying to develop products using skilful combinations of food ingredients and using modern machinery. The number of products available in a large supermarket reflects the success which has been achieved. The very skill though, has led to consumer reaction. The assumptions which had been based on an acceptance of scientific knowledge have been overthrown by the desire to meet the consumer demands for products displaying these negative features of quality.

Historically, these negative features of quality have been controlled by legislation. If there was considered a hazard from a particular additive, then the legislation would be designed to prevent its use - the consumer would be satisfied that the legislation was adequate to provide protection. There has been a considerable change in consumer attitude to this. With additives, many consumers were much more prepared to believe a photocopied sheet giving a list of 'dangerous' additives than they were to believe that the government had a system for ensuring their safety. The same feelings have arisen with pesticides.

The Technical Challenge

What then is the technical challenge?

The legislation which is being developed to meet the needs of the internal market is extensive, but as already indicated, it does not take the controls into any major new area. The scientists and technologists in industry have over many years been able to adapt their techniques to meet the changing demands of the legislation. In practice, these changes have been incorporated into the changing demands of the market place. The past decade, as described above, has seen major changes, not due to legislation but due to shifts in consumer attitudes. Whilst for some products and some markets the legislation may cause major difficulties, the challenge will not come directly from the harmonisation of laws.

The challenge will be to establish an image of quality, justified by maintaining technical skills and resources, so that the consumer will accept that products from a company are meeting all the requirements for safe food. The improved choice will give consumers a major opportunity to try new products and brands. Given the potential for confusion and media coverage of incidents of sub-standard food, a company will be able to maintain (or improve) its market position if the consumers' confidence is maintained.

Strategic Planning for 1992

FOOD ADDITIVES AND FLAVOURINGS: THE EUROPEAN APPROACH

John Horton
Ministry of Agriculture, Fisheries and Food

Three hundred and twenty additives are permitted for use in food in the United Kingdom by thirty-six sets of Regulations and amending regulations. Some people have seen this as a measure of how generous the Government has been to the wishes of the food industry, and it is not until you understand that many other Member States of the European Community allow the free use of many substances as "processing aids" with no controls at all, that it can be seen that in fact the UK's full positive list is far more restrictive. It is important to realise too that, in order to get on the list, every additive has had to undergo not just one rigorous examination, but two. Before the safety aspect is even considered, the application for the approval for a new food additive must first satisfy the searching examination by the independent Food Advisory Committee that there is a genuine need for the additive that will be of benefit to consumers, and cannot be fulfilled by any existing approved additive or by any other means. Once the FAC is satisfied on this, the Committee calls for advice on the safety of the substance for its intended use. This advice is given by a separate independent committee, the "Committee on Toxicity of Chemicals in Food, Consumer Products and the Environment" (COT). This begins the long and expensive process of proving to the Committee's satisfaction that the substance is suitable for the use in food. Only when Ministers have received the advice from the two independent committees, will they consider proposing changes to the law, and these proposals themselves are required by the Food Acts to be subject to public scrutiny before Parliament is asked to approve the new legislation.

This is a slow, complicated, expensive business designed to ensure that only additives of true worth and proven suitability reach the statutory positive list. It is interesting to consider how completing the internal market by 1993 will affect the UK additive and food manufacturer and the consumer.

On the 21st December 1988, the European Council of Ministers agreed a small change suggested by the European Parliament and was then able to approve the European Directive on the use of additives in foodstuffs (commonly called the "Additives Framework Directive"). This Directive expresses the wish of the Council and the Parliament to see a full,

European positive list of food additives and, where necessary, conditions for the use of those additives. UK food manufacturers are used to conditions of use for some preservatives, and a few other additives, but the traditional British approach has been to approve additives for general food use and to assess them on the basis of their safety for such general use. Similarly, we have believed that, if an additive is safe and if its presence is indicated on the label of the food, distinguishing between for example whether it had been incorporated by a food manufacturer as, say, a foam stabiliser or emulsifier, was largely irrelevant and in any case could not be satisfactorily proven in a court of law.

This traditional approach to the absence of conditions of use will change, and with it will come a shift in the emphasis for enforcement of the additives laws from the retail outlet to the food manufacturing premises. However, it is interesting to see that many Member States of the Community already appreciate that, with some food additives, it will not be necessary to set rigid restrictions on use, particularly where there is a generous Acceptable Daily Intake laid down by the Commission's own independent safety advisory committee, the Scientific Committee for Food.

It is interesting, too, to see that the Framework Directive incorporates the two basic principles of satisfying an examination of the twin criteria of need and safety long practised in the UK.

There will be many months' discussions in Commission and Council Working Groups before a proposal is finally ready for the Council of Ministers. It seems unlikely that there will be a great deal of argument over issues of safety - the opinions of the Commission's Scientific Committee for Food are unlikely to differ significantly from the views of other toxicological experts throughout the Community, including our own Committee on Toxicity.

However, there is more than enough room for argument over the need for certain additives. This is where the Community will have to ensure that national regional specialities are permitted to continue to be sold in their traditional markets. However, this will entail all Member States recognising that, with the removal of trade barriers, such specialities have the right to circulate throughout the Community. This is a difficult problem for some member states. For example, apart from the Irish, very few Member States understand the concept of the kipper, or the uncooked British sausage containing bread and appropriate additives. We shall have to ensure that these concepts are understood and appreciated by the legislators in other European countries.

Once the comprehensive full positive list of food additives is agreed, with conditions of use, there has to be a system for introducing new compounds and for reviewing the current list. The Framework Directive foresees the need to adapt the list in the light of new scientific and technological developments, and permits the temporary approval on the territories of national Member States of new food additives. This is where the European Parliament had a significant impact by persuading the Council of Ministers to reduce the period for national approval from three years to two years. It will then be necessary to seek the approval of the Council of Ministers, based on a proposal by the Commission, who in turn will seek the view of the Scientific Committee for Food. Additive and food manufacturers will need to consider carefully whether it would be appropriate to seek national approval in one or more than one Member State before seeking Community approval. There is a risk, after all, that temporary approval would not be continued on a Community basis following the review after two years.

One further area that is envisaged for greater development is that of the specifications for approved food additives. This becomes particularly important as food producers move away from clearly defined, synthetically produced food additives to those which have in some cases been loosely termed "natural". The specifications for such natural extracts are bound to become a focus of attention once the major work of preparing a positive list and conditions of use has been completed.

The use of flavourings in the UK has never been controlled by positive lists, although their use in food is subject to the general provisions of the Food Act. There are some three thousand five hundred flavourings which may be used in foods, but they are used at very small concentrations. Our advisory committees have, however, advised that flavourings should be specifically controlled and this will now be done on a Community-wide basis following agreement last year in the Council of Ministers on a "framework" directive on the use of flavourings in food. This Directive requires the Commission to present proposals to the Council of Ministers for the control of flavourings, and the first stage will be to prepare an inventory of the flavourings used throughout the Community. Work on the inventory has begun. The assessment of flavourings for suitability for use in food requires a different approach to the traditional review of the food additives and work has also begun on a scheme to set priorities amongst the flavourings for toxicological assessment.

It can be seen that Community agreement on the food additives that may be used in foods and on their conditions of use will be a major step forward, removing many technical barriers to trade and increasing the choice for consumers throughout Europe. It is an opportunity for the British Food Industry to demonstrate the marketing power of safe, convenient, attractive food to the increasingly busy and discerning European consumer.

Strategic Planning for 1992

COMMENTS ON THE EC PROPOSALS FOR DIRECTIVES ON COMPULSORY NUTRITION LABELLING [COM(88) 489]

Dr Margaret Ashwell
Science Director
British Nutrition Foundation

Background to the position in the UK

Diet and Health

It is now generally accepted that the diets of Western countries might have some relationship with health. It is possible that some diets might make some people prone to some of the diseases of the affluent society, notably coronary and circulatory diseases, some cancers, diabetes and dental caries. Official and semi-official reports have recommended changes in diet as a measure to promote health. In the UK, the Committee on Medical Aspects of Food Policy (COMA) reported in 1984 on Diet and Cardiovascular Disease and made the following recommendations:

- Fats: Reduce to 35% of total energy, not including alcohol. Only 15% of total energy should come from saturated fats.

- Salt: Intake should not be increased further; consider reduction.

- Sugars: Intake not to be increased further. Could be reduced by some people for reasons apart from CHD (Coronary Heart Disease).

- Fibre: An increase might be advantageous.

The COMA report recommended nutrition labelling as a way of helping individuals to monitor and to moderate their diets. It also recommended that a programme of health education should be established to inform the public about the changes necessary in their diets, and how these could be implemented.

A further report on sugars is expected soon from COMA.

In a survey by the Ministry of Agriculture, Fisheries and Food (MAFF), the National Consumer Council and the Consumers' Association in 1985, nine out of ten respondents thought that nutrition labelling would be helpful. More than half claimed to have made some change in their diet in the previous year, and nearly a third said that someone in their household had some form of special dietary need. While there is clearly still a need for nutrition education, many consumers are now more aware of the fact that foods can affect their health.

Current Guidelines for Nutrition Labelling

Voluntary guidelines were introduced by MAFF in July 1987 and amended slightly in January 1988. The aim was to encourage the provision of information in a standard form so that consumers would be less confused. The guidelines suggest therefore that where nutrition information is given, one of the following formats should be used:

Energy, protein, carbohydrate, fat.

OR
Energy, protein, carbohydrate, fat with a breakdown to show saturates.

OR
Energy, protein, carbohydrate with a breakdown to show sugars, fat with a breakdown to show saturates, sodium, fibre.

Optional additions to the third category are:

Starch in addition to sugars in the breakdown of carbohydrate.

Trans and/or polyunsaturates in the breakdown of fat; monounsaturates may be shown only if polyunsaturates are shown too.

Energy is to be expressed in kilojoules and kilocalories and the other nutrients in grams. The amounts are to be given per 100g or 100ml; in addition, for packs smaller than this or where there are portions the amounts may be per portion or serving. Small packs are allowed to give the amounts on a portion basis alone. The information should appear altogether in one place, in a table with the decimal points lined up, unless the design of the label prevents this. No other information, including visual information, may be given under this "nutrition information" heading.

The EC Draft Directives

Summary of the recommendations

The two linked EC proposals for Council Directives on nutrition labelling have already been summarised in Chapter 6 of this volume, and the reader is referred to pages 154 to 157.

The system is to be voluntary in the first place, although there is provision for some elements to become compulsory "as a result of the current intense scientific activity on the subject of the relationship between diet and health". Any foods which are labelled with nutritional information will have to conform to the rules and the format laid down in the Directive, but foods not labelled must still be allowed to circulate freely. Foods making specific nutritional claims (such as low fat, high fibre) will have to carry nutrition labelling.

Current position

The Draft Directives were published in October 1988. In November 1988, the Ministry of Agriculture, Fisheries and Food (MAFF) circulated a copy of the proposals to a very large number of interested parties and invited comments to be put forward by January 25th, 1989. These comments will form the basis of the position adopted by the UK delegates to Brussels when representatives from all the member countries gather to discuss the Directive and agree on a document that is acceptable to all members. It is very much hoped that this position will be reached by the summer of 1989.

Once the EC Directives have been adopted, it will be necessary for the UK Food Labelling Regulations (1984) to be amended to reflect any changes.

This process could take quite a while since the normal consultation process will apply. It could be several years before manufacturers are legally required to comply with the EC Directive.

Likely responses to the EC Draft Directives

Consumers' general attitude

The Consumers in the European Community Group (CECG) is the umbrella body for 29 UK voluntary and professional organisations with an interest in the impact of European Community legislation on British consumers. Included amongst these organisations are The Association for Consumer Research, The National Consumer Council, The National Federation of Womens Institutes and the National Union of Townswomen's Guilds. Although individual consumer groups will be putting forward their specific views, it seemed sensible, for the purposes of this chapter, to summarise the comments that have been published by the CECG:

- CECG believes that <u>full</u> (sic) nutrition labelling is necessary in order to follow the recommendations of the COMA report.

- A Community-wide scheme of nutrition labelling will have to be <u>compulsory</u>. There must be an agreed timetable for bringing this into effect.

- The information on the label must be <u>usable</u> by the ordinary purchaser, not just the specialist. There must be a programme of <u>consumer education</u> at both national and EEC level to help consumers understand why the information is there and to enable them to use it effectively.

- Member States and the Commission must ensure that the system is <u>monitored</u> and <u>enforced</u> effectively.

<u>Consumers' Specific Concerns</u>

- There should be provision for the voluntary addition of <u>other forms</u> of representation, eg visual symbols or colour coding, in addition to the tabular format.

- CECG <u>welcomes</u> the inclusion of sugars, dietary fibre and sodium in the main list of <u>seven macronutrients</u> to be declared, and the fact that all sugars (sucrose and fructose, glucose and lactose) must be declared together. Given the increased research emphasis on the role of complex carbohydrates in the diet, it may in the future be considered necessary to include them in the main list as well as, or instead of, dietary fibre. The further breakdown of sugars in the optional list seems unnecessarily complicated and CECG would like to see this suggestion dropped for fear of confusing the consumer.

- In the light of the evidence on fats and coronary heart disease, CECG would like to see <u>saturated fats</u> (sic) included in the main list, the amount being given in an indent after total fats. Given the lack of clarity at present on the physiological effects of <u>trans fatty acids</u> and hydrogenated fats, there must be further consideration of how these should be listed; they might in future be included in the part of the list where fats are broken down.

- Kilocalories must be given as well as kilojoules. A Community-wide table for the <u>conversion</u> of grams of nutrients to energy must be <u>agreed</u> and used. This is of greater priority than the establishment of scientifically super-accurate figures.

- There must be agreed <u>conversion</u> figures for fibre. Again, consistency rather than total accuracy is of paramount importance.

- Nutritional information must always be given per 100g or 100ml so that different products can be <u>compared</u>. Information <u>per serving</u> or per portion should be given only <u>in addition</u>, not in place of this.

- Because of the variability in RDA (Recommended Dietary Allowance) between Member States, <u>an agreed list of RDA for vitamins and minerals</u> must be drawn up as soon as possible taking into account recent research findings about these nutrients. 15%, rather than 5%, should be taken to constitute a 'significant amount'; ie that which triggers the inclusion of an item on a label.

- Common methods of food <u>analysis</u> and common tables of nutrient <u>content</u> for foods must be <u>agreed</u> with other Member States to get over the problem of concern about the validity and acceptability about compositional data.

<u>Industry's General response</u>

The Food and Drink Federation (FDF) is the Confederation of UK Trade Associations which acts as a single focus for the issues affecting the whole industry. The FDF has pledged support for the Government's COMA Report on Diet and Cardiovascular Disease and for a uniform system of nutrition labelling.

The Confederation des Industries Agro-Alimentaires de la CEE (CIAA) is the Confederation of the Food and Drink Industries of the EEC. It believes that the main role of the food and drink industry is to make available to the consumers a wide range of products so that they can choose a diet that meets their individual requirements. Consumers must be fully informed about the products they buy, and this information must be provided by industry in the form of labelling within a framework set by law.

For the purposes of this chapter, I have concentrated on the views expressed by these two organisations rather than those of individual companies.

Both the FDF and the CIAA firmly believe that the introduction of <u>compulsory</u> nutrition labelling for food products would <u>be totally inappropriate</u> at the present time; the practicalities of compelling its provision for all food products would be out of all proportion to the possible benefits. Both organisations would support a voluntary system such as that agreed by the WHO/FAO Codex Alimentarius.

Industry's Specific concerns

- Industry would prefer to see a completely voluntary system based on the "<u>Big 4</u>" nutrients as used by Codex (ie energy, protein, fat and carbohydrate). They feel that the Codex requirements are a realistic foundation for the development of nutrition education through the understanding and application of improved labelling. The compulsory format of labelling seven macronutrients <u>might deter</u> many of the smaller manufacturers from making any attempt at labelling whatsoever because of the complexity and costs of the required analyses.

- Industry does not consider that there is a <u>scientifically valid</u> case for the labelling of the seven macronutrients. The case for labelling sodium is of particular concern since industry considers that the scientific evidence relating sodium and hypertension is weak. The cases for labelling sugars and dietary fibre specifically in the compulsory list are also challenged on several counts.

- Industry thinks that the Commission should take the initiative to establish European RDA for vitamins, minerals and possibly protein.

- Industry sees problems relating to the <u>tolerance</u> that would be acceptable for products to comply with legislation about labelling. This is a particular problem for manufacturers making compound products since there would presumably have to be tolerances set for each components of the product as well as for the whole product.

- Industry feels that voluntary nutrition labelling with an extensive compulsory format would put a disproportionate imposition on the producers of pre-packaged goods.

<u>Nutritionists' general attitudes</u>

The British Nutrition Foundation (BNF) is an impartial scientific organisation which sets out to provide reliable information and scientifically based advice on nutrition and related health matters, with the ultimate aim of helping people to understand how they can best match their diet with their lifestyle. The principal functions of the BNF fall under the headings of <u>information, education and research</u>.

As far as its responses to the EC draft Directives are concerned, the BNF welcomes the general concept of nutrition labelling but is concerned that the information should be given on the basis of the following criteria:

i   It can be <u>truly useful</u> in terms of helping consumers to learn about nutrition and achieving the objectives set by COMA.

ii It will 'stand the test of time' regarding the <u>scientific evidence</u> relating diet to health and is not based on passing 'fads'.

iii It is being put onto labels by food manufacturers with a genuine intent of being <u>informative</u> rather than being used in any way as a marketing ploy.

To this end, the BNF would suggest that the EC Directives should firmly and <u>positively encourage voluntary labelling with compulsory format</u>. As far as specifying which items should be labelled, we have no doubts about the 'Big 4' (energy, protein, fat and carbohydrate). We are aware that current scientific thinking as portrayed by the COMA report provides a reasonable argument for including saturated fatty acids and sugars with the "Big 4". However, our concern for criterion (ii) leads us to state that for other items (eg dietary fibre and sodium) about which the scientific evidence is not so clear, it is better not to include them at this time.

In our opinion, it is better, in the first instance, to specify the simplest of all schemes which will aid nutrition education if it is consistently applied. It is important to maintain maximum flexibility as far as the other nutrients are concerned to reflect the possibility that our "best current thinking" could change as new scientific evidence is forthcoming.

The BNF is intrigued by the phrase in the first Directive that "... consideration shall be given to the practicality and effectiveness of nutrition labelling measures compared with other measures through which the same goals could be achieved". We hope that this might refer to the Commission's intent to sponsor Community-Wide Schemes for nutrition education and to sponsor research into the many areas of nutrition that are still desperately needed to clarify some of the relationships between diet and health.

It is axiomatic that the introduction of nutrition labelling will be accompanied by a concerted effort to educate consumers is basic nutrition.

Nutritionists' Specific Concerns

- The BNF notes that the first Directive lays down enabling provisions only, but would like the Commission to clarify its statement that "... it may be necessary for some elements of nutrition labelling to become compulsory". Does this mean that if it is decided that a food (or nutrient) would be the subject of compulsory nutrition labelling, the manufacturer will have to declare some nutrients but need not use the full format suggested? If a food or nutrient is deemed to require compulsory labelling it should surely have to declare a full nutritional profile?

- The BNF believes that the addition of graphical representation should be explored, but that this option should only be pursued for the "Big 4". The addition of graphical representation must be shown to be beneficial for consumers. Too much information could lead to such confusion that it could become counter-productive.

- The BNF believes that when subclasses of nutrients are identified, all constituent classes should be displayed, eg the format suggestion for identifying the subclasses of carbohydrates

Strategic Planning for 1992

should be triggered when sugars as well as starch or sugar alcohols are identified separately.

- The BNF believes in giving kilocalories as well as kilojoules and in giving nutritional information on a <u>per serving</u> basis as well as per 100g or 100ml.

- The BNF believes in the importance of agreeing common methods of food analysis and in agreeing the conversion factors which must be used. The positive encouragement of voluntary labelling would not only provide an incentive for doing this, but it would encourage compositional analysis by manufacturers and thus increase the available databank.

- The BNF believes that an EC agreed list of RDA for vitamins and minerals must be drawn up as soon as possible.

We welcome the idea that the inclusion of a micronutrient in the list should be triggered on the basis of whether it makes a useful contribution to the diet - a distortion in nutritional profile might occur if manufacturers are at liberty to choose which vitamins and minerals they declared.

We believe that 5% might be too small a figure, and that in deciding on an appropriate figure, the EC should remember that the list of micronutrients on the label should allow the consumer to see that eating a wide variety of foods will achieve the RDA and also allow him to identify which foods are good sources of certain micronutrients.

Conclusion

Even within the UK, it is obvious that there is a basic divergence of views between what the representatives of consumers would like to see in the way of nutrition labelling on their food products and what the manufacturers see as practical and scientifically justified. The nutritionists' viewpoint is different again and reflects a balance in a concern for making scientifically sound decisions and making decisions that will help consumers to understand more about nutrition.

The table attempts to summarise what each group would like to see on food labels and compares these with the Codex guidelines and the proposals in the EC draft Directive.

Across the different Member States, there are bound to be some concerns which are similar to those in the UK and some which are completely different, if only because the existing guidelines on nutrition labelling in each country are so different. Greece, for example, has no nutrition labelling at all and products do not always carry a full ingredients list.

In Brussels, there will probably be some general areas of reasonable agreement such as the importance of producing and using unified lists for RDA and the importance of agreeing on methods of analysis and conversion factors. Other points will be much trickier to resolve to the satisfaction of all Member States. In the end, all national positions will be forced to merge into one compromise solution which will supersede all national rules in the goodness of time.

Let us hope that there will be general agreement about the importance of funding more <u>research</u> into the role of different nutrients in the aetiology of diseases and in the importance of helping consumers of all ages <u>understand</u> enough about the basic principles of nutrition. Then they will be able to <u>really use</u> whatever information they eventually find on the label.

Lengthy discussions in Brussels will be expensive; it would be a shame if all the Community taxpayer's money was used in this way rather than in <u>supporting nutrition research and education</u> at grassroots and street level.

TABLE

NUTRITION LABELLING

CODEX GUIDELINES	PROPOSALS in EC DRAFT DIRECTIVE	SUGGESTIONS from CONSUMER REPRESENTATIVES (CECG)	SUGGESTIONS from INDUSTRY (FDF)	SUGGESTIONS from NUTRITIONISTS (BNF)
Energy	Energy	ENERGY	Energy	Energy
Protein	Protein	PROTEIN	Protein	Protein
Carbohydrates	Carbohydrates	CARBOHYDRATES	Carbohydrates	Carbohydrates
Fat	Sugars	SUGARS	Fat	Fat
	Fat	FAT		(Saturated Fatty acids)
	Dietary Fibre	SATURATED FAT		(Sugars)
	Sodium	DIETARY FIBRE		
		SODIUM		

CAPITAL LETTERS eg ENERGY indicates that labelling should be COMPULSORY

Lower case letters eg Fat indicates that although labelling should be voluntary, these items should be included in a compulsory format.

Lower case letters in brackets eg (Saturated fatty acids) indicates that these items should be included in the compulsory format on the basis of "best current thinking" only.

Strategic Planning for 1992

LOWER PRICES AND WIDER CHOICE IN EUROPE "1992"

F.A. Maljers
Chairman
Unilever N.V.

For the consumer, the major benefit which can be foreseen in Europe after 1992 will be less money from the household budget for better products in the supermarket. The consumer can also expect a wider choice of products, partly because many restrictions currently imposed under national food and drug laws will be abolished.

The Europeanisation of eating habits is moving ahead slowly but surely, and may perhaps accelerate slightly when the borders are opened up. In particular this will mean that those products which provide health and convenience benefits will receive more attention. Nonetheless, regional and national preferences will continue to be important. The overall outcome of the single market will be a wider range of more variegated products in each country, coupled with a more uniform supply throughout Europe as a whole. In other words, uniformity of markets will be achieved at the same time as more variety of products.

The fact that the consumer is under-organised remains a political problem. As a consequence there is a risk that relatively small, aggressive groups will find ways of maintaining obstacles to market integration. In the long term, any such failure to achieve a single market would mean a lower increase in prosperity for everyone.

Against this background, the manufacturer's task is to keep well abreast of market trends, to provide new and improved products via research and development and to seize all opportunities of producing as efficiently as possible. Only by achieving these aims can a manufacturer maintain profit margins. Increasing economies of scale mean that the bigger international businesses are best placed to achieve this, provided they have a flexible attitude and are properly structured. At the other end of the market, a growing consumer interest in new product developments also opens up prospects for local companies if they adopt a creative enough approach.

Long-term trend

For Unilever, the unification of the European market is above all the continuation of a trend and not a sudden break with the past. For twenty years now, more and more allowance has been made for unification of the market when taking major investment decisions. However, the situation in each product group differs considerably, depending on such factors as the nature of the production process, market differentiation and the importance of economies of scale.

In the detergents and soaps sector, moves towards specialisation and concentration of production in Europe were initiated quite a long time ago. For food products too, there is a downward trend in the number of production locations.

The ultimate numbers and locations of Unilever factories cannot be predicted as yet, but it seems likely that there will not be as many as the present 200-plus sites in sixteen European countries. Technological advances and the availability of raw materials will also have an influence on these developments. Any such realignments will be implemented as gradually as possible, since social factors play a significant role in change processes.

More centralisation?

A Europe without frontiers will inevitably bring a gradual need for more centralisation within the currently highly decentralised structure of the group, but this will not take place everywhere to the same extent. For example, future production organisation, which is still only being discussed in broad outline at the moment, will require slightly more influence from the centre. On the other hand, marketing and sales will remain close to their national customers, keeping track of market trends and responding quickly to them. But differences will exist between separate product groups; there simply happens to be more diversity in eating habits than in washing habits. There will be a need for limited intervention from the top so as to prevent bureaucracy in the centre and to keep the sense of initiative alive in the operating companies.

For the rest, in the Europe of "1992" all protectionist inclinations will have to be suppressed. This particularly applies to those groups which, though opposed to protectionism in theory, still advocate exemptions for their own group.

FARMING AND 1992: TOWARDS HARMONIZATION

John Young
Senior Economic Adviser
Economics Department of the Corporate Office
Lloyds Bank

Lord Cockfield's 1985 White Paper, Completing the Internal Market marked the beginning of a new initiative to make the EC a truly common market. It identified almost 300 measures necessary for the attainment of this goal and set a legislative timetable to get there by the end of 1992. To speed up decision-making the Community has equipped itself with the Single European Act - a modification to the Rome Treaty which allows most of the 1992 issues to be decided by qualified majority voting, rather than unanimity. The target date quickly became a synonym for the whole programme, which perhaps surprisingly, has aroused a good deal of interest throughout Europe. In this article we examine the background to the 1992 proposals, and attempt to assess their significance for the UK farming community.

Abolishing The Barriers: A Slow Start

When the European Economic Community was established in 1957 it set as one of its major goals the progressive establishment of the common market during a transitional period of 12 years. It succeeded, ahead of target, in eliminating the tariffs between member countries, but, more than a quarter of a century later, there had been little progress in abolishing technical and other barriers to trade. The main non-tariff barriers are:

- different national standards and safety regulations;

- frontier delays and other transport costs;

- different rates of VAT, corporate and other taxes;

- state subsidies to industry and agriculture;

- public purchasing policies favouring particular national producers;

- foreign currency conversions and delays in money transmission;

- exchange controls and other barriers to the movement of funds.

Some of these have legitimate objectives, for example, the protection of consumers, the environment, the stability of the financial system etc, but they can also make it difficult or impossible for foreign firms to penetrate other national markets. For example, it may be too costly for a manufacturing company to carry out special packaging and labelling requirements for an overseas market that accounts for a small part of its turnover, or to go through several different national authorisation procedures so as to sell its product in each country.

The resulting protection has benefitted domestic firms in some countries, but European firms in general have lost out by not having a large single market like their US and Japanese counterparts. Consumers have also suffered through having to pay higher prices.

In the Cecchini Report (subtitled The Cost of non-Europe) the European Commission estimates that by removing these barriers Community output could be raised by 4.5% over the medium term, and consumer prices reduced by 6%.

Standards: Harmonisation or 'Mutual Recognition'?

The initial approach to the problem of different national standards was to try to harmonize them at the Community level, through legally binding Directives. This process however proceeded painfully slowly, with Member States frequently blocking the European Commission's proposals by exercising their veto in the Council of Ministers. Public opinion, at least in the UK, alternated between derision and outrage, at the various attempts to harmonize standards for noise emission by lawnmowers or to agree on what a product had to contain before it was worthy of the description "ice-cream".

Harmonisation

With the 1992 programme the Commission has modified its approach. The aim is to secure mutual recognition of national standards, and to rely on home country control for their implementation. In other words, if a thing is good enough for the Dutch it ought to be good enough for the Greeks, and vice versa, and each country should rely on the other's supervisory authorities to make sure that the goods (and services) it is importing conform to an appropriate standard. The theory behind mutual recognition is that standards need not be identical, so long as they provide an equivalent degree of protection. However, in some cases, the existing diversity of standards has meant that further harmonisation is necessary before they can be mutually recognised.

Harmonisation Measures Affecting Agriculture

The area of animal health and plant hygiene is one in which all parties agree that more harmonisation is necessary. Because of the importance attached to the health and safety aspect there is a reluctance on behalf of governments to accept mutual recognition if this would in any way result in a lowering of standards. This is recognised in the Single European Act, and in fact over 70 of the 279 Directives and Recommendations that need to be adopted and implemented before the end of 1992 are aimed at further harmonising veterinary and phytosanitary controls. Some of the harmonising Directives concern:

- hormone growth promoters;

- production and trade in milk;

- pesticide residues in foodstuffs;

- control of organisms harmful to plants;

- eradication of animal diseases;

- measures against rabies;

- hygiene condition for trade in meat;

- strengthening for controls of veterinary regulations;

- European law on plant breeding.

The aim is to ensure the free passage across borders of plants, live animals and meat, whilst preventing the spread of diseases, and ensuring adequate consumer protection from pesticides, residues and additives.

In this area, the 1992 programme is simply a continuation of the harmonisation towards which the Community was working long before the 1985 White Paper. Nor has the 1992 programme considerably speeded matters. The animal health measures in particular are considerably behind their timetable. The Commission blames the technical complexity of the issues and its own lack of administrative resources for the fact that it has not drawn up all of the proposals that should by now be before the Council of Ministers. The Council of Ministers, in turn, has a backlog of 17 Directives still to adopt. Nevertheless, even though it may be some time after 1992 when these

Directives are finally implemented it is clear that at some time in the next decade Europe will be operating on a harmonised standard.

With UK standards already very high, no additional burden of regulation will fall on British farmers. Since harmonisation will be fairly complete there is also no strong reason to suppose that standards on the Continent will fall short of our own - although there are strongly held differences about what constitutes a higher standard in certain areas. For example, does vaccination, as practised on the Continent give better or worse protection in the case of foot-and-mouth disease than the UK practice of slaughter? However, what is more controversial is the prospect that we will have to rely on other countries' authorities to impose them. In the case of the plant and animal measures the motivation for home-country control is that this is necessary to achieve the Commission's ambition of abolishing frontier controls.

The new harmonised system will rely largely on checks being implemented in the originating country. Under Article 36 of the Treaty, Member States will retain the right to restrict imports for genuine health reasons, and a number of governments, including the UK, are likely to retain the border controls which would be necessary for them to do this, but it will not be possible unilaterally to impose restrictions. It is planned to have a team of Community inspectors who will seek to ensure that standards are properly implemented by the national inspectorates.

Other Directives that at first sight might be thought to affect farming are in practice likely to have little impact.

There are a number of measures concerned with the food processing industry. In this area there are a large number of restrictions caused by different labelling requirements, public hygiene laws etc. France and Germany have in the past banned imitation milk products; Italy has banned the sale of pasta not made wholly from durum wheat; Belgium bans the sale of margarine in butter-shaped blocks. These barriers would be very difficult to defend under Article 36, and they will be broken down eventually by the 1992 Directives and by judgements in the European Court. In 1987 the Court ruled against Germany's use of beer purity laws to stop imports and against France on the milk substitutes issue. This year, it has overturned the Italian stance on pasta. Other actions are pending.

The result of the breaking down of the barriers should be an increase in cross-border trade in processed foods. This may also mean a greater tendency for foodstuffs to be processed closer to the source of supply rather than in the country of consumption. For products not covered by CAP this could change the opportunities for farmers. For products with a guaranteed price, however, there will be less impact.

Tax Harmonisation

The most important tax harmonisation measures potentially affecting the farming industry are the Commission's proposals for approximation of value added tax and excise duties. This would mean harmonised coverage of VAT with two categories of goods and services, each with a band range within which national VAT rates would have to fall. For most goods the band would be 14-20% and, for sensitive items, including food, 4-9%. The implication of this would, of course, be that the UK would have to end its zero-rating of food. This could have some adverse consequences for the farm industry, although the effect on food consumption would be small at the rates proposed.

Perhaps more significant are the proposals on excise duties which would have the effect in the UK of reducing the prices of both wine and beer, but with a larger fall for wine than beer. The fall in absolute price could encourage consumption of all alcoholic beverages, but the fall in the relative price of wine could increase its consumption at the expense of beer, with potentially adverse consequences for barley producers. In this aspect of the 1992 proposals the Commission is unlikely to get its way completely. Decisions on fiscal matters still require unanimity, and the UK is not the only government to oppose the measures. It is possible that the UK would widen the scope of VAT in a limited way, as part of a longer term move towards greater reliance on indirect taxes, but the UK Government is unlikely to go back on its manifesto pledge not to put VAT on food.

MCAs

As part of the 1992 programme the EC governments have already agreed to remove all of the remaining Monetary Compensatory Amounts within the Community. This is potentially the most significant development for UK agriculture since it would require a considerable devaluation of the green pound which would produce a rise in incomes for UK farmers. It remains to be seen whether MCAs actually will disappear. For the UK government it would mean adding to the upward pressure on retail prices at a time when inflation is showing signs of accelerating. For the Community as a whole, there would be an additional cost to the Budget. Furthermore, since the UK is likely to remain outside the EMS, it is not clear whether, or how the Government would try to stabilise farm prices which would tend to fluctuate with the exchange rate.

Conclusion

Aside from the immediate practical consequences the main impact of 1992 may be psychological. As the programme gathers momentum the attention of the UK farm and food industries, like that of the whole business community, will increasingly be directed outwards towards Europe as a whole, and the challenges and opportunities of the single market.

FARM PRODUCE FOR THE COMMUNITY AND THE WORLD

Ralph Howell MP

The development of the single European market is a time of dramatic change for agriculture and the food industry. British producers could be in a good position to benefit from the changes and opportunities presented when the many and various non-tariff barriers are removed.

During the last ten years, reforms to the EC Common Agriculture Policy have reduced the Community surpluses of cereals, milk, butter, wine and other commodities to almost nothing. However, a number of factors are now signalling change. The world population is continuing to rise, and the drought in North America and other dramatic climatic changes will affect the capacity for cereal production of the northern hemisphere. The future agricultural production needs of the world need careful evaluation.

Widespread shortage of food is still the order of the day in many less developed countries. The Communist world has been unable to feed itself fully throughout its existence, and with the disappearance of food surpluses in the advanced world in the last two years, this has created a situation where food is rapidly becoming of paramount importance. Wheat is surely the basis of life, and the management of world supplies is crucial. Having moved away from the gold standard, on to the oil standard, we may find that food will be the most important commodity, and perhaps the next step would be a wheat standard. The creation of massive surpluses, with the resultant depressed prices, is damaging the indigenous agriculture almost everywhere, and particularly that of third world countries. If a mechanism like that of OPEC could be developed for grain; if production could be limited to say 105% of world requirements, and with adequate and properly regulated butter stocks, prices would stabilise and both producers and recipients of aid would benefit.

To take the best advantage of the opportunities offered by the single market, it really is essential that the Community adopts a common currency as soon as possible, and the UK should become a full member of the European Monetary System as a first step. It makes no sense for the nations of the EEC to be working in differing currencies. 1992 should mean an end to green currencies.

The development of harmonised arrangements for trade in food commodities can only benefit the consumer by increased choice, and the producer and supplier by increased efficiency. There is not a problem associated with mutual recognition of health and hygiene standards for food: each State is concerned for the health of its citizens and we should be concentrating on developing a Community outlook; respecting that the standards and values of other Member States are approaching our own.

In the 1990s the UK must not hold back in its contribution to the Community's development. The Government has raised some reservations over the questions of European unity, particularly over fiscal harmonisation. Now that commitment has been given through the signing of the Single European Act, we must be prepared to work towards the development of a Community system of freedom of supply of goods and services, and freedom of movement of people. Full commitment to Europe will enable us to become competitive in world industry, to move towards self-sufficiency in food production and contribute to helping the less-developed regions of the world to care for themselves.

Strategic Planning for 1992

THE POTENTIAL FOR MARKET DEVELOPMENT IN THE TRANSPORTATION OF FOOD AS A RESULT OF THE 1992 PROGRAMME

Ivy Penman
Business Development Director
Tempco Union Limited

A study published by the EEC Commission has estimated that a saving of £135 billion will be made in 1992. This is equivalent to 5% of total EEC GNP at 1988 prices. Such a saving is derived mainly from the abolition of customs duties and corresponding shorter time spent at borders. It is estimated that savings for individual vehicles operating between the Netherlands and West Germany will be £5,000 per year.

The creation of single European standards is leading major multinationals to rationalise and centralise their European production in single plants. The corresponding economies of scale and faster cheaper transportation is leading such companies to centralise production in low cost labour countries. This, in turn, will lead to greater transport activity to the centres of consumption.

What does 1992 mean for food transportation? The benefits of single European production centres for products such as white and brown goods, and cars, can be readily seen since transport costs represent a small proportion of retail selling prices. Food, a low cost product is different - total physical distribution costs average around 18% and can be as much as 35% for certain commodity items. Most EEC countries have their own domestic food manufacturing industries and innovative strategies, such as manufacturing under licence, are other methods of keeping transport costs to a minimum.

In addition, national food tastes tend to be quite different. With the exception of companies such as Coca Cola and the fast growing McDonalds, there are few global food brands.

Harmonisation in 1992 will theoretically open up the European food market. Well publicised examples, such as "Save the British Banger", and German brewers unsuccessful attempts to prevent British and other beers with additives from entering Germany, mean that there will be a great influx of new food products on sale all over Europe, in addition to existing ones. Tremendous transport opportunities will be created, certainly in the short term. Should a product be very successful,

Strategic Planning for 1992

undoubtedly local manufacture will follow, with a corresponding reduction in transport opportunities. Another attraction, certainly to British food manufacturers and retailers, is that EEC consumers spend considerably more on food than the British. The Dutch, for example, spend 40% more per capita; the Germans and French spend even more.

Non-European producers will also benefit from the creation of a single market in 1992. American and Japanese producers, which currently need to market separately to highly individual countries, will be able to import, for example, into English-speaking Holland, then truck through Europe. The Dutch and, to a lesser extent, the Belgians, will be major beneficiaries in 1992. Fruit from Australasia and the Caribbean, meat from Argentina, sugar from the West Indies, is already being shipped into Rotterdam, Antwerpe and Zeebrugge, then transported by road to the various EEC countries. Part cargo discharges in the UK are becoming increasingly rare. Although the advantages of discharging in Glasgow or Liverpool as European access ports, then transportation through the Channel Tunnel, have been expounded at length, it appears increasingly unlikely that either location could compete with Benelux competitors with their specialist handling and storage facilities.

Dutch handlers are also well placed to benefit from 1992, by building on a position of current strength. Currently, 40% of international European road transport originates in the Netherlands, 27% of which is carried by Dutch vehicles. Fresh produce, a major export item for the Dutch, is carried almost exclusively by Dutch handlers.

A major change in the past decade throughout Europe has been the gradual shift from manufacturers' own account transport to the use of third party contractors and common user systems. The UK has set the pace in this area. This has also been taken up and developed by the British multiple grocers who now use third party specialist contractors to operate their distribution systems. Retail concentration in Europe is someway behind that in the UK. Correspondingly, the use of centralised distribution and distribution and specialist contractors is also less developed in Europe (with the exception of France). Should 1992 prompt the British multiples to enter Europe, with their distribution expertise, this could bring about a massive shift away from manufacturers' transport to the use of third party specialists.

However, of greater importance than 1992 is a general European shift in consumption patterns. More fresh and chilled food is being eaten at the expense of canned. Frozen food consumption is growing rapidly. There is a tremendous growth in the use of temperature controlled vehicles. Concern at the proposed lifting of the ban of irradiation in 1992 and the increasingly "Green" nature of European consumers are leading to exciting developments in transportation systems. One of the most interesting is the Freshtainer system, developed in Austria, which can keep fresh produce, flowers, poultry, meat and fish in prime condition during long voyages and land transportations. It can also extend the life of such fresh foods up to 5 times by the use of computer-controlled temperature, humidity and atmosphere levels.

As a result of such development, by 1992 transportation into and around the single market will truly be revolutionised.

1992 - THE OPPORTUNITIES FOR MEAT AND LIVESTOCK

Dr C M Palmer
Chief Economist
Meat and Livestock Commission

The large single market envisaged by the EC Commission will bring new opportunities for both large companies and individuals. It will mean, among other things, a wider range of products available to the consumer, and the transport of goods across frontiers with a reduction in delay and cost.

Specifically, it will in my view, and that of the Britain's meat and livestock industry, present a real opportunity to improve our meat exports.

These currently stand at £550 million, about 300,000 tonnes. That is 13 percent of total UK meat production. One in every six tonnes of beef and veal, and one in every four tonnes of mutton and lamb are exported, as well as growing amounts of pig meat.

The reproductive performance and feed efficiency of British livestock probably have few equals in Europe - or elsewhere, for that matter - and we know the meat industry can improve its marketing to satisfy a European demand for British meat which is highly regarded among continental buyers for its quality and taste. It is, however, not always as competitive as we would like because of the penalties incurred with existing trading barriers. There is, therefore, no doubt that the abolition of monetary compensatory amounts (MCAs) will make British meat even more attractive to continental importers.

In the same way, the removal of the beef and sheep meat export clawbacks through the disbanding of the beef and sheep variable premium schemes, unique to the UK, will undoubtedly bring benefits to exporters, though their replacement by headage payments will also reduce support to some producers.

However, if these prospects are to be realised, Europe's animal health and meat hygiene regulations will first have to be successfully harmonised. The underlying long-term objective, of course, is to raise the animal health and meat hygiene standards in all Member States to the highest possible levels and to eradicate disease, so that free trade may take place between member states.

Various directives and decisions have been agreed since 1985 to try to control the incidence of the more serious diseases. But with 1,100 cases of African swine fever, and eight of foot and mouth disease in the first 10 months of last year, there is a long way to go before it could be said that such diseases have been eradicated.

In the meantime, control on the movement of animals and meat is likely to be based on the concept of disease-free regions or areas, or even disease-free herds. Only where a disease is endemic would national restrictions apply.

The effectiveness of such a radical change in control measures would depend on the control machinery used and the thoroughness with which it were applied. With no border controls, the EEC Commission envisages procedures based on the mutual recognition by Member States of each other's checks, control and inspection, both prior to departure and at the point of destination.

Apart from the inherent difficulty of eradicating diseases and obtaining high health standards, there are some specific areas which give cause for concern for individual Member States. There are doubts as to which group certain diseases will fall into, and consequently what type of controls would be applied.

For example, the British pig industry has spent £20 million in the past five years to eradicate Aujeszky's disease, while other European countries feel that eradication should be achieved on a voluntary 'health scheme' basis.

The delicate balance between the creation of a free market on the one hand, and safeguarding the interests of Member States with high health status on the other, will be difficult to achieve.

Meat hygiene

The EEC Commission also wants to ensure that meat and meat products are produced to common health standards throughout the community.

The standards to be applied to abattoirs, boning and meat processing plants will generally be those which plants are already required to observe if they export to other EEC countries.

As part of the common health strategy, all fresh meat and meat products will have to be inspected in accordance with common rules from 1 January 1991, and a standard charge will be made for this.

Proposals have also been published to harmonise the standards for production and trade in minced meat.

Technical Barriers

A number of technical barriers to a Single Market are also particularly evident in the food industry, where national rather than Community legislation can control the use of specific ingredients, packaging and labelling. This can lead to diverse requirements in different Member States, making it difficult for manufacturers to compete abroad, or even preventing trade in some products across national boundaries.

The EEC Commission has now changed its approach to food legislation, moving away from compositional directives and concentrating on introducing a programme of food labelling to give information to the consumer on ingredients, and to set general food safety and hygiene standards.

There are labelling implications for speciality products and "protected" names such as "Parma ham". It is believed that, as a consequence of harmonisation, the production of these articles may possibly no longer be restricted to a particular region or Member State. Given adequate information on the label, a Parma-type ham could be produced and marketed anywhere in the EEC.

This development might be viewed as a threat or an opportunity for the UK meat products industry. Export opportunities for "British Charcuterie" products will be able to be exploited to the full but, on the other hand, UK producers of these foods must prepare for increased competition in the form of imports.

This competition may take the form of imported products, such as sausages, which are associated in Britain with reserved names and are therefore subject to additional UK domestic legislation, such as minimum meat content. The imported product may have no such legislative burden in the country of production.

In addition, because there is no language barrier between exporter and importer; the name "sausage" does not require additional qualification purely on the grounds of consumer information. The consumer may be misled into assuming the product has the same minimum meat content as a sausage produced in the UK.

However, I am happy to say that the spectre of such hybrids as a "Euro-sausage", conforming to an EEC recipe, has now receded.

One area of potential significance for the UK industry concerns Quality Assurance Schemes (QA); the development of which the Meat and Livestock Commission gives high priority.

Under Article 30 of the Treaty of Rome, Member States are prevented from maintaining "quantitative restrictions or measures having equivalent effect" which represent barriers to free trade. Rulings in the European Court of Justice have extended this principle to cover discrimination between home-produced and foreign goods and restrictions on the basis of technical standards or labelling requirements.

On this basis some officials in the EEC Commission criticise certain QA schemes, and while these criticisms should not be levelled against present schemes in the UK, other Member States are known to be considering the use of loosely organised "quality clubs" as a defence of the home produced item. There is a danger of the standing of QA schemes in general being devalued, to the detriment of credible schemes such as those in operation in the UK.

The EEC Commission has also published proposals for directives on quick-frozen food (which seeks to impose maximum temperature requirements), food inspection and nutritional labelling of food, while proposals are awaited for directives to control the use of irradiation and on new foodstuffs obtained by biotechnical processes.

As to the fiscal barriers to free trade, the current proposals on VAT are that each country will apply two rates - a standard rate of between 14 and 20 percent for consumer goods and a reduced rate of between four and nine percent for basic necessity items, which would include food.

If enforced, this would have a great impact in the United Kingdom and the Irish Republic, where food is zero-rated.

For all these reasons, it seems to many of us that the full single market programme is unlikely to be achieved by the end of 1992. But there is also little doubt that the EC Commission's push towards a single market will continue and that many, if not all, of their plans will eventually become a reality.

Strategic Planning for 1992

IMPACT OF THE SINGLE MARKET ON THE MEAT MANUFACTURING INDUSTRY

Bacon and Meat Manufacturers' Association

The impact of the single market on the meat manufacturing industry is three-fold:

- the completion of regulations which require all stages of meat production to conform to EC standards of buildings and product and personal hygiene;

- the completion of framework directives governing the composition and labelling of meat products;

- the expansion of trade in new and exciting products into and from the UK.

The cost of bringing abattoirs, meat plants and processing plants up to EEC standards will be enormous; and though heavy investment is taking place or planned, a number of businesses will cease to trade. There is also a great deal of clarification needed before we are in a position to develop confidently our export of products to the rest of the Community in terms of what rules on compositional standards may be set up to complement or modify the Cassis de Dijon ruling which states that a product legally marketed in one Member State cannot be debarred from entering another.

One certain aid to the acceptance of our products will be evidenced by a high degree of professionalism in their manufacture, composition and labelling.

The BMMA has made great strides in setting up a self-regulation programme whereby its members are demonstrating to independent inspectors that they have established and are maintaining standards well up to the requirements of the law as it stands. This will be a positive stepping out point to move to the much more stringent demands of the EC.

A particular possible threat lies in the way in which common standards are enforced. Some countries, particularly the new entrants, understandably have a long way to go to reach established EC standards, which may give them an unfair advantage in competing in the same market as ourselves.

THE DANISH PIGMEAT SECTOR AND THE EC INTERNALMARKET

Danish Bacon and Meat Council

General Remarks

In the Community the agricultural sector has been based on the Common Agricultural Policy - that is to say that this sector already has a free Single Market without restrictions as we know them from the industry.

On the other hand we have during the last 10 years seen a higher degree of protectionism due to the general over-production of goods and the general economic recession.

Despite the fact that the agricultural sector in principle has a free market, the introduction of the Single Market in 1992 means that the Commission now has the intention to create the optimal free European market with total free movement of goods.

The agricultural sector has learned to live with the Agricultural Policy. Nevertheless, the White Paper presented by the Commission contains about 70 proposals which directly and indirectly relate to the pigmeat sector. These proposals mainly concern legislation on food and veterinarian issues.

Generally speaking, the Danish pigmeat sector sees the realisation of the single market as a positive challenge. This has to be seen against the background of the structure of the Danish pigmeat industry, which is characterised as an exporting industry.

So the establishment of the totally free market is an overall positive development. The establishment is however also cause for scepticism in relation to the level of harmonisation - if the result is harmonisation on a low level.

Veterinary legislation

In relation to the harmonisation of the veterinary legislation the Danish pigmeat industry has a major problem.

For many years Denmark has spent millions of Danish kroner to improve and maintain the national veterinary standards; with good results so that Denmark today has a high veterinary status. But with the harmonisation there are now fears that the free movement of goods and animals will destroy this status and thereby destroy many years' hard work. There is a potential risk of the introduction of contagious diseases such as foot-and-mouth disease and other diseases such as TGE and Aujeszky. This might result in economic losses on the production side as well as in relation to our exports. For the farmer the economic risk can be of a disastrous nature, so although Denmark supports the principle, the intention of harmonisation gives cause for concern.

Besides the direct threat to the producers' economy there is the fear for the Community export to third countries - which can only continue when the Community can guarantee the high veterinary status.

To sum up, the harmonisation of the veterinary legislation might, in the extreme consequence, result in a decline in the Danish veterinary standards.

Food legislation

In connection with the food legislation, we also foresee the fear that the legislation might be on a rather low level.

This has to be seen against the background of the Commission's policy of making almost no harmonisation, but relying on mutual acknowledgement of the food legislation in the individual Member States. This policy is almost the same as making chaotic conditions for the production and export of foodstuffs.

According to the Single European Act, national governments can introduce further rules for the production of foodstuffs if the Member States find the Community legislation insufficient. If the Commission maintains the present policy concerning food legislation there might - at least in Denmark - exist a possibility of imposing stricter rules to the production of foodstuffs in Denmark than in the rest of the Community. If this happens the production of foodstuffs in Denmark will be under circumstances that distort the conditions of competition compared with foreign production.

Perspectives for the future

The establishment of the single market will influence the pigmeat sector both directly and indirectly. The direct effect will be in the shape of the proposals concerning veterinary and food legislation, and indirectly the sector will be influenced by legislation and developments in other areas of the society.

The coming years will therefore be characterised by:-

- fewer but bigger food companies;

- a higher degree of market transparency;

- changes in the traditional channels of distribution;

- concentration of economic resources for development and research;

- internationalisation of firms.

Strategic Planning for 1992

EC HOME MARKET 1992 - PROBLEMS FOR THE SWISS FOOD INDUSTRY

FIAL
(Federation des Industries Alimentaires Suisses)

Free Trade - Food Law

The free trade between Switzerland and the EC is mutually affected by differing norms in the area of food laws. These differences are not because of diverging concepts but because of different health and consumer policies. Food laws of the EC and Switzerland are broadly comparable.

The differences lie mainly in the regulations regarding:

- composition (admission or prohibition of ingredients, additives, minimum and maximum content); and

- labelling of products.

In general the differences in composition are more important than those of labelling, as the labelling has to be different because of the different languages.

The "standards" of the Codex Alimentarius are the basis for a world wide harmonisation of food law. However, changes in national or EC law respectively have not been introduced in the same way. Switzerland has at times deviated more from the Codex than the EC.

Regarding the regulation of composition, differences between Switzerland and the EC are mainly in additives.

Switzerland has its own additive regulation (SR 817.521; of 20.01.1982, as amended on 19.04.1984, 11.02.1986 and 04.11.1987). This regulation includes:

- positive lists of basically permitted additives (12 categories);

- application lists defining permitted additives in individual foodstuffs and their maximum limit.

In the EC the regulation of additives is principally also by positive lists. There are directives for 4 additive categories (colouring materials, preservatives, and antioxidants as well as emulsifiers/stabilisers/thickening and gelling agents). This directive only gives a listing of permitted additives. The specific application in individual foodstuffs (type and amount of the permitted additive) is the responsibility of the individual EC Member States and is therefore regulated in different ways. This causes difficulties in trade for some sectors (soft cheeses, sugar products etc).

Additives permitted by the EC are given an E number for their identification. This practice is also used in Switzerland.

There are also various differences regarding labelling regulations between Switzerland and the EC.

These differences were recently shown by the Swiss National Committee of the Codex Alimentarius which compared the Codex-Standard for labelling of prepackaged foods of the Swiss Food Regulation (LMV) and the EC Directive.

In this context the E labelling of prepackaged goods should be mentioned. Packages processed in the EC according to the regulations of the EC Directive for harmonisation of legal requirements regarding processing certain products with respect to weight and volume may carry the exactly defined E sign. Within the EC, products labelled in this manner are not subject to spot checks at borders. In its regulation for labelling and the corresponding Technical Regulations (SR 941.281) Switzerland uses a different system for statistical spot checks of prepackaged goods. Both systems are based on the mean value system and can be regarded as the same. Therefore the E labelling can be used for Swiss prepacked foods for the EC, and in principle there are no spot checks at the border. In practice, however, there have been occasional difficulties when exporting to England.

Agricultural Policies - Balance of Raw Material Prices

Differences in the agricultural policies of Switzerland and the EC mean that raw material needed by the processing industry (milk and milk products, sugar, flour, eggs, plant fats, fruits and vegetables) are subject to different conditions of procurement. The political means used in our country include import bans, transport systems and price supplements. As safeguarding the right of agricultural wage parity has to be maintained through prices for agricultural products, the prices in Switzerland are significantly above those in the EC.

The resulting differences in cost prices for industrial processing on both sides of the border lead to an artificial disortion of competition. The EC (in 1966) Switzerland (in 1976/1981) and other EFTA countries have provided legal conditions, so that their processing industries have equal access to raw materials at home and abroad. These regulations have been implemented in trade contracts in Article 9 and protocol 3 of the Free Trade Agreement between EC and EFTA countries, as well as in Article 21 paragraph 1 (c) and appendix D of the EFTA Convention; both legal documents allow internal reductions as well as reimbursements at the border.

The EC policy in this area is incorporated in Regulations (EEC) 3033/80, 3034/80 and 3035/80 of 11 November 1980, and the Swiss regulation is incorporated in the Federal Law on Import and Export of Agricultural Products of 13 December 1974 (SR 632.111.72), with the appropriate regulations.

The system used at present is not free of distortions in competition, and is to the disadvantage of the Swiss producer by causing:

- generalisation of standard recipes (average recipes) and incomparability of Swiss recipes in comparison to those of the EC. This applies particularly since the EC has created a new raw material matrix following the introduction of the harmonisation system;

- delayed effects of changes in the price relation between home market, EC and world market;

- lack of consideration of the advantageous conditions for EC processing firms when calculating the EC reference price; such advantageous conditions (export subsidies, internal reduction in prices etc) can arise especially when calculating a realistic sale price at times of surplus;

- interest costs because of considerable "time lag" between procurement (and payment) of raw materials and receipt of payment inform of exports;

- individual processed products not to be subject to the regulation of the Federal Law on import and export of agricultural products.

Strategic Planning for 1992

INTERNATIONAL PROFILE OF THE GREEK FOOD INDUSTRY

Fouli Dimou
General Director
Federation of Greek Food Industries

Today in the European Community - our large home market - 320 million consumers spend 17% of their budget for household expenses to cover their nutritional needs.

Approximately eleven million farmers and animal breeders are involved everyday and in every corner of the Europe of twelve in the production of millions of tonnes of agricultural products such as wheat, milk, oil, fruits and vegetables and much more.

However, for many years now the needs of the European consumer have not been met through the satisfaction of his hunger only. His needs go along with the continual progress in standards of living and conditions of work, with new consumer habits, with everything involved in the daily marathon of man for further acquisitions.

Over 25 million workers of the EC are today employed in factories and industrial units for the production and distribution of a huge variety of processed foods to the door of the consumer. The European consumer is becoming more and more demanding. He is not content with hygienic and nutritious food alone. He wants enjoyable food which is fresh and at the same time well-maintained, long-lasting and better tasting. He wants food that is not only tasty, but has attractive packaging and price. In other words, the European today demands the best quality at the lowest price.

This, then, is the role of the food industry to offer products adapted to the needs of even the most demanding consumer.

The food industry, processing in one way or another over two thirds of agricultural production, is called on to play a broader socio-economic role in contemporary Europe.

The Greek food industry, having only recently moved on from its infancy, is no longer a mere observer of developments beyond its unprotected boundaries. The food industry originally appeared in the 1960s and since then, its rampant development has rendered it the most significant branch of Greek processing. Today its contribution to the developing Greek economy is manifest:

- the leading industry in production value, producing 19% of the gross product of the whole of the processing sector;

- the greatest number of units consisting of 16% of the units of the whole of the processing sector;

- the second largest industry in terms of employment, employing 17% of the total work force of the whole of the manufacturing sector;

- the second largest industry, in terms of added value, contributing 24% to added value of the processing sector;

- the second largest industry in terms of turnover, realising 16% of total sales of the processing sector;

- the second largest industry in terms of investments realising 13% of the total gross investment of the whole of the processing sector.

The Greek food industry exports 14% of all exports in the processing sector and 9% of total of Greek exports.

The achievements of the Greek food industry in the last few years have indeed been impressive, taking into account Greek circumstances.

However, when comparing the national income of the Europe of twelve with that of Greece, the major effect of having signed the Treaty has been to open the door to a market 80 times larger than that contained within the boundaries of this tiny state. As Europeans, we are participating in the biggest single market in the world, but if we compare ourselves to the largest national economy within the European Community we are a tiny regional economy earning only one twentieth of the Germany national income.

The per capita income of each Greek is less than half the income earned by most Europeans.

It is a characteristic that the average German has more extra spending power over and above the average Greek than the Greek has available to spend in total. These limitations of the Greek economy promoted the Greek food industry to take on quite an intense outward-looking attitude right from the beginning. However, technological developments in the continually changing international environment demands our country's greater involvement in the game of international competitiveness. The commercial cost-conscious view is that Greece must be used as the "back door" for those who wish to gain access to other neighbouring markets through big grants. Incentives and much lower labour costs are not valid any more.

The Greek food industry is now something extremely different and exciting. If the income earned by the average Greek is enough to maintain his economic circumstances, then the average German has more than that to spend on something else. Most Greek people can manage the basic essentials of life and a few can afford a few extra comforts. So the German consumers added purchase must be not only for something more but for something superior. These superior goods are high added value products on which the Greek food industry has now focused its attention.

This qualitative differentiation of the outward-looking attitude of the Greek food industry has now become the main characteristic of its international profile.

An example of this international image is Greek yogurt, made from French milk and bought by the German consumer.

The quest for raw materials is not always an easy one. The climatic conditions of our country, the morphology of its soil and the various weaknesses of its agricultural structures do not facilitate the supply of raw materials in the quantities and quality needed by the Greek food industry. The attempt at restructuring the agricultural sector directly involves the food industry. Often surplus EC products find a way out through the Greek food industry which, despite its comparatively small size, contributes to the support of the income of the European farmer.

The mobilisation of science and technology for the continual improvements of the quality of Greek raw materials and, in turn, for the improvements of the quality of the final product create a close dependence of the Greek food industry on European know-how, European mechanical equipment, European technology, and in this way contribute to broader economic cooperation with its counterparts.

Finally, the production of goods with European specifications suitable for free circulation in each member state, but also for third countries, concentrates the efforts of the Greek food industry on complete harmonisation of Greek food legislation with that of the Community. This contributes to the wider attempt made today at a Community level for the abolishment of intra-Community technical barriers and for the completion of the Internal Market.

The readiness of the Greek food industry and its determination to play a primary role internationally was made evident recently with the investment proposals. Within the IMPs (the Integrated Mediterranean Programmes) of 25 billion drachmas, Greece aims to reinforce its international personality within the Europe of twelve and beyond these boundaries.

FOOD PACKAGING MATERIALS - THE DEVELOPMENT OF LEGISLATION IN THE EUROPEAN COMMUNITY

Ministry of Agriculture, Fisheries and Food

The European Community took its first action on food contact plastics during the early 1970s.

Council Directive 76/893/EEC on the approximation of the laws of the Member States relating to materials and articles intended to come into contact with foodstuffs was implemented in Great Britain by the Materials and Articles in Contact with Food Regulations 1978. The Regulations controlled, among other things, migration into food from materials and articles and the labelling of such materials and articles. They required that food contact materials should be manufactured in such a way that they would not transfer their constituents to foods in quantities which could endanger human health or bring about a deterioration in the organoleptic characteristics of the food or an unacceptable change in its nature, substance or quality.

The spur to legislative action was evidence that certain foods packaged in vinyl chloride polymer and copolymers could become contaminated with measurable quantities of this monomer, which at the time was causing concern amongst toxicologists. The Community therefore decided to set a limit on the amount of vinyl chloride allowed in plastic food contact materials. Thus EEC Directive 78/142 "on the approximation of the laws of the Member States relating to materials and articles which contain vinyl chloride monomer and are intended to come into contact with foodstuffs" was introduced. This was implemented in the UK by the 1980 and 1982 Materials and Articles in Contact with Food Regulations, requiring that the quantity of residual monomer in vinyl chloride polymers and copolymers does not exceed 1mg/kg of material or article, and that the food contact materials and articles manufactured with vinyl chloride do not transfer the monomer to food. Methods of analysis and detection limits were also prescribed.

A summary of EC Directives is at Table 1. The EEC Commission's work on vinyl chloride let them to consider the whole field of plastics. The Materials and Articles in Contact with Food Regulations 1987 - currently in force - contain in addition a permitted list of substances that may be used in the manufacture of regenerated cellulose film (RCF). The Regulations implement elements of Council Directive 83/299 EEC and Commission Directive 86/388/EEC relating to RCF intended to come into contact with food. The 1987 Regulations also consolidate that 1978 Regulations as amended in 1980 and 1982. They came into operation on 2 October 1987.

(All of the Regulations mentioned apply to Great Britain but not to Northern Ireland, where separate but similar legislation was introduced.)

The following proposals on plastics are at various stages of development.

a) Commission Working Paper III/3473/88

   Proposals for a specific Directive on plastic materials and articles intended to come into contact with foodstuffs.

b) Commission Document III/192/84

   Latest revision - a draft positive list of plastics additives.

Framework Directive

A new Framework Directive (89/109/EEC) replacing Directive 76/893/EEC has recently been adopted. The only significant difference is a procedural one which will permit agreement on future specific directives, usually at EEC Commission level, by qualified majority rather than unanimity. It lists groups of materials which are to be covered by specific directives. These are expected to include limits on migration, and list substances permitted to be used in the particular material. Once a positive list has been fixed, no other substance can be used. However, new substances can be added to the list if there is general approval by the Community or following authorisation by a Member State for use in its own territory.

Rules for testing migration of constituents of plastics

Council Directive 82/711/EEC lays down the simulants to be used and the testing conditions to be employed with plastics that are intended for general usage. Council Directive 85/572/EEC specifies which, if any, of the simulants need to be used for plastics that are intended to come into contact with a single foodstuff or a specific group of foodstuffs.

It is intended to enact these two Directives laying down the basic rules for testing migration in UK law at the same time as the Community positive lists of substances to which they apply. (Each Member State must implement them no later than the time they implement the first Community positive list).

Plastics Directive

There are currently two proposals for "specific" Directives under discussion; the first, on plastics, is worth examining in some detail. The proposal is contained in a Commission Working Paper (III/3473/88) and comprises a limit on overall migration and a positive list of monomers and other starting substances. This Directive is expected to be adopted this year with implementation into UK law about a year later.

It is proposed that plastic materials and articles shall not transfer their constituents to foodstuffs in quantities exceeding 10 mg/dm^2 of surface area of the material or article (overall migration limit). However, there are derogations built in; e.g. on migration: at the higher level of 60mg/kg of foodstuff for containers of between 0.5 and 10 litres and for containers whose contact surface area cannot practically be estimated.

The simulants and test conditions to be used are specified in Directives 82/74/EEC and 85/572/EEC. The sample is to be placed in contact with the simulant in a manner representing actual usage conditions, i.e. only those parts of the sample intended to come into contact with foodstuffs shall be in contact with the simulant. There are separate test procedures laid down where repeated contact with foodstuffs in intended.

If it is technically impossible to determine overall migration using existing analytical methodology, the overall migration test need not be conducted, but a generic specific migration limit of 60 mg/kg would be applied. Specific migration tests would need to be conducted on all constituents of a particular plastic and the sum of individual migrations must not exceed the overall migration limit.

The second feature of this proposal is a positive list of monomers and other starting substances. All such substances have been evaluated by the Commission's toxicological advisory committee, the Scientific Committee for Food (SCF).

Of almost 450 substances evaluated, the SCF has been able to express a definitive opinion on fewer than one third. Thus over 300 substances are currently listed in Annex II and further information is required on all of these within three years.

These substances should be re-examined not later than five years after the entry into force of the Directive. If no information is provided, it is probable that they will be proposed for deletion from the Directive.

Plastics Additives

The second "specific" Directive covers plastics additives. This is expected to be adopted in 1990 and implemented into UK law in the following year.

The EC Commission has made good progress with compilation of a positive list. As with monomers, all substances are being evaluated by the SCF. Draft SCF opinions are available on the majority of additives and, once again, it appears that a large percentage will be classified in Annex II.

Future EC programme

With the introduction of the Plastics Directive and lists of monomers and additives, work on plastics would still be far from complete as substances used in a large number of applications are excluded from the scope of the current lists. Thus future positive lists need to be drawn up for monomers and plastic additives used in:

a) surface coatings obtained from resinous or polymerised products in liquid, powder or dispersion form (eg varnishes, lacquers, paints);

b) printing inks;

c) adhesives and adhesion promoters;

d) epoxy resins;

e) silicones;

f) plastics obtained by bacterial fermentation.

The Commission will also need to decide what action should be taken on colourants, which are currently defined outwith the additives lists, and on aids to polymerisation. The Commission may follow the Council of Europe Experts' Committee which enumerated a set of general principles to be applied to colourants because they decided it was impracticable to draw up a positive list.

Many other materials will need to be covered by EC Directives - elastomers and rubber, paper and board, glass, metals and alloys, wood and cork, textiles and possibly others - by the target date for the completion of the EC internal market, 1992. Of these only paper and board has so far been given any consideration at EC level so clearly there is much work ahead.

TABLE 1 - FOOD CONTACT MATERIALS DIRECTIVES

a. Council Directive 76/893/EEC -	the general or framework Directive on materials and articles intended to come into contact with food.
b. Council Directive 78/142/EEC - Commission Directive 80/766/EEC Commission Directive 81/432/EEC	relating to Materials and Articles which contain vinyl chloride and are intended for food contact use.
c. Commission Directive 80/590/EEC-	determining the symbol that may accompany materials and articles intended to come into contact with food.
d. Council Directive 82/711/EEC -	laying down the basic rules necessary for testing migration of the constituents of plastic materials and articles intended to come into contact with food.
e. Council Directive 83/229/EEC -	on the approximation of the laws of Member States relating to materials and articles made of regenerated cellulose film intended to come into contact with foodstuffs.
f. Council Directive 85/572/EEC -	laying down the list of simulants to be used for testing migration of constituents of plastic materials and articles intended to come into contact with foodstuffs.
g. Council Directive 89/109/EEC -	the revised general or framework Directive on materials and articles intended to come into contact with food.

EUROFI

The following titles are published by Eurofi:

A GUIDE TO EUROPEAN COMMUNITY GRANTS AND LOANS
A comprehensive manual on all EEC grants and loans with regular updates.

EEC CONTACTS
Directory of contacts for EEC and EEC related questions.

LEGAL INDUSTRIAL ESPIONAGE
A source book and guide to finding company information.

EUROPEAN BUSINESS REPORTS - SPAIN AND PORTUGAL
For the international corporate decision maker, giving assessments of business opportunities, investment climate, market intelligence and key contacts in Spain and Portugal.

MONEY FOR RESEARCH AND DEVELOPMENT
An entirely new guide to funds for research and development in an easily digestible format.

MOLE: BUSINESSMAN'S GUIDE TO THE GOVERNMENT
A subject directory of key contacts in Whitehall and Westminster.

MIND YOUR LOCAL BUSINESS
A practical guide to information for Local Authorities - essential reading for everyone in local economic development.

INDEX TO DOCUMENTS OF THE COMMISSION OF THE EUROPEAN COMMUNITIES
An annual key word index providing a simple guide for tracing by subject all publicly available COM Documents published yearly.

WOMEN DIRECTORS
Directory of Who's Who in the world of Women Directors, containing the names, business addresses and details of over 1,500 UK Women Directors.

For further information please contact:

Eurofi plc
Guildgate House
Pelican Lane
Newbury
Berks
RG13 1NX

Tel: (0635) 31900